SUPERSIZE
YOUR SMALL BUSINESS PROFITS!

*How to Survive the Current Recession
and Manage Your Small Business Profitably
During Turbulent Economic Times*

BY FRANK T. KASUNIC

Order this book online at www.trafford.com
or email orders@trafford.com

Most Trafford titles are also available at major online book retailers.

Printed in Victoria, BC, Canada.

ISBN: 978-1-4269-1730-1 (sc)
ISBN: 978-1-4269-1729-5 (dj)
ISBN: 978-1-4269-2329-6 (e)

Library of Congress Control Number: 2009936931

*Our mission is to efficiently provide the world's finest, most comprehensive book publishing
service, enabling every author to experience success. To find out how to publish your book, your
way, and have it available worldwide, visit us online at www.trafford.com*

Trafford rev. 11/11/2009

 www.trafford.com

North America & international
toll-free: 1 888 232 4444 (USA & Canada)
phone: 250 383 6864 ♦ fax: 812 355 4082

This book is dedicated to my family, my good friends, and struggling small business owners everywhere.

God bless them all!

QUOTES FROM "SUPERSIZE YOUR SMALL BUSINESS PROFITS"

Regarding Goal Setting - *"I cannot stress enough the importance of goal setting. It sets the tone and direction of your corporation. It allows you to set objectives that are consistent with the overall goals that you have established. And, like a lighthouse beacon on a dark and stormy night, it keeps you on the right track to achieve those goals."*

Regarding Family Succession - *"Business acumen is not transferred through the genes, but is forged in the hot fire of tough business experience and difficult decision-making."*

Regarding Arbitration – *"If you have a good case and a good attorney, don't put your fate in the hands of a "Rent-a-Judge" arbitrator if you can possibly avoid it."*

Regarding your Board of Directors – *"Once you begin to manage through your Board of Directors, you will feel the power that you get from being proactive and being out in front of your business decisions. It is a welcome change from being reactive and always feeling like you're behind the eight ball in everything that you do with your business. And, once you have tasted the economic rewards of real participative corporate management, you'll never go back to the old way of doing things."*

Regarding Outside Advisory Boards – *"The most substantial management difference separating a small business from a large business is the availability of in-house expertise. Having an Outside Advisory board is a great way for a small business to close that gap without having to spend a lot of time and money to do so."*

Regarding your Company Reputation – *"Your Company's reputation and customer service are joined together like a hand in a glove."*

Regarding your Business Assessment – *"If you don't know where you're at today, how can you possibly know where you're going to be tomorrow?"*

Regarding an Achievable Business Plan – *"The supporting assumptions underlying the financial projections must be tied to specific and realistic company goals and objectives. Without this underlying foundation in place, your business plan is nothing more than a fancy piece of paper signifying nothing!"*

Regarding Financial Projections – *"Adopt the policy of having a "living budget and forecast".* Simply put, this means that your quarterly budget and forecast should change with substantial changes in the economic climate in your area and your company's current business conditions.

Regarding Financial Analysis – *"Financial analysis is like doing a postmortem on dead meat"!* If all you do is analyze past performance and do not utilize the results of that analysis to improve future results, you are truly wasting your time!

Regarding accurate Financial Statements – *"If your company's financial statements are inaccurate because your financial controls are virtually nonexistent; your company is like a ship without power and without a rudder. You don't know where you are, you don't know where you've been, and you certainly don't know where you're going! And if you don't know where you're going, any errant wave will get you there. However, you may not like the journey and you certainly won't like the destination, when you are dashed against the financial rocks of bankruptcy."*

ABOUT THE AUTHOR – FRANK T. KASUNIC

Frank has been a CFO, Controller, VP Finance, Secretary/Treasurer, a financial consultant, and at times Marketing Manager, Operations Manager, and acting President for 25 different companies. These companies have ranged from small startup companies to medium-sized and large companies, and have spanned several different industries. Frank's occupational experience gives him a broad base of knowledge in the following industries: securities, financial planning and consulting, insurance, real estate, transportation, retail sales, agricultural development, and manufacturing. He has proven himself to be a senior financial and administrative manager with the ability to analyze organizations over a broad spectrum, and then determine, implement and achieve results oriented performance objectives.

Frank's areas of expertise include accounting, finance, administration, budgets and forecasts, short-term and long-term strategic planning, treasury management, investments, and the management and equity funding of startup and turnaround companies. His accomplishments include managing a turnaround company from an equity position of only $16,000 to over $3,700,000 in three years. He implemented Performance Evaluation and Review Techniques (PERT) and Critical Path Method (CPM) workflow analyses in a critical audit situation resulting in substantial savings for the company. He then directed an information systems conversion from EDS to IBM. Frank has also engineered an IPO for 10% of a company's stock, and has generated other equity funds utilizing joint ventures and private placements.

Frank's professional certifications have included the following: a Certified Public Accountant (CPA) certificate, a Certified Financial Planner (CFP) certification, a Series 7 and 24 Securities License,

Health & Disability and Property & Casualty Insurance Licenses, and a Real Estate Salespersons License. Frank has a B.S. (Bus) degree with a major in Accounting from the University of Idaho, an M.B.A. from Golden Gate University, and all coursework completed for a Ph.D. in Information Science at Claremont Graduate School.

Prior to entering the business world, Frank spent about seven years with the United States Air Force as an aircrew member and instructor, achieving the rank of Captain prior to his honorable discharge in 1970.

Frank is a highly motivated and creative chief financial officer who possesses diversified talents, skills and experience. He utilizes these skills to prioritize and focus on the key critical areas that make for business success. Yet, he is hands-on enough to be able to direct daily operations to a successful conclusion. His leadership style is motivational, and he invokes a high degree of team spirit and loyalty in his staff. He displays a can-do attitude and sets realistic and achievable goals and objectives. More importantly, he usually implements those objectives before the scheduled completion date.

INTRODUCTION

I have been Chief Financial Officer and at times Marketing Manager, Operations Manager, and acting President for 25 different companies. These companies have ranged from small startup companies to large companies and have spanned several different industries. As a result of my extensive experience with many different companies, there is no doubt in my mind that small companies have a set of management problems that are not shared by larger companies. For purposes of this book, any company that employs less than 250 persons or has gross revenues less than $100 million dollars will qualify for inclusion as a small business. While this definition of a small company may seem a bit arbitrary, larger companies are typically compartmentalized, having many areas of in-house expertise. Smaller companies have a much more abbreviated and functional management team comprised of several officers and managers. Generally speaking, small business managers do not have access to a wide range of specialized expertise from within their own organization. This is the most significant factor that separates managing in small companies versus large companies. You will also find that there are many textbooks and other business books and publications devoted to the problems and opportunities of medium and large size companies. However, there is a scarcity of practical books that address the manifold problems of a small business owner or manager in a simple, no-nonsense and realistic way. Small business management has to address almost all of the problems that exist in a large business, but the management team is not equipped to do so without some outside professional assistance. In this book, I discuss how a small business can access knowledgeable professionals without having to pay an arm and a leg to do so.

A small business does have one great advantage over a large business enterprise and that is its flexibility and speed of its response to change and innovation. Also, a small business manager does not have to burrow through several layers of bureaucratic management to get things done! Properly utilized, this freedom, flexibility and quickness to respond to change can result in a competitive advantage for the well managed small business.

My intention in this book is to cover a number of broad functional areas that represent common problems in small businesses. I will identify the problems or opportunities, define them and offer a few no-nonsense ideas, actions and solutions for your consideration. The areas to be addressed are as follows:

1. **THE GREAT RECESSION OF 2009 AND BEYOND -** Actions that you can take relatively quickly in these turbulent economic times to increase your sales and gross margins, reduce your expenditures and improve your cash flow from operations.

2. **ORGANIZING YOUR BUSINESS FOR SUCCESS -** Everything from the type of business organization you choose, organizing and building your management team, hiring the best managers and terminating your underperformers, and managing through your Board of Directors is covered in this segment.

3. **ASSEMBLING YOUR TEAM OF ADVISORS -** How to form an Outside Advisory Board and the manifold advantages that the Board brings to your company, how to choose the right Corporate Attorney, the pitfalls of Arbitration, and how to select the right CPA firm.

4. **BUSINESS CONTINUATION PLANNING -** This section contains separate chapters on Disaster Planning and Business Succession covering two critical planning areas for small businesses where the planning is either inadequate or is not done at all. The importance of purchasing Key Person Insurance and funding Buy/Sell Agreements with Term Life Insurance is also discussed.

5. **SUCCESSFUL BUSINESS PLANNING -** In this section, I examine Goal Setting, Developing Objectives, Key Result Areas and Management by Objectives as an integral part of your overall planning process. I then summarize a blueprint for creating the end result of all the preceding activity, which is your Business Plan.

6. **ANALYZING YOUR FINANCIAL STATEMENTS -** This section includes a general discussion of the importance of accurate and timely Financial Statements and an introduction to the Income Statement, Balance Sheet and Cash Flow Statement.

7. **INCREASING YOUR SALES AND IMPROVING GROSS MARGINS** – I outline several ways to increase your revenue and gross margin percentage and reduce your cost of sales with separate chapters relating to each major topic.

8. **CONTROLLING AND REDUCING EXPENSES -** I then discuss a number of ways to reduce your expenses with separate chapters providing more information about the suggested expense reductions.

9. **MAINTAINING POSITIVE CONTROL OF YOUR ASSETS** – The reporting and control of current assets like Cash, Accounts Receivable, Inventories, and Current Liabilities as key components of working capital are discussed, along with the reporting and control of Fixed Assets to include real property and office and production equipment.

10. **CHANGE MANAGEMENT -** The various types of changes facing most businesses are discussed along with how to plan for and implement all types of changes. I also discuss the reasons for employee resistance to change and what you, as a manager, can do to overcome this resistance and successfully implement change.

11. **SUMMARY** – This is a brief overview of the book and a glimpse into the future for small business owners and managers.

12. **FORECAST** – A brief glimpse into the future of this deep recession, and ways to protect yourself and your business from its ravages.

13. **IT'S NOT TOO LATE!** – A listing of recession related protective measures you can take now to protect yourself and your business in these turbulent times.

WARNING! This book is not your average business college text filled with theories, unworkable ideas, citations, notations, and appendices. It is experiential by design, and is chock full of workable solutions for the problems faced by small business owners and managers. I have dealt with most of the business problems described in this book personally and have resolved them successfully. Ideally, the book will fill some of the gap in the literature regarding the profitable management of your small business in turbulent economic times. In this book, I have provided a considerable number of practical no-nonsense ideas and suggestions that should help you, as a small business owner or manager, to profitably manage your business. You should be able to implement at least a few of these suggestions to increase your sales and gross margins, decrease your expenses, and implement sensible controls that will enhance your profitability. If you are successful in achieving this, then the purpose of my book will be fulfilled!

Contents

SECTION 1

THE GREAT RECESSION OF 2009 AND BEYOND

CHAPTER 1

HOW TO COPE WITH THE
GREAT RECESSION OF 2009

RECESSION PROOF YOUR SMALL BUSINESS

When I first started writing this book in July of 2008, I didn't plan to include this chapter. However, as we approached the end of the year, it seemed like a natural addition to a book that is devoted to making and saving money for small businesses like yours. It is estimated that small businesses with less than 100 employees represent more than 50% of the jobs in the United States. According to the Financial Times, "The U.S. will see 62,000 companies go bust next year (2009), compared with 42,000 this year (2008) and 28,000 last year (2007), according to a report by Euler Hermes, part of German insurer Allianz". Assuming that the median number of people working at those companies is 50, at least another three million people could be out of work in 2009. This dire prediction will get a lot worse because GM and Chrysler have gone into bankruptcy this year. The multiplier effect of these huge business failures has yet to be fully absorbed by our economy.

There are actions that I have categorized and listed below that you can quickly implement to maintain your profitability and help insure that your small business is not one of the 62,000 projected to go out of business in the United States this coming year.

PAYROLL RELATED SAVINGS

1. **Cut Staff** – This is an excellent time to trim the fat and lay off or terminate marginally productive employees. With mandatory and voluntary benefits included, you will save about 130% of the salary of every full time employee you terminate.

2. **Eliminate Your Overtime Expense** – Except for special circumstances, all overtime must be eliminated. Those circumstances involve true emergency situations, and small amounts of planned overtime that will eliminate the need to hire another employee. Remember that overtime hours, assuming a 150% hourly cost, add up to nearly 200% of the hourly rate with benefits.

3. **Lay Off Your Payroll Person and Contract with an Outside Payroll Service** – I have recommended this action for small businesses because you win 2 ways. First, you reduce the direct costs of processing the payroll. Secondly, you substantially reduce the administrative costs associated with the payroll. See my Chapter on "PAYROLL PROCESSING COST REDUCTIONS" for more information.

4. **Reduce the Hours That You Are Open for Business** – With less business, do you really need to be open all those hours? If you operate a retail enterprise, analyze the amount of business you generate by the day and by the hour during each day. **Seek to eliminate unproductive days or hours that you are currently open for business.** An example would be a Monday where only 4% of your business is being generated. Obviously, you need to be closed on that day. This will save you employee costs and utility bills.

5. **Declare a 5% to 10% Salary Reduction** – Reduce your employees' salary and hourly rate by 5% to 10% depending on the severity of your financial distress. This will save you an additional 20% of the wages you have saved in mandated employee benefits such as FICA, Unemployment Insurance

and Workers Compensation Insurance plus any employer provided benefits tied to compensation.

6. **Reduce Vacation Time** – If you have an overly generous vacation policy allowing as much as 3 or 4 weeks, consider the financial effect of reducing the vacation period to 2 weeks maximum. It may or may not be worth the effort, depending on the number of your employees that are receiving 3 to 4 weeks of vacation.

7. **Eliminate Voluntary Sick Pay Benefits** – If you provide voluntary sick pay benefits, which are generally used by employees as additional vacation or time off, eliminate this benefit entirely.

8. **Reduce or eliminate the 401k employer match** – Now is not the time to be supporting a rich benefit package, when you are fighting for the survival of your business. Change the employer match paragraph in your 401k plan document and reduce or eliminate the 401k employer match percentage (This is not a big deal to do from a paperwork standpoint). Communicate the change in writing to your employees and implement the change in your next payroll.

9. **Start a Cafeteria Plan** – If you don't have a Section 125 Cafeteria Plan, initiate one effective next month to start saving on payroll taxes for your company and your employees!

10. **Eliminate Employer Provided Section 79 Group Life Insurance** – These are tough times. The only time this benefit pays is when an employee dies, so your current employees will not miss it, unless they have passed away at their desk and you haven't noticed! As a no-cost alternative, substitute the employer provided group insurance with an elective employee paid group plan where the premiums can be deducted from their payroll checks.

11. **Reduce Health and Dental Insurance Benefits and Increase Deductibles** – In conjunction with your insurance broker, and

with written communication to your employees beforehand, swap your current plan for a plan that provides inexpensive basic coverage with higher deductibles.

12. **Partially Self-Insure Your Employee Health Plan** – Although I am not a fan of partial self insurance for health plans (See Chapter 37), there is an exception. Adopting a partially self-insured health plan can defer about 90 to 120 days of cash flow related to your health insurance costs.

13. **Increase Employee Contributions to Offset the Cost of Their Health Insurance Coverage** – Determine how much you can expect your employees to contribute to their health insurance coverage relative to your critical business need to cut costs. Your employees may have to cover all of the cost of their health insurance if your survival and their jobs are at stake. If you have just started a Cafeteria Plan, assuming an overall tax savings of about 20%, your employees will only be out of pocket about 80% of the increase in their contributions. They will also be much more receptive to reducing the overall costs of their health care plans (See paragraph 11 and my Chapter on The Insurance Game).

14. **Hire Independent Contractors** - By hiring independent contractors, you will save the employer's share of all the mandated employee costs such as Social Security and Medicare taxes, state and federal unemployment taxes, and Workman's Compensation Insurance plus all of the voluntary benefits you pay on behalf of your full time employees. However, have your corporate attorney insure that your independent contractors don't qualify as employees. If they do, you won't want to deal with the back taxes, penalties and fines that you will have to pay, so be careful with this one!

PREMISES RELATED SAVINGS

1. **Renegotiate Your Lease Costs** – Believe me, in today's commercial real estate market, anything is possible. Among the things you can negotiate are several months of free rent,

reduced rent and/or cams and other items such as CPI annual lease cost escalators. See Paragraph 16 in Chapter 33 about No Nonsense Expense Reduction.

2. **Reduce Utility Costs** – If you own or lease a stand-alone building, consider having an energy audit performed by your utility company. Usually, the utility company will perform this service free of charge. Implement all of the inconsequential cost items they suggest, as your energy savings will substantially exceed your cost. Your utility company may well reimburse some of your cost. If you rent or lease your building, you may want to negotiate with your landlord to reimburse your cost.

3. **Do Your Own Janitorial Work and Save** – Fire your outside janitorial service and have one of your minimum wage employees take on that responsibility.

EQUIPMENT RELATED SAVINGS

1. **Eliminate Unnecessary Cell Phones** – No employee should be issued a cell phone unless they absolutely have to have one to conduct business.   This is one of the biggest bills in your telecom budget and has a great tendency to grow out of control!   Reduce it to an absolute minimum.

2. **Renegotiate Your Cell Phone Contracts** – None of the companies that provide cell phone service want to lose your business. It's just too profitable to for them to walk away from and it's the perfect time to renegotiate!

3. **Authorize Car Allowances Instead of Cars** – Adjust the employee car allowance to approximate the amount of business usage of the employee's personal car. When you consider the full amount of vehicle expense including depreciation, fuel, maintenance, taxes and licensing, and insurance that your company pays for, you will save more than 50% of these costs by moving to car allowances for employees who have a company car. To further enhance your cash flow, sell the

company vehicles that you no longer need to your employees at a discounted price.

OTHER IMMEDIATE EXPENSE REDUCTIONS

1. **Negotiate Pricing With Your Vendors** – You can negotiate lower product pricing, banded volume discounts, storage, freight costs, product advertising assistance, and cash purchase discounts or extended payment terms with your vendors. See Paragraph 1 and 2 in my Chapter on "COST OF SALES REDUCTION"

2. **Reduce Travel Expense** – Use Web Conferencing, pre-planned open ended phone calls, and dual purpose travel to reduce your travel time. For the travel that you have to do, assign the responsibility of Travel Director to an office employee to coordinate travel, insure all travel is approved, and secure the lowest prices available on transportation and lodging. See Paragraph 14 in my Chapter on "NO NONSENSE EXPENSE REDUCTIONS" for more information.

3. **Examine your Property & Casualty Insurance for Cost Reductions** – If you haven't conducted a P&C Insurance review lately, now is the time to do so. You may be able to reduce or eliminate some of your coverage, or partially self-insure by increasing your deductibles if it makes sense to do so. Contact your broker and arrange for a full review of all of your current insurance coverage.

4. **Utilize Proprietary Product Pricing Strategies to Increase Your Margins** – If you are selling proprietary products that no one else in your area sells, you can actually increase your prices on these products without losing any significant amount of sales. I would recommend a small 2 or 3% increase that will not greatly upset your customers to be made effective as soon as possible. (See Chapter 25)

5. **Utilize a Low Cost Pricing Matrix to Increase Your Margins** – If you sell low cost products priced under 2 or 3

dollars, initiate a low cost price matrix to further increase the sales price of your low cost proprietary or non-competitive products. (See Chapter 25)

6. **Initiate Extended Warranty Sales** – If you sell products where customers normally purchase an extended warranty, this is a great way to increase your sales and profits. You can take 60% to 80% of your extended warranty sales to gross profit. And, your cash flow is increased by 100% of your extended warranty sales less your sales commissions. The rationale for this recognizes the fact that you normally won't have to pay any warranty claims until the original manufacturer's warranty of 90 days to one year has expired.

7. **Rationalize Unprofitable Products and Use Contract Manufacturing** – If you are manufacturing unprofitable products, stop manufacturing those low volume, high cost, unprofitable losers as quickly as you can. If you need to stock certain legacy products because of customer requirements, consider contract manufacturing with an appropriate mark-up of your sales price to cover the product cost, freight, handling expenses and a reasonable profit. (See Chapter 32 regarding "COST OF SALES REDUCTION SRATEGIES").

8. **Reduce Your Product Inventory** – Keep your inventory lean and mean by selling or returning to the manufacturer any obsolete, damaged or excess non-moving inventory. Don't order more inventory than you need to fill customer demand unless significant discounts of at least 10% and favorable payment terms are offered on fast moving inventory. This will improve your cash flow significantly.

9. **Negotiate your Freight Costs** – Since fuel costs have dropped sharply, it's definitely time to renegotiate your freight costs with your carriers. If, for whatever reason, they are not negotiable, procure bids from other carriers.

10. **Purchase Discounted Supplies and Forms** – Order economic quantities of forms and supplies for at least a 10% discount,

and negotiate storage with your vendor. Also, inquire about prompt payment discounts and special payment terms. (See Chapter 43)

11. **If Your Income Tax Payable is Less Than Your Estimated Payments, File Your Income Tax Early** – File your Income Tax Return early to receive your refund as quickly as possible. Also, if you had a net loss in 2008, do not pay any estimated tax for 2009 until you are sure you will have income to report. (See Chapter 50)

SUMMARY

By no means is this a comprehensive list of all the things that you can do in the immediate future to improve your profitability and cash flow. However, most of the items on this list can be implemented quickly to improve your financial condition.

SECTION 2

ORGANIZING YOUR BUSINESS
FOR SUCCESS

CHAPTER 2

CHOOSING YOUR TYPE OF BUSINESS ORGANIZATION

TYPES OF BUSINESS ORGANIZATIONS

There are basically seven types of business organizations from which to choose. These are a sole proprietorship, a general partnership, an LP or limited partnership, an LLP or limited liability partnership, a "C" or general corporation, an LLC or limited liability corporation, and an "S" corporation, which is simply a "C" or an LLC corporation which has filed for "S" corporation status with the IRS.

I. **Sole Proprietorships** - A sole proprietorship owned by one person is the simplest and most common type of business entity. Any small business that has not legally established itself as another type of business will be treated as a sole proprietorship.

ADVANTAGES OF A SOLE PROPRIETORSHIP:

1. Sole proprietors have the maximum amount of independence and autonomy, which is attractive to entrepreneurs. Basically, a sole proprietor is responsible for and makes all of the business decisions.

2. Sole proprietorships do not have to file separate income tax returns. In addition, some business taxes are less for sole proprietorships than for other types of business organizations.

3. Accounting is simplified. **Caution: This often becomes a disadvantage if the accounting for the business is not kept up to date and separated from the individual affairs of the owner.**

4. Operating your business is simpler in a sole proprietorship. Other business types often have to deal with complex and time-consuming governmental and regulatory requirements in operating and reporting on their businesses.

5. Start-up costs are minimal. You don't need the services of an attorney. And only a few documents are required by federal, state, or local agencies to start the business. However, you will still have to file a "fictitious name statement", a business license, and if you have employees, you will need a federal and state Employer Identification Number (EIN), a certificate of Workman's Compensation coverage, and other licensing and zoning requirements that are necessary to do business at your location.

6. Any business losses can be used to offset other income on your personal tax return.

DISADVANTAGES OF A SOLE PROPRIETORSHIP:

1. **CAUTION: The chief disadvantage of operating your business as a sole proprietor is that <u>you have unlimited business and personal liability</u> for anything that your business does or doesn't do. Your business creditors, your employees, and anyone injured directly or indirectly by your activities can sue your business and you as an individual for any amounts not covered by insurance. This means that all of your business and personal assets are at risk!**

2. Raising capital for a sole proprietorship can be difficult, if not impossible in today's credit environment. Lenders are extremely reluctant to extend credit to the individual owners of sole

proprietorships. Those who do require the individual owner to sign pledges of assets as collateral, as well as business and personal guaranties in the event of a loan default.

3.   Although a sole proprietorship can be sold, it can continue for only as long as the owner is still living. When the owner dies, the assets and liabilities of the business become part of the owner's estate.

Recommendation: Once a sole proprietorship has operated profitably for a while, the individual owner must seriously consider incorporating his business. While incorporating a business is more complex and costly than starting a sole proprietorship, it protects the business owner and his family from lawsuits and other business liabilities. Also, many financing opportunities are available to corporations that are not available to sole proprietorships. And, in these days of tight credit availability, that is an extremely important consideration.

II. General Partnerships - General partnerships must have two or more partners who are all responsible for all the business activities. The partners share assets and liabilities, profits and losses, and are presumed to be jointly responsible for all the operations of the business.

ADVANTAGES OF A GENERAL PARTNERSHIP:

1.   All of the partners in general partnership avoid double taxation because the partnership is not taxed as a business entity. Each partner includes pro-rata business income and losses as on their individual income tax returns.

2.   You can raise capital more quickly in a General Partnership, as compared to other types of businesses.

3. In a general partnership, an unlimited number of general partners can combine their resources, knowledge and expertise to benefit the business operation.

DISADVANTAGES OF A GENERAL PARTNERSHIP:

1. **CAUTION: The chief disadvantage of operating your business as a general partnership is that you not only have unlimited business and personal liability for anything that you do in the business, you also have unlimited liability for any of the business actions of the rest of the general partners. In a general partnership, all of the partners are jointly and severally liable for the actions of any or all of the partners. This means that all of your business and personal assets are at risk for any business action that is undertaken or, if required to be completed, not completed by you and your partners.**

2. Your partners may have different expectations or goals for the business, leading to personal disputes among the partners.

3. Partners may not share equally in the amount of time and capital resources contributed to the business enterprise

4. It may be difficult to attract new general partners representing additional capital.

Recommendation: Because of the fact that you can be held liable for the acts of any of the partners, jointly and severally, I would highly recommend that you stay away from general partnerships. However, if you absolutely have to become a partner in a general partnership, you should engage a lawyer to draw up a general partnership agreement. The agreement should cover at minimum the death, disability, or withdrawal of a partner, sale of a partnership interest, buy/sell agreements among the partners, designation of the managing partners, dissolution of the partnership, capital contribution requirements, profit and loss sharing percentages, timing requirements for financial statements, audits, and tax returns to be filed, a designated partner for tax matters, a designated CPA firm to do the tax returns and perform the audits, and anything else that you or your attorney determine that should be included in the general partnership agreement. Once the agreement has been finalized, ensure that all of the general partners have signed and dated the document and had their signatures notarized for recording. Then, instruct your attorney to have the document recorded in your local jurisdiction, most likely the county containing the partnership's legal address. The general partnership agreement is your only protection as a partner in general partnership. Consequently it is extremely important to ensure that the document is carefully crafted, is comprehensive and protects your interests as a general partner.

III. A Limited Partnership (LP) – A Limited Partnership is a type of business organization with at least one or more managing general partners who have unlimited liability with regard to the operations of the business, and one or more limited partners, whose liability is strictly limited to the amount of their investment, even though they can participate in partnership profits.

Note: There is one important exception to this general rule. If a limited partner acts in the capacity of a general partner, they become a general partner because of their management activity.

ADVANTAGES OF A LIMITED PARTNERSHIP

1. Its a lot easier to raise capital in a limited partnership, since the limited partners (investors) liability is limited to the capital they have invested in the business.

2. General partners of the limited partnership are free to run the business without the interference of the limited partners.

3. Limited partners can come and go without having to dissolve the limited partnership.

DISADVANTAGES OF A LIMITED PARTNERSHIP

1. **Caution: General partners of a Limited Partnership have the same personal liability as if they were partners in a general partnership. (See the general partnership caution above for more details). In addition, the general partners have a high degree of fiduciary responsibility to the limited partners. This can become a legal minefield in the event that one or more of the limited partners decide to bring suit against the general partners.**

2. Since the limited partnership type of business organization has been abused in the past, there are many state and federal requirements that do not apply to other types of organizations.

Recommendation: The general partners of a Limited Partnership have the same liability issues as they would in a general partnership. In addition, they face potential legal action relating to their management activity from the limited partners.   Therefore, I would strongly recommend consideration of an LLC (Limited Liability Company) that better protects all of the LLC members without giving up all the advantages of a Limited Partnership.

IV. A Limited Liability Partnership (LLP) - A limited liability partnership, or LLP, is a fairly new type of business entity. It shares many of the characteristics of a limited partnership, but gives each member of the LLP an equal voice in managing the business, as in a general partnership. Unlike a general partnership, an LLP protects members from personal liability. However, their investment in the LLP is entirely at risk.

ADVANTAGES OF A LIMITED LIABILITY PARTNERSHIP

1. Profits and losses of the LLP are passed through directly to the partners. Therefore, there is no "double taxation" of partnership income.

2. Generally speaking, a Limited Liability Partner actually has limited liability. The LLP partners are only personally liable for their own negligence or that of an employee working under their direct supervision. The LLP partner is not personally liable for the negligence of anyone else involved in the LLP.

DISADVANTAGES OF A LIMITED LIABILITY PARTNERSHIP

1. Individual partners in an LLP can bind the partnership to written, and to the extent of state law, oral business agreements without the consent of the other partners.

2. Money and property contributed to the LLP by the partner is owned by the partnership unless stated otherwise in writing, and the partner is not entitled to its return or remuneration unless it is specifically covered in the partnership agreements.

3. LLPs are not recognized in every state, and the transfer of ownership can be a nightmare of legal complexities

Recommendation: If you are considering the formation of an LLP, why not step up to a Limited Liability Corporation (LLC). It has most of the advantages of an LLP, and none of the disadvantages.

V. "C" Corporations - The most common corporation is a "C" corporation or general corporation. C corporations may have an unlimited number of stockholders. A "C" Corporation structure is generally chosen by companies that plan to have over 30 stockholders, that have no need for any kind of specialized type of organizational structure, or plan on having a public stock offering at some time in the future.

ADVANTAGES OF C CORPORATIONS

1. There is less risk of an IRS audit, compared with a sole proprietorship.

2. There is substantially limited personal liability for business debts and legal suits.

3. You can deduct the cost of your benefits as a business expense.

4. There is no limit to the number of shareholders C corporations can have.

5. C corporations can raise additional funds through the sale of stock.

6. The shareholders of a C corporation don't have to be U.S. citizens or permanent residents.

7. C corporations use their own cash to pay any taxes on the corporation's profits.

8. C corporation owners do not have to pay individual taxes on profits unless the corporation pays a cash dividend to the owners.

9. A significant small business tax advantage is that with C corporation taxation, the first $100,000 in corporate income is taxed at preferential corporate tax rates that are generally lower than the tax rates assessed on the individual owners of an LLC.

DISADVANTAGES OF C CORPORATIONS

1. C corporations potentially can face "double taxation" as they pay income tax based on corporate taxable income, and the shareholders have to report distributions of dividends as taxable income on their individual tax returns.

VI. "S" Corporations - S corporations are simply regular C corporations or limited liability corporations (LLCs) that have elected Subchapter S Corporation (S Corp) status by filing Form 2553 with the IRS. In order to qualify for S corporation status, there must be: 1) less than 75 shareholders, 2) the shareholders must be individuals, estates or certain qualified trusts, who consent in writing to the S corporation election, (3) the shareholders can't be non-resident aliens, and (4) an S corporation can't issue preferred shares of stock with special liquidation, dividend or conversion rights.

ADVANTAGES OF AN S CORPORATION

Electing S corporation status with the IRS enables the corporation to avoid "double taxation" by having S corporation income treated like the income of a partnership or sole proprietorship. The S corporation income is "passed-through" to the shareholders who report the income or loss generated by the S corporation on their individual tax returns.

DISADVANTAGES OF AN S CORPORATION

By electing S corporation status with the IRS, you have limited the corporation with regard to the number and type of shareholders, and the types of securities that the corporation can issue. Almost by definition, you cannot undertake public offering of stock in an S corporation.

VII. A Limited Liability Corporation (LLC) - A Limited Liability Company (LLC) is basically a combination of a partnership and a corporation. An LLC combines the tax advantages and management flexibility of a partnership with the liability protection of a corporation. Forming an LLC has become a popular alternative for sole proprietors and partnerships that have thought about forming a corporation in order to protect their personal assets. LLCs also avoid "double taxation" because the income of the LLC itself is not taxed at the company level. Instead, taxes on profits and deductions of losses are computed at the individual level on the personal tax return of each LLC member (owner).

Note: LLC owners can elect to have the IRS tax the LLC as a sole proprietorship, partnership, C Corporation, or S Corporation. Owners make this election with the IRS after the company is formed in the state of incorporation.

ADVANTAGES OF AN LLC

1. The chief advantage of a Limited liability Corporation is exactly what the name of the corporation implies. The owners (called 'members') of an LLC have limited liability for business debts or legal suits. If the LLC is properly structured and managed, each owner's personal assets will be protected from lawsuits and judgments against the business, so each owner's liability is limited to the amount each has invested in the company.

2. LLCs avoid corporate "double taxation" because the income of the LLC is not taxed at the company level. Instead, The LLC income or losses are "passed-through" to the members (owners), who report the income or loss generated by the LLC on their individual tax returns.

3. Owners of a Subchapter S Corporation ('S Corp') are required to be citizens or permanent residents of the United States. There is no such requirement for a general, or 'C,' corporation or for an LLC, unless that LLC elects S corporation status with the IRS.

4. Normal business expenses such as an owner's salary and benefits are qualified deductions for an LLC, before the income is allocated to the owners for tax purposes.

5. An LLC, like an LLP, has unlimited flexibility in the allocation of profits and losses to its ownership interests, ("member interests").

Therefore, the owners of an LLC are free to allocate the company's profits and losses however they see fit.

6. LLCs are a recognized business structure in all 50 states and the District of Columbia.

DISADVANTAGES OF AN LLC

1. Although some states allow single member Limited Liability Companies (LLCs), the LLC must have at least two members to elect partnership classification for federal tax purposes.

2. LLC earnings are generally subject to self-employment tax.

3. State law may limit the life of the Limited Liability Company.

4. As a partnership, if 50% or more of the capital and profit interests are sold or exchanged within a 12-month period, the Limited Liability Company (LLC) will be terminated for federal tax purposes.

5. Limited Liability Companies (LLCs) can't take advantage of incentive stock options, engage in tax-free reorganizations, or issue Section 1244 stock.

6. LLC businesses that operate in more than one state may not receive the same tax treatment from state to state. Some states don't tax partnerships, but they do tax Limited Liability Companies.

7. Conversion of an existing business to a Limited Liability Company (LLC) may trigger unwanted recognition of gain for tax purposes on the appreciated assets of the existing business.

SUMMARY AND RECOMMENDATION

Unless you have a specific and overriding reason to form an LLC, I would recommend that you organize as a regular "C" Corporation. This gives you the ultimate flexibility as to how you can organize and capitalize your business. If you want to avoid corporate "double taxation of dividends" or pass on a net loss to your shareholders, you can always elect Subchapter S status if you qualify, by filing Form 2553 with the IRS after you have formed your corporation.

CHAPTER 3

ORGANIZING YOUR COMPANY FOR MAXIMUM PROFITS

In this chapter, we will do more than simply provide you with a sample small business organization chart. It is critically important to structure your organization so that your managers are not stepping on each other's toes. In an unstructured organization, you are never sure who is responsible for what. Consequently your managers will waste a lot of time and energy waging turf wars over extending their authority and spreading gossip. In this kind of an organization, your managers are not focused on the overall corporate goals and objectives. In fact, they may not even know what the corporate goals and objectives are, let alone how their department can assist the company in achieving those goals. It is much more profitable for you as the owner, president or general manager of a small business to properly define your organization so that turf wars, gossip and idle chit-chat are kept to an absolute minimum. Therefore, your management team needs to know what each individual manager is responsible for and who they report to regarding their duties and responsibilities. This means that you as president and general manager must have a list of duties and responsibilities for yourself and for each manager reporting to you. Assuming that you have a comprehensive list of duties and responsibilities, you need to create a position description for each of your managers.

A TIME-SAVING IDEA - Assign your managers the task of writing their own job descriptions. Tell them to make those job descriptions as comprehensive as possible. Also, let them know that you will be comparing their job descriptions with your own detailed listing of duties and responsibilities for each manager. You will find out in short order how much they know about the tasks they should be performing. You'll also find that your detailed list needs to be updated with other managerial tasks that are currently being performed. Compare these job descriptions to look for duplication of duties, tasks that should be performed by another manager, tasks that need not be performed, and tasks that are not being performed by any manager. Once you have completed the comparison, it's time to sit with each of the managers, and complete their job description. Have your managers sign their job description to signify that they are in agreement with the duties and responsibilities that you have jointly listed. Keep your managers job descriptions in a desk file, have a copy placed in their personnel file, and give them each a copy for their own records. The value of this action will become apparent when you have your first performance review with your managers.

Once your managers have completed the process of creating their own job descriptions, have them assign the same task to their team members. Continue the process down the organizational chart until all of your employees have job descriptions. Make it crystal clear to your employees that in a small company it is virtually impossible to list all of their tasks in a job description. Therefore they should understand that there is an additional undefined task for every manager and employee in your company. So that there is no misunderstanding, put the following wording into the job description ("and whatever else you're asked to do or that needs to be done").

HOW TO STRUCTURE YOUR ORGANIZATION

There are many different organization chart formats that can apply to a small company structure. The format that is best for you will depend upon your industry, the goods and services that your company supplies to your industry, and the overall size of your company within that industry. I have presented a typical small-company organization chart below. It is by no means comprehensive, but it does give you an idea of what a top down small company organization chart might look like.

A TYPICAL SMALL COMPANY TOP DOWN ORGANIZATION CHART

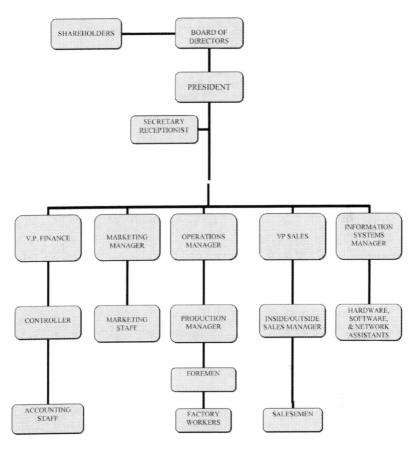

SUMMARY RECOMMENDATION

I highly recommend a top-down organizational structure for small businesses. This structure should be based on function, with all of the functional top level managers reporting directly to the President. In the preceding organization chart, that includes the VP Finance, Marketing Manager, Production Manager, Sales Manager, and the Information Systems Manager. All second line managers and supervisors reporting to these managers should have job descriptions that are functionally related to the overall job descriptions of the first line managers.

CHAPTER 4

BUILDING YOUR MANAGEMENT TEAM

GENERAL MANAGEMENT QUALIFICATIONS FOR SMALL BUSINESS MANAGERS

In a large business enterprise, the management team has an army of specialists reporting to them. However, in a small business, there is no doubt that a key manager must not only be a specialist in his area of expertise, but a generalist capable of managing other related areas. As an example, let's compare the responsibilities of Controller or CFO in a large and small company regarding taxation. In a large multinational US company you may have a tax department comprised of several divisions. One of these would be US federal taxes, another would be US state taxes, a third might be Canadian and provincial taxes, and a fourth might be International Taxation, having subdivisions by country. For a large company, this list of divisions is by no means comprehensive. However, in a small company, taxation is simply one of the many tasks that the controller or CFO is burdened with. Also, there is no in-house expertise that he can rely upon to assist in the performance of this important task. This is why I have always been amused and sometimes irritated by the search firm that first advertised on behalf of a small business for a corporate controller. The advertisement always included the requirement "and with Big 8 (the 8 largest CPA firms) Experience." By the way, this advertisement was copied by many other search firms over the past 30 or 40 years. But what does "Big 8 Experience" mean when you're hiring a CFO or controller for a small business? We can assume that a CPA who has worked for a large public accounting firm has the following professional credentials and experience:

1. External audit knowledge
2. Internal audit knowledge
3. General US tax knowledge
4. General accounting knowledge
5. Some industry knowledge related to those businesses in industries that the CPA has audited.

Now let's take a look at the additional areas of financial management expertise that might be required of the CFO or controller in a small business environment.

1. Business experience related to your company
2. Tax knowledge specific to your company
3. Cash management expertise
4. Treasury management expertise
5. Human Resources expertise
6. Pension and profit sharing expertise
7. Employee benefits knowledge
8. Experience dealing with unions
9. Experience in dealing with legal matters
10. Regulatory and compliance expertise in that industry
11. General corporate management expertise
12. Management information systems expertise
13. Computer hardware, software and networking expertise
14. Telephones and telecommunications expertise
15. Corporate Secretarial experience
16. Business short-term and long-term strategic planning experience
17. Experience in purchasing the various insurance coverages required by the company
18. The ability to work effectively with a closely held shareholder or family group
19. A creative approach to business that allows the candidate to "think outside the box"

Of course, a CFO or Controller candidate for your company will probably not possess all of these qualifications or experience. However, as most of this expertise is needed in a small company, it is critical that the President, the Board of Directors, and the owners make an enlightened evaluation of the members of the management team that they are recruiting in light of the additional criteria outlined above.

Other more general considerations concerning the education level and experience of any of your managerial candidates might include the following:

1. Do the candidates have any formal education in the management of a business? (BS (Bus) degree, an MBA, or some equivalent amount of formal training and education.)

2. Do the candidates have any other specific formal education regarding the overall management of their respective departments?

3. What level of actual management experience do the candidates possess in a general management capacity, or management experience specific to the company and their job descriptions?

I have found that all too often little or no attention is paid to the professional qualifications of managers in a small business, with the possible exception of the CFO/Controllership position.

SUMMARY

The objective here is to have an overall approach to hiring a professional, experienced and well rounded management team that will significantly contribute to the overall success of your business. With that objective in mind, read my next Chapter on "HIRING THE BEST MANAGERS".

CHAPTER 5

HIRING THE BEST MANAGERS

HIRING THE RIGHT PEOPLE TO BE YOUR MANAGERS

I've learned a few important lessons about hiring managers in my business career over the past thirty-eight years. Hiring the right people to fill your management positions is absolutely critical to the success of your business. And, believe me, it's a jungle out there when it comes to hiring managerial talent. There are several things that you can do to put the odds in your favor. The following suggestions garnered from my own experiences may assist you in making the right hiring decision.

1. Create a detailed job description for the management position that you are seeking before you start your employment search.

2. Examine your organization to determine whether there is an existing employee who has the qualifications and can be promoted to this position. If you can justify this, it is absolutely the best way to go. Promoting from within saves time and money, and can substantially improve employee morale. If you don't believe this works well, just ask Proctor & Gamble, one of our most successful large companies that employ this hiring strategy!

3. Use your job description to place a well-crafted employment advertisement in the nearest newspaper with good circulation to attract potential candidates. The best day to run your ad for this purpose is usually a Sunday morning edition of the newspaper. If you have not yet terminated the current manager,

ask your newspaper classified representative to run a numbered box ad that requests a resume from the applicant and does not divulge the company name.

4. Today, the Internet is an excellent source of information about potential applicants for managerial positions. For managerial positions paying over $100,000, there is a free listing for employers at TheLadders.com. For lesser paid positions requiring a listing fee, Monster.com and CareerBuilder.com are recommended. And don't rule out a free listing on Craigslist.com for non-managerial positions.

5. If at all possible, let your management employees and others who may be able to assist in locating a potential candidate know that you are conducting an executive search.

6. Executive employment agencies, generally speaking, do not have your best interests at heart. Stay away from them if you can. Most of these agencies are simply interested in making a match where none exists, and collecting a rather large fee for their meager services. Agency fees vary from about 20% to as much as 35% or more of the first year salary for the management position that you are hiring. Generally, the agencies want all of their fees paid up front on the employee's hire date. To secure that commission, when it suits their interest they will sometimes manipulate, conceal and even at times fabricate the truth about the candidate's background, qualifications and references. This kind of representation is not in your best interests as an employer, and it is really not in the candidate's best interest if they are truly looking for a long-term employment situation.

7. If you have to use a search firm or an executive employment agency to find a suitable management candidate, be aware that the commissions, the guarantees of candidate suitability, the length of any guarantees, and the deadline for payment of any fees or commissions are all negotiable items. Remember that you are the customer, and if they want your business you are in the driver's seat and you can dictate the terms accordingly.

8. You can almost count on the fact that little or no technical testing has been done by the average search firm or agency.

9. You can also count on the fact that the background and reference checks have only been done on a cursory basis. In some cases, not all of the references have even been contacted.

10. So what's it all mean to you as an employer? You must be prepared to do your own technical or other testing. You will also have to verify employment history and education credentials, check DMV and criminal records, and do your own reference checking. These items must be completed by your company before you hire the candidate. It makes no difference whether you have located the candidate on your own or you have utilized a search firm or agency to identify candidates on your behalf.

11. If you currently have a relationship with a firm that does background checks, have them check and verify Social Security numbers, driver's license and criminal records, education credentials listed by the candidate, credit information and other matters of public record. In one situation, we were lucky enough to have a company that was affiliated with our workman's compensation provider, who could offer all of these services to us free of charge or at a substantial discount.

12. Ensure that you do the reference checking yourself. You'll be amazed at the information you can develop by having an open-ended conversation with the listed references.

13. Have the candidates come to your office for a preliminary interview. The candidates should bring with them a resume and a list of references.

14. Have the candidate complete your company's Application for Employment Form before starting the interview. This will give you an opportunity to review the Form along with the resume before you begin the interview.

15. After the initial interview process, if you think there is a possibility of hiring this candidate, you can have them sit for any technical or other exams that you require the candidate to take. At the same time, you can ask the candidate for a list of references if you don't already have a copy.

16. If you have no interest in the candidate, don't waste any more time in the interview process. Cordially end the interview and let the candidate know that you will be continuing the search process.

17. If you are interested in seeing the candidate again, let the candidate know that you will be back to them in the next several days with a decision to either see them again for a final interview or eliminate them as a candidate.

18. If everything about the candidate checks out well, to include all reference and background checks which normally take several days to complete, review the status of your hiring process. You may have several candidates that look promising. Depending upon the results that you have achieved during the candidate selection process, you can then schedule final interviews.

19. Let the candidates know that the final interview may be lengthy and schedule an appropriate amount of time for that interview. Remember that it is very important to you and your company that you make a good hiring decision. Don't let anyone or anything rush this process.

EXAMPLES OF PROBLEM CANDIDATES THAT WERE NOT HIRED

In one situation, a managerial candidate was presented to a prospective employer by an employment agency. Initially, based upon the information presented to the employer by the agency, the candidate appeared to be a potential hire. Supposedly, all of his background and reference information had been checked by the agency. However, the candidate appeared to be quite nervous during the interview, even though the company personnel conducting the interview had done everything they could to put the candidate at ease. After the interview, by thoroughly checking the candidate's references, the company discovered a number of undesirable things to include potential fraud, which would eliminate the candidate from consideration. In fact, the escapades of this candidate could have filled a small book that might have made it on the bestseller list!

In another situation, a company located a job candidate for an accounting supervisor position through its own advertising. The candidate had completed a significant number of college accounting courses and had stated that her goal was to become a CPA. So far, so good! After having the candidate complete an accounting and bookkeeping test, the results were so poor that it was hard to believe that the candidate had taken any accounting courses at all! Then, to add insult to injury, the candidate wanted to argue about the validity of the test that she had failed. Obviously, this individual was not hired! This example shows the importance of testing to determine the knowledge level of the candidate that you have under consideration for a managerial position.

CONSIDER USING A "TEAM INTERVIEW" TO HELP ASSESS YOUR CANDIDATES

Basically, a "team interview" is an interview requiring the participation of more than one company employee. When you get to the level of four or five company participants, it is also called a "panel interview". For small companies, I would recommend an interview team of three managers at the most. However, one of the team members must be designated as the manager in control of the interview process. This team member will normally be the manager that the candidate will be reporting to. It will be the responsibility of the interview team manager to keep the interview process on track and on time.

How to Conduct a Team Interview – The following suggestions will assist you in conducting your team interviews:

1. Obviously, you will want to pre-qualify your candidate prior to the team interview. Otherwise you will be wasting a lot of valuable management time.

2. Have the team members develop several specific questions for the candidate from their perspectives. They should also develop several general questions that will open up a two way conversation with the candidate. The interview manager should prepare an initial general question that will act as an "icebreaker" and get the interview off to a good start.

3. The interview manager should make a selection of the questions to be asked, and establish the general order of those questions. This will help the interview move along in a general format that encourages the candidate to talk.

4. The interview manager should insure that the focused nature of the questions does not stifle the purpose of the interview, which is to get the candidates talking about themselves.

5. Encourage interview team participants to take notes during the interview.

6. The interview manager who is probably the hiring manager should let the candidate know that the interview is a team interview. The candidate should also be given the names and titles of the team members.

7. The interview manager should insure that an inordinate amount of stressful questioning is not intimidating the candidate. After all, you may want to hire this candidate! You want to have the candidate leave with a good impression of your company, whether they are hired or not.

8. The interview manager should convene a short meeting after the interview to assess the results of the interview and come up with a consensus view of the candidate.

The Benefits of a Team Interview - When a team interview is executed properly, it will accomplish several things for your candidate selection process, as follows:

1. A team interview will, by its nature, develop additional information about the candidate, prompted by more varied questions from the team members.

2. The team interview will place more stress on the candidate, and allow you to observe the reactions of the candidate to stressful situations.

3. The team interview can save time if the candidate would have to be seen by two or three management employees.

4. The team interview allows the company to view the candidate from several different perspectives, contributing to a more informed and better hiring decision.

5. A team interview tends to narrow the focus of the interview on the candidate.

Considering all of the positives and negatives of team interviewing, you can gain important additional insights about the candidate utilizing this process. You will also get a preview of the candidate's reactions to the other team members, and their reactions to the candidate that may affect your hiring decision.

A Personal Experience Regarding Team Interviewing – When I left the Air Force as a Captain in 1970, I interviewed with and was hired by Ross Perot's company, Electronic Data Systems (EDS). As a candidate, I was introduced to the EDS team interview process. Believe me, it was a tough interview. At the time, EDS used the "skeet shooting" approach to team interviewing and I was the target! While it irritated me at the time, that interview provided EDS with a lot of information about my character and fortitude. They needed that information, because the position I was being recruited for was a very demanding one. This experience introduced me to the team interview process, and I have been a proponent of it, with some modifications, ever since.

THE INTERVIEW PROCESS – GET THEM TALKING!

In my experience, the biggest mistakes made by management in the interview process are as follows:

1. **Not allowing enough time for the interview** – If the interview time is too short, there is no way that you will be able to find out enough information about the candidate to make an intelligent hiring decision. Assuming that you have pre-qualified the candidate, you should schedule at least one hour or more for the final interview.

2. **Not allowing the candidates to give you enough information about themselves** – You need to hear directly from the candidates about their experience, work ethic, judgment, and initiative, past job-related problems, corporate culture, and compensation requirements.

3. **Not having a planned approach to the interview** - During the final interview, you should have questions ready that will make the interview open-ended. Your purpose is to encourage as much discussion as is legally permissible. The things you find out during this interview will sometimes amaze you. You may find that the candidate doesn't really like the job you are hiring them to do, or perhaps the candidate has a plan to move out of state, or to change their career path in the near future. But believe me, you'll find out nothing of the sort if you simply conduct a perfunctory interview.

4. **Not observing legal requirements regarding the questions that may be asked during the interview** - There are legal restraints concerning age discrimination, sexual orientation, physical disabilities, family status and other hot button items. Stay away from any discussion of these items, unless the prospective candidate volunteers the information. After

hearing what they have to say, tell them that these are not your candidate selection criteria items, and should not be discussed further during the interview.

What questions can we use to get the job candidates talking about themselves that are not off limits? – With the resume of the candidate on my desk, I have used the following open-ended questions to encourage the candidates to respond without time limitations.

1. **Ask the candidates about their work history** – What were your duties and responsibilities in your last position? Did you like your job? What part of your functions did you like the best, and which did you dislike the most? Have the candidate repeat this process for at least the prior 2 positions. At the same time, you can be checking the candidate's resume for any gaps or inaccuracies in their responses.

2. **Ask the candidates what they know or have found out about your company** – This will tell you how much research they have done about the company and it relates directly to their initiative and motivation.

3. **Ask the candidates about the average number of hours per week they worked in their last positions** – You can also ask whether they liked the weekly hours worked in their previous positions and what average work time they have anticipated in this position. This will give you a good idea of the candidate's contribution and work ethic.

4. **Ask the candidates to tell you what they would do with the money and with their careers if they won $1,000,000 tax free in a state lottery** – This will tell you a lot about the judgment of the candidate and their real feelings about their careers.

5. **Ask the candidate to tell you about their greatest accomplishments and their greatest failures in a business environment** – You will learn a lot about the scope of the

candidate's responsibilities by the way this question is answered.

6. **Now ask the candidate to talk about their greatest strengths and weaknesses** – There should be some correlation in their answer to the question above, and you will learn more about the candidate's candor in answering this question. Beware of candidates who have expressed no weaknesses. Either they are blind to them or they are covering them up.

7. **Ask the candidate why they applied for this position** –Does their response suit your company's needs, or are you simply going to be a way station on their career path?

8. **Finally ask the candidate where they expect to be in your company after 5 or 10 years** - Are their career goals at your company realistic or are they "over the top". If so, you may not be looking at a long term employee.

A POST INTERVIEW CHECKLIST - THINGS YOU SHOULD YOU DO AFTER HIRING A CANDIDATE

1. If you require drug testing, ensure that the candidate knows that, as part of the hiring process, he or she must pass a drug test before actually starting work.

2. Have the candidate complete and sign all the necessary forms to do any additional background checks. These can be DMV and criminal record investigations, Workers Compensation claims records, credit checks and any other investigations that are required for managerial position candidates.

3. Let the candidate know in writing that these checks and investigations must be completed to the satisfaction of the company as a requirement for continued employment.

4. Also, inform the candidates that any intentional falsification of the information provided by the candidate in their job application, resume, references or other information provided

by them to the company, will result in the termination of their employment.

5. Ensure that the candidates understand that they are "at will" employees. Make it crystal clear that there is a probationary period which is typically 90 days. During that period they can be terminated for any reason. After the 90 day probationary period, there is no guarantee of any future employment with your company beyond the next paycheck.

6. Have your new managers sign for your Employee Handbook, indicating that they have read and understood its contents.

7. Welcome new managers to your organization! Distribute a memo to all staff officially notifying them of the new management hires along with some of their background information. Personally escort your new managers around your organization and introduce them to the other managers and employees. Arrange a facilities tour for your new managers. Have an informal meeting with the new managers' departments to introduce them and to show your support for them.

8. Create a press release for your local newspaper with background information about the new manager. There is nothing like getting "free advertising" for your company, and it makes the new manager feel important to you and your organization.

9. Discuss with your new managers all of the elements of their job description. Have them initial two copies: one copy for the personnel file, and one copy for your desk file.

10. Utilize the job description to conduct their 90 day probationary period review and regular reviews thereafter. Put the new employee on notice as to exactly where they stand. If they are not performing up to your standards, let them know in writing what their deficiencies are and what they need to do to improve their performance.

11. The 90 day probationary period is not cast in stone! If it makes sense to both parties, the new employee's 90 day probationary period can be extended for a reasonable amount of time thereafter. After the completion of the unsatisfactory 90 day review, inform the employee in writing about the reason for the extended probationary period, what the employee must do to improve their performance, and the date that the extended probationary period will end.

12. If any bonus or incentive programs have been extended to the employee, discuss those programs with the employee and why they may have failed to qualify for the programs.

THE EMPLOYEE HANDBOOK - YOUR GUIDELINE TO SUCCESSFUL EMPLOYEE RELATIONS

Every business should have a well crafted employee handbook that establishes the "rules of conduct" for your employees. A good employee handbook should have at least the following information:

A   A welcome letter signed by your company president. This makes the employee handbook a personal invitation for your employees to follow the guidelines set forth within the handbook.

B   A general business biography and mission statement for your employee to read and reference.

C   General contact information for your business and hours of operation.

D   Common sense business rules to include at minimum:
  1) Time and Attendance Policy.
  2) Zero Tolerance Policy for employee theft.
  3) A statement regarding your Drug and Alcohol Policy.
  4) Your company's appearance standards.
  5) Information about payroll requirements and scheduling.
  6) Your Americans With Disabilities (ADA) Policy.
  7) Your company's Non-discrimination Policy

8) Your probationary period, typically the first 90 days.
9) A statement regarding at-will employment.
10) Your company's Sexual Harassment Policy.

An informational page describing your company benefits, eligibility requirements and how to apply for those benefits.

Have your staff review the handbook and job descriptions with your new employees and have them sign a receipt for both items, along with other new employee information. **Also, have your attorney review your employee handbook for legal compliance annually.**

SUMMARY

As you can see from reading this chapter, you are not relieved of your responsibility to do your own due diligence when hiring a manager. Take anything said about the candidate by a recruiter with the proverbial grain of salt! They serve their own interests best, which is to generate a commission for themselves. If the candidate is applying for a professional position, don't hesitate to have them sit for a test of knowledge in their area of expertise. They must pass that test in order to merit further consideration. Have the resume of the candidate verified by personnel, with particular emphasis on their work background and educational achievements. You should personally check for yourself by telephone the references given by a candidate who will be reporting to you. Don't hesitate to ask the references to talk in general terms about the candidate. You will be amazed at the information that will be volunteered by references given the right prompting! Treat the interview process as a key, critical element in your hiring decision. Do whatever it takes to get the candidates talking about themselves! If you adopt most of these suggestions, you will be significantly ahead of the competition in hiring and retaining the right kind of managers.

CHAPTER 6

TERMINATING
UNDERPERFORMING MANAGERS

You might ask why the subject of hiring and firing managers is discussed in adjoining chapters. These tasks are opposing bookends that, if performed properly, work together to accomplish the same objective. That objective is to have the best management team working for you that you possibly can. Believe me, no matter how careful you are in the hiring process, you will end up hiring candidates that will not perform up to your standards and will have to be replaced. My own success rate in hiring is one outstanding long-term employee resulting from three candidates hired into the company. The problem here is that most managers have no problem in quickly hiring candidates for their open positions without a thorough review of the candidate. However, most of the same managers have significant problems when it comes to terminating one of their managers or employees. And, a fair percentage of those managers who have the intestinal fortitude to terminate their employees when necessary, don't know how to do it properly. Terminating an employee is one of the toughest things that you have to do in business. Also, unless you enjoy that kind of thing, it is extremely stressful for both the manager and the employee. With that in mind, I offer you the following suggestions that may assist you in the unpopular but necessary task of firing or terminating your managers or employees.

1. In the case of poor performance, the employee should have been given in writing at least one opportunity to improve their performance as part of an overall review.

2. In the case of theft, lying or other outrageous behavior, the employee should be dismissed as soon as practical after a thorough investigation has been documented and completed.

3. All dismissals, firings or terminations should be discussed with the president and the affected managers before making a final decision.

4. Once the decision to terminate employment has been finalized, you should contact your company attorney and review your termination procedures as applied to this situation.

5. Steps should be undertaken to replace the terminated employee immediately after the date of termination, if possible.

6. You should prepare for the termination meeting in advance, by knowing what you are going to say and how to say it.

7. You should have pertinent documentation available at the termination meeting, such as employee job descriptions, employee performance reviews, written warning letters and other written communication that the employee has already received copies of.

8. Schedule the termination meeting at the end of the business day. I have found that the best day and time for scheduling a termination is Friday after 5:00 p.m.

9. In no case should you allow the employee to have access to their employee file.

10. You should have another individual present at the termination meeting such as the individual's manager or a personnel representative. If you are a male terminating a female employee, try to ensure that the other company representative at the termination meeting is a female.

11. If the employee requests the reasons for their dismissal, and you have been advised by your attorney that there is no problem

in discussing those reasons, tell the employee the reasons for their termination honestly, directly and without rancor.

12. Have a listing available of the company property that must be returned by the employee. This might include such items as company vehicles, office, desk and door keys, company credit cards, cell phones, uniforms and any other company property assigned to that employee.

13. Allow any employees being terminated sufficient time to remove their personal property. If this cannot be done immediately, schedule a time for this to be done after business hours or on the weekend with a designated employee there to monitor the removal of any personal property.

14. The manager in charge of the termination and any other company representatives attending should compile notes regarding the termination meeting and date and sign them.

15. Management should verbally communicate the fact that the manager or employee has left the company to all of the managers and employees who need to know.

16. Management should avoid at all costs making any defamatory statements about the employee who has been discharged either inside or outside of the company.

TWO EXAMPLES OF STRESSFUL TERMINATION MEETINGS

In one situation, an individual had engaged in credit card fraud. The evidence was clear and convincing. A morning termination meeting was arranged to complete the termination process. The meeting was attended by two company representatives. The employee finally admitted to engaging in fraud. Then the employee became quite emotional with fits of crying bordering on hysteria. The employee begged and pleaded to be able to keep their job. The employee was offered a ride home, as it did not appear that this individual was capable of driving safely, given the emotional state that was being displayed. Finally, after another 30 minutes of this kind of hysterical display, the employee decided to go to their car and drive off the premises. This kind of termination presents a formidable challenge to the management participants. Given the emotion of the situation, it is tempting to take the easy way out and offer the employee continued employment on a probationary basis. But the best thing to do is to stick to your guns and quickly terminate any employee who has already committed fraud.

In another situation, there was considerable animosity between an employee and his manager. The employee threatened the manager with bodily harm, and admitted that to the company representatives investigating the incident. Consequently, the employee was dismissed but not before making more threats of physical violence against the manager. The manager had to be hidden in a safe place while the employee was walked to his vehicle and was observed driving off the premises. This timely action avoided what could have been a serious physical confrontation.

SUMMARY

Even though employee terminations are difficult for managers and employees to endure, when you have made up your mind to terminate a manager or employee, and you have located a suitable replacement, be like Nike. Just do it, but do it the right way!

CHAPTER 7

MANAGING THROUGH YOUR BOARD OF DIRECTORS

What a novel idea! In too many small businesses, the Board of Directors is a Board that only exists on paper. These "Paper Boards" are lucky if they hold a meeting once a year. And when they meet, they are simply doing the perfunctory housekeeping items that must be done to keep the corporation active from a legal standpoint. In an organization like that, typically nothing of substance is approved by the Board in advance or even contemporaneously with the transaction. Just about everything is approved by the board after the fact, and in many cases the approvals of actions taken during the year come after the year-end. These ex post facto "Board" approvals simply provide cover for actions already taken. Yes, we know that you may own all or a substantial part of the company, but operating a corporation in this fashion will eventually present you with serious problems. So why not take a little more time, avoid the problems, and use your Board of Directors to assist in the management of your company.

HOW TO START MANAGING THROUGH YOUR BOARD OF DIRECTORS

1. **After you have completed your business plan**, inform your management and staff that you will be holding your Board of Directors meetings once every calendar or fiscal year quarter at a specific time, location and date approximately 3 weeks after the end of each quarter.

2. This should give you and your staff plenty of time to complete and analyze the quarterly financials and compare those with your budgets and forecasts.

3. All of your corporate objectives which have been assigned to a manager or an officer, including the president should be analyzed at the end of each quarter and graded for completeness, quality of work, creativity and adherence to budget. (There is nothing like leading from the front!),

4. All officers and managers responsible for the achievement of your corporate objectives should be in attendance at the meeting to report on the success or lack of success in meeting these corporate objectives.

5. The meeting should start with a review of any old unfinished business. If possible, a summary action plan should be created at the meeting to assign responsibilities and complete any unfinished business. If that is not possible, a follow-on meeting should be scheduled with the participants who are involved with the unfinished business, for the express purpose of creating a detailed action plan to complete this business.

6. The president should then give a summary of the company's financial results for the quarter, along with an explanation for any substantial deviation from the financial plan.

7. The department managers should then be called upon to give a detailed analysis of their department's actual performance, compared with the departmental financial projections for the quarter. Any substantial positive or negative variations should be given a satisfactory explanation. This should apply to all officers and managers involved in the management of the business, whether they are family members or not. All of your managers must understand that you are going to manage this company through the Board of Directors and all managers must and will be held accountable!

8. If there has been significant overall deviation from the quarterly budget and forecast, and it appears that this deviation, whether positive or negative, will continue into the future, I would advise that you amend your financial projections for the upcoming quarters that are going to be affected. After all, it's your budget and forecast! You shouldn't have to be stuck with something that you created months ago, and that you know is inaccurate.

TIP: *Adopt the policy of having a "living budget and forecast". Simply put, this means that your quarterly budget and forecast should change with significant changes in the economic climate in your area and your company's current business conditions.* You, along with your CFO and the rest of your management team, must work together in a collaborative effort to amend your quarterly financial projections for the next 4 quarters. A due date must be assigned for the completion of this project.

9. The department managers should then be called upon to discuss any new business or developments in their department, or that may have an effect upon their department.

10. The president will then have an opportunity to discuss any new business relating to the corporation, how any of the departmental managers will participate in this new business, and submit the new business to the board for its approval.

11. A period of open discussion should be held to encourage participation from all managers. This should encourage managers with any ideas that may generate revenues, reduce expenses, or assist the corporation in other intangible respects to come forward with those ideas.

12. Prior to the close of the quarterly meeting, any other items deemed appropriate to discuss should be brought before the Board.

SUMMARY

Once you begin to manage through your Board of Directors, you will feel the power that you get from being proactive and approving business decisions with the assistance of your Board in advance of their implementation. It is a welcome change from being reactive and always feeling like you're behind the eight ball in everything that you do with your business. **And, once you have tasted the economic rewards of real participative corporate management, you'll never go back to the old way of doing things again.**

SECTION 3

ASSEMBLING YOUR
TEAM OF ADVISORS

CHAPTER 8

CREATING AN OUTSIDE ADVISORY BOARD

WHAT IS AN OUTSIDE ADVISORY BOARD?

An Outside Advisory Board (Advisory Board) is a combination of company management, usually the President and Chief Financial Officer, and outside advisors familiar with the company but not employed by the company. The outside advisors generally include a representative from the company's corporate legal counsel, the company's CPA firm, the company's primary insurance broker, a financial planner representing the ownership interests, and one or two industry executives who have experience in related industries that are not directly in competition with the company. The outside advisors can also include managers with general business experience, start up company experience, growth company experience, advertising and marketing experience, computer networking and telephony experience, and experience raising capital in the financial markets.

HOW DO I CREATE AN ADVISORY BOARD?

1. Start with your corporate attorney firm and discuss the idea with them. Once they understand the concept, you can ask them to draw up a document for your Board of Directors to approve the creation of the Advisory Board.

2. Have your corporate attorney insure that the document indicates that the Advisory Board is in an advisory capacity only, and has no liability for the acts of the company or its Board of Directors.

3. Insure that your list of potential Advisory Board members represents a diversity of business experience that will supplement the experience of your staff. This expertise could include legal, accounting, marketing, financial planning, insurance, computers and networking, start up and growth company experience, and experience in securing equity funding.

4. Select the members that you would like to have on your Advisory Board, and contact those individuals to see if they are willing to serve on that board.

5. Inform your property and casualty broker in writing that you want your Officers and Directors, and Errors and Omissions coverage to be extended to the outside members of your Advisory Board, in the unlikely event that suit is brought against an outside member of the Advisory Board. Insure that a copy of this change in policy coverage is provided to you by your broker.

6. Set a schedule for your Advisory Board meetings, to be held in conjunction with and immediately after your quarterly Board of Directors meetings.

WHAT ARE THE ADVANTAGES OF HAVING AN OUTSIDE ADVISORY BOARD?

1. You are not limited with regard to the kind or amount of expertise that your Advisory Board members possess.

2. You are not limited, except by the practicality of size, in the number of Advisory Board members that you can have.

3. You are the beneficiary of multidisciplinary expertise, yet you are only paying for a few hours of the Advisory Board member's time each quarter.

4. Having all this expertise available to you at one time will save you time and money.

5. You won't have to spend additional time updating your corporate attorney, accountant, insurance broker, financial planner and other professionals who are on your Advisory Board and currently doing business with your company about the your company's current activities.

6. In a number of instances, you will be able to call upon members of your Advisory Board for advice without being "on the clock" for billing purposes. This is a great opportunity for a small business owner to "pick the brains" of the Advisory Board members without being "on the clock" for fee billing purposes!

HOW TO CONDUCT ADVISORY BOARD MEETINGS

1. Schedule your Advisory Board Meetings quarterly, and well in advance of the proposed meeting date, so that you get maximum attendance from your Advisory Board members. The meeting date should be about 21 days after the end of the quarter. Set the meeting time for 9 a.m. to avoid potential conflicts with other time commitments that your Advisory Board members may have.

2. Provide your Advisory Board members with an agenda for both the Board of Directors meeting and the Advisory Board meeting at least 10 business days in advance of the meeting date.

3. Organize your Board of Directors meeting agenda to enable your Advisory Board to be in attendance for the last part of your Board of Directors meeting. This portion should be informational and in summary form, so that you do not waste the time of your Advisory Board members. However, they will still have the availability of all the managers and directors at the meeting in case they have questions.

4. Schedule a general brainstorming session for the purpose of improving the profitability of your business as the last topic on the Advisory Board agenda. You will be amazed at the wealth of good ideas your Advisory Board members can generate.

HOW SHOULD I COMPENSATE MY ADVISORY BOARD?

You will probably have to pay your CPA and your attorney their normal hourly rate for two to three hours of their time. Your insurance broker and financial planner earn commissions from whatever products they sell and will consider their attendance as a cost of doing business. Your other outside Advisory Board members should be compensated much like your attorney and your CPA. The total cost of your quarterly Advisory Board meetings will range from $2,000 to $3,000. Your total annual cost should only be about $10,000 to $15,000.

SUMMARY

I have stated previously that the most substantial managerial difference separating a small company from a large company from a management standpoint is the availability of in-house specialist expertise. Creating an Outside Advisory Board is a great way for a small business to close that gap without having to spend a lot of time and money to do so. After you are able to assess the considerable benefits that your Advisory Board members will provide to you and your company, I am sure you will agree that it's a small price to pay for the needed expertise that you will receive in return!

CHAPTER 9

CHOOSING YOUR
CORPORATE ATTORNEY
AND OTHER ATTORNEY SPECIALISTS

In a small to medium-sized company, the CFO or Controller will have to assume in part the internal role of general corporate counsel. This is because normally, there will be no lawyer on your staff. If the CFO is also a Certified Public Accountant (CPA), that individual will have had some training in and exposure to business law. However, this training is of such a generalized nature that in no way is the CFO equipped to render specific legal advice in place of a qualified lawyer. Therefore it is very important that you establish a good working relationship with an attorney firm that can efficiently and effectively act on your behalf in general corporate matters.

CHOOSING AN ATTORNEY

This is the most important decision you will make to control your legal costs and have a successful relationship with your attorneys, whether they are specialists or general corporate counsel. Here are several factors you may want to consider.

   A. **Industry Experience** - Select an attorney with experience in your industry as your corporate general counsel. You may pay a little more for experience, but if your attorney completes an assignment in half the time and delivers a better product than an attorney with no experience in your industry, a somewhat lower hourly rate is not going to make up the difference.

B. Communication – Choose an attorney that you can talk to and communicate with. You want understandable communication in plain English, not legal jargon.

C. References – Get company references with contact names and telephone numbers from the attorney firms that you are considering, preferably in your industry, and don't be afraid to check them thoroughly.

D. Costs – The following are some cost considerations when selecting your corporate attorney firm. You will want to meet with and receive bids from several firms before you make a final decision.

1) Do you want your corporate attorney firm on a retainer basis or an hourly billing? Unless you have a lot of legal work, I would recommend an hourly rate, with a fixed fee for special legal projects.
2) Will the hourly rate include paralegal assistance and other overhead items, and if not, how will these items be billed?
3) Will the attorney firm submit a bill for payment monthly, will the invoices be current, and will they identify all the costs?
4) Will the attorney firm negotiate a fixed project fee?
5) Will the attorney firm be using novice attorneys (I call them junior G-men) at your expense? Remember that there is no billing credit for your participation in their training. More importantly, your hourly billing will be substantially increased because of their inefficiency. Usually, this is not a big consideration with small attorney firms having only several attorneys.
6) Request that all the items that you have agreed to with your prospective attorney must be included their engagement letter.

E. Attorney Specialists - When you require an attorney who specializes in a specific area of the law, i.e. securities law, hire an experienced securities attorney, not a corporate general counsel. Use the same selection criteria above to make your specialist selection decision.

F.   **Make your attorney a "team member"** – Ask your attorney candidate to be a member of your Outside Advisory Board. If the answer is no, consider engaging another attorney who will serve on your Outside Board.

ATTORNEY SPECIALISTS

There are many instances, as a corporate officer or owner, where you will require specific and professional legal advice from your attorney. These occurrences can be subdivided into two broad areas as follows:

1.   There are general corporate matters that should be addressed by your corporate attorney.

2.   There are legal matters relating to real estate, insurance, pension planning, securities law, personnel matters, bankruptcy, real estate and many others that should be handled by an attorney with a depth of experience who specializes in those areas of the law. You certainly wouldn't want to have the family doctor perform brain surgery on you. Why then would you expect a general corporate attorney to be able to handle an intricate and complex securities matter? You can certainly have your corporate attorney recommend an attorney or an attorney firm that specializes in securities matters, as an example. But even with a good recommendation, you can find yourself embroiled in some very peculiar situations when you deal with attorney firms.

AN EXAMPLE OF AN OUT OF CONTROL ATTORNEY ENGAGEMENT

It's difficult to have to comply with all of the disclosure items that intricate security laws require you to make as part of a public offering of your company stock. To assist us, we had engaged one of the more prestigious legal firms in Los Angeles specializing in securities law. We thought that we were making excellent progress until we reviewed a draft copy of the offering circular. Our lawyers had inserted a number of self-serving statements that basically relieved them of any liability regarding the issuance of the offering. However, the same statements virtually convicted the company's management and directors of engaging in potential securities fraud! We refused to sign the document, and they refused to continue without having the company accept these self-serving statements. Believe it or not, we actually had to hire another securities attorney to represent us with the original securities firm that we had engaged! Because they were then dealing with another securities law firm that they had some respect for, they eliminated these self-serving statements, and finally completed the offering circular. Of course, we did not complete this engagement on time and the cost far exceeded what we had budgeted. Needless to say, I learned a lot from this frustrating experience and did not make the same mistakes again when dealing with specialized legal firms.

NOTE: This is an excellent example of the importance of getting several attorney recommendations from trusted sources and having a personal interview with the primary attorney who will be assigned to your engagement. Determine if the attorney is someone who seems to be reasonable and that you feel can work with. You can then ask for a free estimate of the fixed price for the project and the time required to complete the engagement. If you shop around, you can find the right attorney to complete your engagement on time and at a reasonable price.

SUMMARY

Choosing your attorneys wisely is a critical factor in terms of controlling your legal costs and having a successful relationship with your attorneys, whether they are specialists or general corporate counsel. Ask your corporate counsel to be a member of your Advisory Board. Whenever possible, ask your attorney for a no-charge fixed fee cost estimate for any substantial legal assistance that you require and the estimated time to complete the assignment. If you decide to proceed, have your attorney incorporate everything you've agreed to in an engagement letter before beginning the engagement, to avoid any potential misunderstandings.

CHAPTER 10

ARBITRATION – THE GOOD, BAD AND THE UGLY!

Arbitration has been hyped as the greatest advancement to our legal system since the Laws of Hammurabi were codified in ancient Babylon! Currently it is very fashionable to have an arbitration clause in almost every contract you sign. Arbitration was supposed to deliver a speedy, low-cost and just outcome in matters of civil dispute. However, in many arbitration cases, the reverse outcome has occurred. Arbitration (also known among lawyers as "Rent-a-Judge") has become a slow and costly procedure that has no guarantee of a fair outcome, and generally can't be appealed. The following list outlines the substantial flaws in the arbitration system of jurisprudence.

1. **Costs of Arbitration** - There are arbitrator's fees and expenses to pay, the costs to schedule a hearing room and other costs of arbitration to consider, particularly in complex cases requiring expert witnesses. Contrast that expense to a legal system where the judge and courtroom are provided free of charge, and witnesses can be subpoenaed.

2. **Limited Discovery** – Because of restrictions of the full range of discovery, all of the rules of procedure and evidence may not be properly applied.

3. **Limited Cross-Examination** – Generally, there is limited cross-examination of witnesses during an arbitration hearing.

4. **Requisite Experience** - An arbitrator who is not a lawyer may not have the requisite specialized legal expertise to conduct the arbitration.

5. **Punitive Damages** - Punitive damage awards are unlikely to be granted, and are not enforceable in some jurisdictions.

6. **Arbitration Appeals** - It is either difficult or next to impossible to appeal an arbitration decision, because appeal and judicial review are severely restricted.

7. **Arbitration Awards** - Arbitrators generally make their awards without written opinions or other supporting documents. There is also an observed tendency among arbitrators to award something to each party if they are unsure about an equitable decision.

8. **No Public Record** - Arbitration awards are generally not made public. Therefore, there is no public record of arbitration awards to serve as a guideline for arbitrators.

An Example of an Arbitration Case Gone Wild – Some time ago I was introduced to arbitration as a potential witness for a company where I was employed as VP Finance. The arbitration revolved around an insurance broker who was receiving commissions on insurance products that he had sold. He was also billing for services that were normally provided free of charge and that he had not provided in any event. The arbitration was lengthy and costly. Since I was a CFP (Certified Financial Planner) and a CPA at the time, I could have provided expert evidence as a witness, but was never called to testify. Even so, we had strong defenses against the claim the broker had made regarding further payment due to him for services contracted for but not rendered. Because of this, I felt pretty confident about our prospects to win this arbitration. When the decision was rendered, I was absolutely flabbergasted. Not only was the broker awarded his fees for doing absolutely nothing, but he was awarded an additional amount for contract termination and interest on the contract balance! And, worst of all, this outrageous decision could not be appealed! If we had tried this case in court, it would have taken half the time, cost half as much, and we would probably have obtained a fair and equitable judgment.

SUMMARY

The moral of this story is quite clear. If you have a good case and a good attorney, don't put your fate in the hands of a "Rent-a-Judge" arbitrator if you can possibly avoid it.

CHAPTER 11

CHOOSING A CPA FIRM

DO I REALLY NEED A CPA FIRM?

You can certainly continue to operate your business without engaging a CPA firm to perform a review or an audit of your annual Financial Statements. After all, there is a moderate cost for this service, and the audit will tie up your financial department for several days. These are the negatives, but they are offset by a substantial number of important positives as follows:

1. **Audits act as a deterrent to employee fraud** - The very fact that you have an annual audit is well known to your employees. This fact alone will diminish employee fraud, simply because they know that you are having outside auditors review your financial information.

2. **Audits are designed to detect major fraud** – If your auditors are properly conducting the audit, they will discover any substantial fraudulent activity. However, be aware that there is a popular misconception that audits will detect any fraud. This is incorrect because normal audits are not Cash Proof Audits, which examine all transactions relating to cash. These types of audits are all encompassing, are expensive to conduct and usually are not requested by the audit clients. So bear in mind that normal audits will probably not uncover minor fraud or petty theft.

3. **Annual CPA Audits or Reviews of your company's financials may be required by your banks, finance companies, and others** – Most banks, franchisors, and finance companies now

require an Audit or Review to initially secure financing. If you are bidding on larger governmental contracts, this could also be a bid requirement. Some of your large vendors may also require audited or reviewed annual Financial Statements to help justify extending credit to your company. The above creditor requirements for audited or reviewed statements are usually continuing and ongoing.

4. **Financial Statement Annual Audits provide a degree of assurance and reliability from outside auditors to other owners, creditors, and investors** – As a managing owner or partner, you have a substantial due diligence requirement to your other owners, partners, creditors, or investors. Having an audit performed by an outside unaffiliated CPA firm relieves you of some of this responsibility.

5. **Do you intend to take your company public within the next 3 to 5 years** – If so, you should contact your auditors now to schedule a year-end audit. You will need a minimum of three years of audited (not reviewed) statements in order to qualify for a public stock offering.

6. **Determination of company value for buy-sell agreements or key person insurance policies** - If any shareholders want to sell their share of the business, or if a key owner dies or is involuntarily retired because of health problems, the buy-sell agreements generally require that an outside audit be performed as of the date called for by the agreement. These audits are much easier and less expensive to complete if you have had a prior audit completed within the last 12 months. In that case, you are currently engaging a CPA audit firm and they are already familiar with your business. Therefore, they can react to your request much more quickly and at a substantially lower cost than starting from scratch. (See Chapter 14 – Using Term Insurance to Fund Key Person and Buy-Sell Agreements)

WHAT SELECTION CRITERIA SHOULD I CONSIDER WHEN ENGAGING A CPA FIRM?

1. **Proximity** - Interview CPA firms that have a local office. There is a lot to be said for the convenience of having your CPA reasonably close to your location. Proximity also enables your CPA to act as one of your outside Board members and saves you travel time and expenses when you have an audit or request other on-site CPA services.

2. **Size** - Look for a smaller CPA firm. You will get more senior CPA staff time from a small firm working on your audit or other assignments. This contrasts with recent hires or non-CPAs provided by the larger CPA firms. The lack of experienced personnel on site not only costs you money in terms of audit inefficiency, but it places an additional time burden on your financial and accounting staff. You don't want to be placed in the position of having to effectively train junior staffers for a large CPA firm. As a small company, you can't afford to be in that position. If a large CPA firm is local and fits all the other criteria, have an agreement with them before the audit starts as to the quality and experience of staff that they will have on site. Do this before the audit begins.

3. **A Personal Story about my first audit experience** – I was representing a major Canadian brokerage firm as their V.P. of Finance. We were being audited by one of the "big eight" CPA firms at the time, and we had scheduled a "box count" which involved counting all of the physical securities that were on premises. Our audit firm sent over 2 fellows who were just out of college, and quite frankly didn't know a stock from a bond. They were so green and inexperienced that we began calling them the "junior G-men". I remember saying after the box count that we could have shown these two novices Monopoly game deeds to Boardwalk and Park Place, told them that it represented 1,000 and 500 shares of IBM, and they would have believed us! The moral of the story is that just because you hire a large CPA firm and pay more than you should have to for a first rate job, it does not necessarily mean that you will get what you paid for!

4. **Experience and Reputation** - Select a CPA firm that has been in business at least several years and has a good reputation and experienced staff.

5. **Industry Expertise** - Select a CPA firm with audit experience in your industry. Again, there is no substitute for experience. You also want the availability of a CPA audit manager who has expertise in your industry.

6. **Flexibility** - Choose a CPA firm that is flexible with regard to assignments and scheduling.

7. **Affordability** – Choose a CPA firm that will work with your financial and accounting staff to reduce the cost of the audit by having internal staff create audit working papers internally prior to the on-site review or audit.

WHAT SHOULD I EXPECT FROM MY CPA FIRM?

1. **Accuracy** – Your annual audited Financial Statements should accurately portray the financial status of your business as of the audit date.

2. **Timeliness** – Your audit should be completed efficiently and the audited financials should be delivered to you on time.

3. **Fixed Fee Pricing** – The audit price should be negotiated prior to starting the engagement at a fixed price agreed to by you and the CPA firm in the engagement letter.

4. **Internal Control Assessment** – As part of the audit report, you should receive an Internal Control Letter which addresses the strengths and weaknesses of your internal control procedures. Make sure you tell your auditor that you consider this a very important part of the audit, and if they discover significant weaknesses, instruct them not to "sugarcoat" the report. Your company must address the weaknesses in its internal control procedures, so let the chips fall where they may.

5. **Business Improvement Recommendations** – Your CPA should be willing to communicate general recommendations for the improvement of your business that have been observed as a result of the audit. **This has a value far beyond the cost of the audit, yet many CPAs are hesitant to make these suggestions.** Again, let your CPA firm know that you value their business insight, recommendations, and ideas for your business and that you fully expect a written or verbal report from him in that regard at the end of the audit. **Don't let your CPA off the hook regarding a Business Improvement Assessment Report!**

6. **Tax Returns** – After the completion of the audit, no one is in a better position than your CPA firm to complete and file your corporate income tax returns. They should have collected on site, almost all of the information necessary to complete your tax returns. So take advantage of this fact and have the cost to complete and file your tax returns included in your audit fixed price estimate.

TIP – If there are no other considerations, you might also consider having your business CPA firm file your personal tax return. They already have in their possession all of the business information necessary to file this return. This should result in a leaser cost to file your personal return.

SUMMARY RECOMMENDATION

I would definitely recommend that you engage a CPA firm to do you annual audit and tax work. You will not only gain the comfort of having an outside third party CPA firm certify the accuracy of your financial statements, but your tax returns will be professionally prepared as well. Your banks, franchisors, major vendors, and other lenders will probably insist on your company engaging a CPA firm to perform this work annually in any event. And, if you ever decide to do a public offering of your company stock, you will need three consecutive years of audited statements to comply with SEC requirements.

SECTION 4

BUSINESS CONTINUATION PLANNING

CHAPTER 12

PLANNING FOR DISASTERS

DO YOU HAVE A DISASTER RECOVERY PLAN?

This is your starting place for disaster planning. Do you have any sort of disaster recovery plan? If you don't, according to a recent survey you can join the 73% of other small business owners who don't have a disaster recovery plan either. If you are among the other 27% who do have a plan, perhaps this chapter will give you some new ideas as to what you can do to protect yourself and your business before, during and after a disaster.

WHAT KIND OF PLANNING CAN YOU DO BEFORE A DISASTER STRIKES?

This is a great question because almost all of your planning must take place before a disaster strikes or is imminent. Let's cover a few of the things that can ensure the continuity of your business in the event of a disaster, regardless of type.

1. **Do you have Business Interruption Insurance coverage?** If you don't have this critical insurance, the first thing I would do upon reading this is contact your property and casualty broker and arrange for a meeting to secure this vital coverage.

2. **Do you have sufficient property and casualty insurance to cover the current replacement cost of your physical location and all of your equipment?** Your physical property coverage should be reviewed for adequacy with your broker each year.

3. **If you have business interruption insurance coverage, is the amount of insurance adequate to continue your business during the disaster recovery period?** To determine this, you need to know when your coverage was last updated. Then, along with your chief financial officer or controller, you need to compute the amount of cash that will allow your business to continue to operate for three to six months without significant revenues. Again, contact your broker and have the amount of business interruption insurance coverage adjusted accordingly.

4. **Do you create an adequate backup for your computer system programs and transactions on a daily basis?** Don't let anyone fool you. Your computer programs and data should be backed up daily on magnetic media such as portable tapes, CDs or USB flash drives.

5. **Do you currently utilize offsite storage for your daily backups?** If you don't, you are missing a key element in your disaster recovery strategy. Your off-site storage can be as simple as taking your backup tapes or discs to the bank when you make your daily deposit, and storing them in your safe deposit box.

6. **Are you aware that there are currently a number of online backup services that you can utilize for a relatively modest fee?** Although it's redundant and since the expense of the service is inconsequential, **I recommend that you contract with an online backup service to save your programs and data daily**. Along with your daily backups on tape or disc that you store off-site, this gives you substantial additional protection in the event of a disaster. There is nothing like having two backup alternatives in case one of them fails!

7. **Have you identified another location that can accommodate your business, in the event that your primary location becomes unusable after a disaster strikes?** If you are lucky enough to have multiple locations, you should consider a

backup plan that anticipates any of your locations becoming unusable, with one or more of your other locations potentially acting as a backup. However, companies that have only one location face a much bigger problem. What kind of size, services, capabilities and facilities must an alternate location have in order to be considered a viable backup location? Selecting an alternate site should be fairly easy for a service company, such as a CPA firm or an insurance brokerage company. Service companies might simply be able to rent a hotel conference room with Internet and telephone services readily available to them and quickly set up shop. However, companies such as a full-service auto dealership or a manufacturing company have a host of other things to consider when selecting an alternate location.

8. **Have you seriously considered computer Hot Sites for disaster recovery and transaction data continuity?** Hot site services for small businesses are available from a number of vendors at a reasonable cost. The hot site contains a duplicate of your computer system, including a mirror image of your last backup. After a disaster, if time permits, you can instruct your computer manager to download a current backup of your computer data to your hot site. After a disaster has occurred, the availability of the hot site should allow your business to relocate with a minimum of downtime or transaction losses. If you have an alternate physical site immediately available, your hot site can be up and running within a matter of hours after the disaster has occurred.

The items listed above are critical to the survival of your business in the event of a disaster. Therefore, I strongly recommend you complete these items before you address the development of a comprehensive disaster plan. In any event, most of the items above would have to be addressed before you could complete your disaster recovery plan. I will outline below some of the more important elements that should be included in your disaster recovery plan.

PREPARING YOUR DISASTER RECOVERY PLAN - WHAT SHOULD IT CONTAIN?

There are a number of important elements common to any well-written disaster plan. They are as follows:

1. A general statement of policy regarding your company's disaster response.
2. Personnel evacuation procedures, with a list of fire extinguishers and locations.
3. Equipment shut-down procedures, with a complete list of all equipment that should be shut down or turned off, time permitting, and with any special instructions attached.
4. A listing of any highly hazardous chemicals or explosives, showing locations, quantities, and any special instructions regarding same.
5. Computer program and data save procedures, if time permits.
6. Company reorganization plans in the event of a disaster.
7. Communication protocols in the event of a disaster (Who is assigned to contact fire departments, police departments, emergency response teams, etc. with a listing of all emergency phone numbers and contacts, if applicable)
8. Organization of the Crisis Management Team
9. Contact listings for the crisis management team members.
10. Contact names and phone numbers for critical vendors and customers who should be notified as soon as practical.
11. A media response kit.
12. Any other information regarding instructions that may be specific to your company and that you feel would be helpful in a disaster situation.

THE FUNCTIONS OF THE CRISIS MANAGEMENT TEAM PRIOR TO ANY DISASTER

During the disaster planning phase, the crisis management team should be responsible for the following items:

1. The establishment of the scope and objectives for company's Disaster Recovery Plan.

2. The development of the Emergency Action Plan for all of the company locations.

3. The overall assignment of duties and responsibilities for team members and other employees who will be involved in disaster recovery. This should include a list of replacements for Crisis Management Team members in the event that they are injured or are otherwise unavailable.

THE FUNCTIONS OF THE CRISIS MANAGEMENT TEAM DURING A DISASTER

1. The number one priority of the Crisis Management Team is to ensure the safety and well-being of all the company's employees.

2. Once priority number one has been secured and confirmed by a headcount, the Crisis Management Team should ensure that all emergency phone contacts have been made.

3. If time permits, the team will confirm that all equipment shut down procedures have been followed, and that a computer data save has been completed on portable magnetic media.

4. If you have the time, the Crisis Management Team should hold a preliminary disaster evaluation meeting on the site. If time does not permit this, the team should schedule a preliminary disaster evaluation meeting as soon as practical at a specific time and place.

THE FUNCTIONS OF THE CRISIS MANAGEMENT TEAM AFTER A DISASTER

1. If you have held your preliminary disaster evaluation meeting, schedule a follow on meeting on the disaster site, if possible.

2. Establish a plan for maintaining disaster site security.

3. Ensure that your alternate site of operations is not damaged and can be utilized.

4. Ensure that you have an action plan to establish your communications links at your alternate site.

5. Determine what equipment, if any, can be removed from the disaster site and transported to your alternate site.

6. If you are utilizing a hot site computer service, ensure that they are aware of your alternate physical site location and have made arrangements to have your computer system functioning normally as soon as possible.

7. Set a date and time schedule at the disaster site or your alternate site for your crisis management team and other employees to be assigned specific disaster recovery tasks and regular employment duties.

8. Insure that all of your critical suppliers, vendors and customers have been contacted. Let them know that you will be calling them back with a specific plan or other information as soon as you have it available.

9. After your preliminary disaster evaluation meetings, you must formalize a detailed recovery plan, complete with estimated costs and a time schedule for completion as soon as possible.

10. If, for any reason, the disaster site has become unusable and the alternate site of operations is only temporary, a new location will have to be selected. Again, estimated costs and time schedules must be prepared.

11. The time schedules and costs associated with the original site recovery or a replacement site should be presented to the Board of Directors for their approval. The approval should be subject to the concurrence of the insurance companies providing your property and casualty coverage and your business interruption insurance.

SUMMARY

While it is impossible to develop a comprehensive disaster recovery planning list without knowing your business operation more intimately, this chapter will give you and your managers a good idea of what the disaster recovery planning process entails. And, as a perfect example, the recent hurricane season of 2008 should give you all the incentive that you need to start and complete your disaster recovery planning as soon as possible.

CHAPTER 13

BUSINESS SUCCESSION FOR SMALL FAMILY BUSINESSES

SMALL FAMILY OWNED BUSINESS ORGANIZATIONS

In the United States it is estimated that 75% of small family businesses are operated by the founder who owns a majority or all of the company. It is also estimated that there is no concrete plan for succession in the majority of small family businesses. This presents a significant problem if something unexpected happens to you, the owner/manager. Therefore, if you own and operate a small family business or if your company has no plan for succession, the following ideas are worthy of consideration.

MAINTAINING BUSINESS OPERATIONS IN THE FAMILY

If family succession is the desire of the owner, obviously nothing is going to sway that decision one way or the other. However, there are a number of questions regarding the family members under consideration that may affect the way in which this decision is implemented. I have outlined a number of these as follows:

1. Do any of the family members under consideration really have the desire to undertake the overall management of the company as president?
2. Will any of the family members commit to the time necessary to successfully manage the business?
3. Have any of the family members professionally trained for this position?

4. Do any of the family members have the requisite experience for this position?
5. Do any of the family members have a business degree in accounting, marketing or business administration?
6. Are any of the family members currently working in the business in some capacity?

From my own experience, there is a great tendency in owner managers to overestimate the abilities of their offspring. Sons, daughters and other relatives who couldn't hold on to a decent job outside the company are given significant positions of authority along with fat paychecks in family-owned companies. I have seen situations so egregious that the company would have been better off hiring in a qualified professional manager, and sending the family member home with pay! Therefore, I offer the following statement for your consideration. **Business acumen is not transferred through the genes, but is forged in the hot fire of tough business experience and difficult decision-making.** Your business should not end up being a family playground when you are gone. If you want your business to continue to thrive and benefit your family financially, operate your business based on a profit motive utilizing sound business principles.

OPERATING A FAMILY BUSINESS LIKE A BUSINESS

You may be lucky enough to have a family member who is a worthy successor. Therefore, you have made the decision to "keep it (the management) in the family" and are searching for the best way to professionally manage your business. To avoid personally offending any family members involved in the management of the business, give serious consideration to the following suggestion. **Manage your company through your company Board of Directors**! While it might seem like a novel idea, it can actually eliminate or substantially reduce the effect of personalities and family ties on corporate decision-making. Consider having the Board of Directors initiate or take the following management actions.

1. Approve all vision statements, mission statements and goals set by the company.
2. Approve all the company objectives necessary to achieve those goals.
3. During the quarterly board meetings, track the progress of each individual manager, whether they are family members are not, in achieving those objectives.
4. The individual managers should report to the board on their progress in attaining their objectives.
5. The individual managers should also report to the board regarding the financial performance of their departments during the last quarter as compared to the projected financial plan for the next quarter.
6. Each individual manager, whether they are a family member or not, should be held accountable to the board for their performance over the last quarter.
7. Each individual manager should submit an overall activity plan for the coming quarter to be approved by the board.

By actually using your Board of Directors to manage your business, you will tend to depersonalize the business decisions and actions taken by the board. To some degree, this process should take some of the emotion out of making employment decisions involving family members.

IF THERE ARE NO FAMILY CONSIDERATIONS, HOW DO I DEVELOP A SUCCESSOR?

There are many ways to develop your successor, providing that you have someone on staff that is promotable to the position of president. If you have a general manager, this would seem to be the most likely candidate to be considered as a successor. If you don't have a general manager, you may have a marketing manager, a chief financial officer or another corporate manager whom you feel would be a likely candidate for your position. If you are convinced that no one on your management team can be trained to assume your position, you need to give this potential problem considerable thought the next time you recruit a manager. Obviously, you should be looking for a manager who does have the qualities and qualifications to be your understudy.

Once you have identified a manager who has the potential to assume the responsibilities of the presidency, there are several things that you can do to train and develop your successor.

1. Ensure that your potential successor takes full advantage of any management training opportunities and other industry training directly related to your business.

2. Occasionally, there are opportunities to be in charge of your management staff when you are off premises or on vacation. Let your successor and the rest of your staff know that he or she will be in charge during your absence, and will assume most of your duties and responsibilities.

3. During these periods where your successor will be temporarily in charge, discuss with him or her beforehand the items that need to be completed in your absence.

4. After you return, review all of the assigned items with your successor, whether they have been completed or not. Use this opportunity as a training session and let the successor know what you would have done differently, and why.

5. Take the time to rate your successor's performance, and let the successor know the results of your rating.

6. Take your successor with you on visits with your important customers and vendors. Solicit feedback from these sources about their opinion of your designated successor.

7. When opportunities present themselves to you for public speaking, have your successor address the group in your stead. Then, rate their performance for content, style and presentation.

8. Whenever you are engaged in a task that you feel is important for your successor to understand and know how to perform, invite the individual in for an on-the-job (OJT) training session. This training method is conservative of your time, as you would have to complete the task in any event, and is great training for your successor.

9. Schedule periodic reviews with your successor monthly, but in any case not less than quarterly, to evaluate their progress in achieving the benchmarks that you have set for their attainment of the successorship position.

10. Lastly, if you think that your potential successor is worthy of consideration, schedule some time each week to discuss important considerations regarding your position. Also, plan to have the discussion open-ended, as there are more items that your successor may want to discuss with you.

SUMMARY

As you have the opportunity to accomplish the items listed above, you'll be better able to assess whether your potential successor actually has what it takes to assume the role of president. **By the way, the methodology above also works well for family members!**

CHAPTER 14

USING TERM LIFE INSURANCE TO FUND KEY EMPLOYEE INSURANCE AND STOCK PURCHASE AGREEMENTS

WHAT IS TERM LIFE INSURANCE?

Typically, Term Life Insurance will provide death insurance in the amount of the face value of the policy for a specific fixed term of 5 to 30 years. After the fixed term, the premiums rise drastically. Term life insurance has been decreasing in cost ever since the insurance companies stopped using the 1958 CSO (Commissioners Standard Ordinary) tables of mortality and started updating these tables with current mortality statistics. By the way, a number of life insurance companies used these outdated 1958 tables well into the 1970s, even though most of us knew that we were all living longer! Today, term life insurance has become very competitive and is relatively inexpensive to purchase, providing the individual is in reasonably good health.

WHO IS A KEY EMPLOYEE?

The loss of a key employee can negatively affect the financial results of a business. A Key Person is anyone in the organization whose death or disability would produce the following results:

1. The disruption of normal business operations.
2. The loss of customers or profits.
3. The loss of specialized employee knowledge or skill-sets.
4. The impairment of the company's ability to secure financing.

5. The obligation of the company to have to repay debts or redeem stock.

Some examples of key employees are business owners, presidents, general managers, chief financial officers, sales managers, and specialized creative talent to name a few. If any of your key employees are that critical to the continued success of your company, carefully consider the retention ideas listed below.

KEY EMPLOYEE RETENTION AFTER RETIREMENT

The best Executive Information Systems (EIS) ever designed, after five years of effort, only captured 85% of the knowledge of an expert manager! Don't make the same mistake that so many companies do and assume that there is no middle ground between retirement and full time work for a key person approaching retirement. That key person can still be an asset to you, assisting your company even in retirement. You simply have to structure an arrangement that will work to the benefit of both parties. Those arrangements are only restricted by the creativity and circumstances of both parties. However, here are a few ideas for your consideration.

1. Have the key person join your Outside Advisory Board.
2. Assign the key person necessary tasks that will justify several days of work each month.
3. Set up an "on demand" consulting relationship with the key person.
4. If the key person has retired out of your geographic area, establish a phone consultation arrangement utilizing Cisco's Webex Teleconferencing Service. It's almost like having them in your office!

Recommendation: Don't let a key person who is retiring walk out the door with an intimate knowledge of your company's operations. Negotiate an arrangement beforehand to access that knowledge when you need to!

KEY EMPLOYEE INSURANCE

Many small to medium-sized companies insure their fixed assets and inventory, but fail to insure one of their most valuable assets: key employees. A Key Person Insurance Policy will insure the organization against the loss of employees important to the success of the business. Each policy will cover the death or disability of a key employee. The employer pays the policy premium and is the beneficiary of the policy. If a key person dies or becomes disabled, the company receives the policy benefits tax-free. However, the insurance premium payments made by the company on this policy during the period that it is in force are not tax deductible.

RECOMMENDATION FOR PURCHASING KEY EMPLOYEE INSURANCE

Although there are many ways to fund this protection, **I recommend the purchase of inexpensive term life insurance with a disability rider for Key Employee Insurance coverage, as this is the least expensive method for the company to consider, and most conservative of cash flow.** Purchasing term life insurance with a disability rider is a simple process that involves an application and a medical exam. *Since the coverage is the same regardless of the insurance company providing it, don't pay any more for it than you have to. Do insure that the life insurance company that you choose is rated "A" or better by A.M. Best, an insurance company rating service. Have your broker shop around for the best term life premium rates.*

BUY-SELL AGREEMENTS

Almost any owner of a closely-held business will benefit from a funded cross-purchase or repurchase buy-sell agreement. The business is usually the source of the owner's income and is most often the largest asset in a business owner's estate. Death or disability of a business owner or partner can leave the business partners and their families in an untenable financial position. All small businesses, including corporations, LLCs, sole proprietorships and partnerships, need to create buy-sell agreements and provide for the funding of them. A buy-sell agreement should be developed by your attorney and, at minimum, cover three important problem areas and provide a solution for each.

A BUY-SELL AGREEMENT MUST:

1. Establish a purchase price for the deceased, disabled or retired owner's interest.
2. Contain a restrictive clause that prohibits the transfer of stock or interest in the business to other owners or family members not part of the buy sell agreement.
3. Clearly identify the company as the purchaser of the owner's stock upon the death, disability or retirement of the owner.

SUMMARY RECOMMENDATION FOR FUNDING BUY-SELL AGREEMENTS

Term Life Insurance with a Disability Insurance Rider offers the most cost effective solution for funding a Buy-Sell Agreement.

A Disability Insurance Rider will pay the death benefit if the policy owner becomes disabled. Upon the death or disability of the insured, cash is immediately available to the entity or surviving owners to purchase the owner's interest. This will provide the former owner's family or estate with the cash necessary to pay estate settlement costs and taxes. In addition, insurance proceeds are typically income-tax free to the recipient. Insurance proceeds can satisfy the obligation to purchase stock included in most buy-sell agreements, without placing a financial strain on the buyer. However, there is a wide choice of insurance products available including term, whole life, universal life and survivorship insurance. These choices allow for great flexibility in product design, funding requirements, and cost. To determine which insurance product is best for you and your company, you should consult with your insurance broker and your attorney.

SECTION 5

SUCCESFUL BUSINESS PLANNING

CHAPTER 15

SETTING CORPORATE GOALS

There is a decided difference between setting goals and setting objectives. Your corporate goals establish the intermediate to long-term direction of your company. Objectives establish, at least in part, the ways and means to achieve your goals. Although both strategies are very important, it only makes sense that setting goals must precede the establishment of objectives.

GOAL SETTING - WHERE DO WE BEGIN?

There is an ancient Chinese proverb that says "If you don't know where you're going, any road will get you there." As a company, if you don't have any clear cut direction or corporate vision, you will not be nearly as successful as your competitors who know where they're going. **I cannot stress enough the importance of goal setting. It sets the tone and direction of your corporation. It allows you to set objectives that are consistent with the overall goals that you have established. And, like a lighthouse beacon on a dark and stormy night, it keeps you on the right track to achieve those goals.** You and your managers need to spend some uninterrupted week-end time away from the office to reflect upon the following areas:

1. **What Is Your Vision for Your Company?** This is the time to look deep into your crystal ball and gaze at the future! What do you see your company achieving 10 to 20 years from now? You have the opportunity to create an inspiring vision for your company. But don't get too wordy. Limit your vision statement to just a few sentences.

a. **Create a company mission statement.** A mission statement is a clear and definable goal that is easily remembered. A good example of this would be the current goal of the Chinese space agency. China has set a goal to walk on the moon in the year 2024. And let's not forget one of the most memorable mission statements ever spoken when John F. Kennedy in a speech to a special joint session of Congress on May 25, 1961 said **"I believe that this nation should commit itself to achieving the goal, before this decade is out, of landing a man on the moon and returning him safely to the Earth."** Do you believe that we would have successfully accomplished this mission in 1969 without President Kennedy dedicating our country to the achievement of this visionary mission statement in 1961? I don't think so! Well, this is your opportunity to create a short, well-crafted and farsighted vision statement for your company.

b. **An example of a specific mission statement -** When I was hired by this company, there was no safety program, no safety committee, no safety handbooks and no company emphasis on safety at all! Over time, I authored safety handbooks and initiated several safety programs. At the same time, I encouraged the company to provide safety equipment to employees, such as OSHA approved work boots, eyeglasses and goggles without charge. We then formed a safety committee to address safety issues throughout the company. During the safety committee's first year of operation, we developed a following mission statement. **"At ABC Company, safety is serious business".** Notice that this motto (mission statement) is short, to the point and expresses the company's concern about safety. To drill this motto deep into the employee's consciousness, we used it on most of our safety literature. Also there was hardly a time when we held a safety committee meeting regarding anything relating to safety that I did not ask the participants to repeat our safety motto. In this case, our motto repetition increased safety awareness, and safety awareness created a safer working environment.

2. **Where Are You At Today?** If you don't know where you're at today, how can you possibly know where you're going to be tomorrow? To develop and analyze this necessary planning information, I suggest that you perform a company assessment utilizing the following outline:

    a. Determine your company's current status with regard to your industry, your products and services, your location and physical plant, your customers, your vendors, your competitors, your company's overall performance, and your current financial situation as determined by your balance sheet, profit and loss statement, and statement of cash flows.

    b. Analyze your company strengths in each of the above areas, and rate these strengths from one to ten, ten being the strongest.

    c. Analyze your company weaknesses in each of the above areas, and rate these weaknesses from a negative one to ten, ten being the weakest.

    d. Identify the challenges to improvement in each of these areas.

    e. Identify opportunities for improvement in each of these areas.

    f. Are there any current plans, formal or not, to improve or strengthen these areas? If so, commit these plans to writing so that they may be analyzed.

    g. Are there any challenges or opportunities for the company that have surfaced recently and have not yet impacted your financial statements? If so, identify and analyze these new events. **Don't be caught flat-footed!**

3. **Where Will You Be Tomorrow?** In order to successfully undertake the task of setting future goals, you must be committed to do the following things:

THE PREPARATION PHASE

a. With your managers' assistance, complete the items in paragraphs 1 and 2 while at work, where you'll have financial data and other information readily available.

b. Once you have completed these items, distribute this information to your managers.

c. Challenge yourself and your managers to bring to the table a list of company and departmental goals, and establish a due date for the completion of this assignment.

d. Review the goals submitted by you and your managers and eliminate potential conflicting or duplicative goals. Then, classify and prioritize the remaining goals.

e. Provide a comprehensive listing of the merged and prioritized goals by company and by department to each manager to be reviewed by them before the focus meeting. To ensure that this review is complete, have your managers return a copy of the listing to you with any comments or requested changes. **TIP - If you see nothing in the way of comments from any one of your managers, you can make an assumption that they have spent no time on the review process.**

f. Schedule a weekend goal focus meeting in your conference room if you don't normally work on the weekends. Otherwise, schedule the goal focus meeting offsite so that you will not be constantly interrupted. Distribute an agenda for this meeting. All of this work, (a. through f.), should be accomplished prior to your goal focus meeting. This will help you to create a serious atmosphere for your meeting and make it as productive as possible.

Now that you have completed the preparation phase, you are ready for the meeting phase, which is most exciting and creative part of goal setting.

THE MEETING PHASE

a. ***Follow your meeting agenda. Start with defining corporate goals first.*** This will help to ensure that your departmental goals are consistent with your corporate goals. The next four requisites will relate to John F. Kennedy's goal of landing a man on the moon. President Kennedy said in a joint session of Congress on May 25th 1961 **"I believe that this nation should commit itself to achieving the goal, before this decade is out, of landing a man on the moon and returning him safely to the Earth."** We will segment this goal into four parts to illustrate each of the following four requisites.

b. ***Set specific goals, even though they may relate to a general objective***. The more specific your goal is, the higher the odds that it will be achieved. <u>Example</u>: **"landing a man on the moon"**

c. ***Align your goals with your vision of the company's future***. They must be consistent with the company's mission statement and other goals and objectives. <u>Example</u>: **"and returning him safely to the Earth."**

d. ***Set a definite time frame for the accomplishment of your goals***. <u>Example</u>: **"before this decade is out".**

e. ***Incorporate measurable performance into your goal setting requirements.*** <u>Example</u>: **"I believe that this nation should commit itself to achieving the goal"**. By making the commitment to achieve the goal of landing a man on the moon within nine years, there is an implied need to measure the progress towards the achievement of this great goal. Kennedy gave a speech on September 12th 1962 where he detailed the financial commitment to achieve this goal and said ***"During the next 5 years the National Aeronautics and Space Administration expects to double the number of scientists and engineers, to increase its outlays for salaries and expenses to $60 million a year; to invest some $200 million in plant and laboratory facilities; and to direct or contract for new space efforts over $1 billion - To be sure, all this costs us all a good***

deal of money. This year's space budget is three times what it was in January 1961, and it is greater than the space budget of the previous eight years combined. That budget now stands at $5,400 million a year--a staggering sum". Again, the more specific you can be with regard to measuring your goal, the more the likelihood that you will meet or exceed it.

f. **Set your goals high, as Kennedy did.** Even if your goals are somewhat out of reach, you will make much more progress striving for lofty goals than if you had set easily attainable goals.

g. **Your goals must be realistic, and achievable.** In retrospect, the goal set by the John F. Kennedy of landing a man on the moon was certainly achievable because we are able to accomplish that moon landing in 1969, one year ahead of schedule. However, when the goal was set in 1961, I'm sure that there were quite a few skeptics who would have questioned whether the goal was realistic or not.

h. **Encourage participation! Goals that seem unrealistic at the start may, after discussion, seem very achievable.** Allow for some consideration of goals that have been suggested by the meeting participants. You may be surprised at the range of possibilities presented by your managers that you have never thought about before.

AN EXAMPLE OF THE IMPORTANCE OF GOAL SETTING

In a Board of Directors meeting for a public Life Insurance Company, we were faced with two challenges, either of which had the potential to bankrupt the Company. One of these related to the company's sale of group accident and health insurance in several states. The premium business looked fantastic until the claims started arriving. It became evident that this book of business was sold at a much lower premium than it should have been. The premiums didn't even cover the current claims, let alone the administrative cost, future loss reserves and a reasonable profit. The goal challenging the board was "How do we close out this book of business before it closes us?" Since I had a fair amount of experience purchasing insurance in other industries as a customer, I suggested that we stop paying claims. All the other directors were aghast at the idea and they were convinced that the state insurance commissioners involved would put us out of business. So initially, they were not willing to consider it. However, we did manage to bring the idea to the table for discussion again. When I was asked how we could accomplish this and still stay in business in those states, my answer was a simple one. Once we stopped paying claims, it would not be long before our customers themselves terminated the business. At that point, we would still have enough financial resources to pay all of the valid outstanding claims immediately. Therefore, a goal that appeared to have been impossible to achieve quickly became a reality, and a major obstacle to the company's survival was removed.

THE FOLLOW-UP PHASE

1. Agree on a common set of company goals.
2. Commit these goals to writing, and prioritize them by company and by department.
3. Distribute the list to your managers for a final review.
4. Conduct a follow up meeting with all of your managers. Present your company vision and mission statements and goals to the managers.
5. Conduct an open ended discussion concerning the implementation of these goals.
6. Let your management team know that they will be expected to develop action plans for their departments, based upon the management by objectives (MBO) process which we will cover in the next chapter.
7. Have the Board of Directors approve your vision and mission statements at their next board meeting.

GOOD THINGS HAPPEN WHEN YOU DEFINE YOUR COMPANY VISION AND SET REALISTIC GOALS

In the mid-1980s the two partners of a small southeast CPA firm finally took some time off for a weekend planning session. They discussed their current business operation and the challenges that were hindering them in achieving the degree of business growth they desired. After introspectively looking at their business, they determined that 10% of their clientele was causing 90% of their problems. Having to spend a substantial amount of their time resolving these problems did not allow the partners sufficient time to add profitable new business. And, once the partners' additional time was added to the cost of the problem accounts, they became either unprofitable or marginally profitable. After digesting this information, the partners set two related goals. One goal was to eliminate the bottom 10% of their clientele each year. The other goal was to take the time that was saved by the elimination of their problem accounts, and use that time to find and attract profitable new business. They not only achieved their goals, but after substantially increasing their business and hiring many more CPAs, they became one of the largest regional CPA firms in the Southeast!

GOAL SETTING - CONCLUSION

You have now completed the most important part of your planning process. You have created the corporate vision and mission statements for your company, and established future corporate and departmental goals which have been agreed to by your managers. In the next three chapters, you will learn how to develop goal oriented objectives and utilize the MBO process to attain them.

CHAPTER 16

SETTING OBJECTIVES

Okay, you've now completed the fun part of planning in the last chapter. You have set your company strategy, created a vision statement, and outlined the goals that you want your company to achieve over a specific timeframe. Visualize it this way. You have created an image of a house that you want to build. However, not much will get done unless you have a detailed set of architect's house plans. The critical task of setting objectives is much like the architect drawing up those detailed house plans. The management task of properly defining your objectives is absolutely critical to your success in achieving your goals. In fact, it's so important that I have devoted this chapter to cover the basics of setting objectives.

WHAT ARE OBJECTIVES?

An objective is a detailed step-by-step plan containing a timeline for accomplishment which enables you to achieve a goal. It is a blueprint for accomplishing a goal over a specific period of time. Setting an objective is not a static process. It is an iterative process, requiring continual monitoring to determine if you are both on time and on track to accomplish your objectives. By the way, an iterative process can be compared to adjusting the sights of a new gun using a bench rest. You fire five shots at a bull's-eye for effect. Then you look at the target. If all five shots hit the center of the bull's-eye you don't need any further adjustment. However, that is not usually the case. If you find the center of the shot grouping is above and to the right of the bull's-eye, you adjust your gun sights accordingly. Then you fire five more shots at the bull's-eye for effect, and go through the same process until you have achieved your objective and the center of your shot grouping is in the center of the bull's-eye. This is the definition of the iterative process. You continually fine tune your planning until you have achieved your objective. Since, in reality, your objective is moving at varying rates of speed and direction, the iterative process is a continuing one.

WHAT ARE THE DIFFERENT TYPES OF OBJECTIVES?

There are basically four different types of objectives. They are Strategic Objectives, Creative and Innovative Objectives, Improvement Objectives, and Routine Operational Objectives, all of which we will briefly discuss here.

1. **Strategic Objectives** - Strategic objectives are long-term objectives designed to maintain and improve the company's competitive position by increasing market share at the expense of the competition. This can be accomplished by technological innovation, product differentiation, cost advantages, better merchandising, better warranties and customer service, more durable products, better delivery systems, and better product support, thus creating increased company and product value in the eyes of the customer. Strategic objectives concentrate on achieving a sustainable competitive advantage, and translating this into increased market share for the company's products and services.

2. **Creative and Innovative Objectives** - Creative objectives relate to the process of developing fresh new ideas that will significantly enhance the value of the company's products and services. Obviously creative ideas and objectives will generally precede innovative objectives. Innovative objectives usually start with creative ideas and contain ways to implement those ideas. Keep in mind that new ideas alone, without implementation, will not create any value for your company. Innovation objectives are "where the rubber meets the road", turning today's ideas into tomorrow's reality.

3. **Improvement Objectives** These objectives relate to an improvement in the way we perform existing operations or

procedures, as compared with innovation objectives which are related to the implementation of creative new ideas. Improvement objectives require modifications to standard operations or procedures which will result in one of the following outcomes.

A. **Increased revenues directly or indirectly**. As an example, you set an improvement objective to significantly improve your technical sales training, resulting in increased sales and more satisfied customers.

B. **Decreased expenses**. For example, in a manufacturing environment you could set an improvement objective to institute a Zero Defects Program, which would reduce the number of manufacturing errors and scrappage.

C. **Increased customer satisfaction**. As an example, you could set an improvement objective to significantly improve your sales catalog and brochures, resulting in increased sales and ease-of-use for customers, and higher customer satisfaction.

4. **Routine Operational Objectives** Routine operational objectives are related to the improvement of normal business operations and processes. Routine objectives can be large or small in scope. They can also be mandated by government, a response to your competitor's actions, or initiated by company management. These routine objectives can be implemented in production, transportation and delivery, merchandising, distribution, customer service and support, finance, accounting, human resources and any of your other operational areas. A good way to plan for the implementation of routine objectives is to identify Key Result Areas (KRAs) in all of your departments. After you have identified your Key Result Areas, you will then develop Key Performance Indicators (KPIs) for each KRA. The Key Result Area process is important enough that I have dedicated the following chapter to a more detailed description of it.

These four types of objectives above are not all-encompassing in scope, overlap to some degree, and certainly could be catalogued differently.

The important thing to remember is that you should include a representative number of strategic, innovative, developmental and routine objectives in your company business plan.

COMMON ELEMENTS OF PROPERLY DESIGNED OBJECTIVES

Let's make an assumption that your strategic planning sessions have produced realistic and attainable goals. If that is the case, you are ready to establish the tactics that are specifically designed to attain your goals. The first step in your tactical planning is to define your objectives both in terms of the expected results and the timeframe for completion. Remember that objectives are not goals. A company goal, by itself, can be a bit nebulous. As an example, let's say that one of your goals to increase sales volume by 10% in the coming year. That's a great goal and is probably realistic and achievable, but it is not an objective. Remember that objectives must be detailed step-by-step plans with a timeline for completion. With that in mind, let's examine the critical elements that your objectives should contain.

1. *First and foremost objectives, like goals, must be realistic.* For example, in 1961 if John F. Kennedy had set a goal of a man reaching Mars by the end of the decade, and returning home safely, it would have been totally unrealistic. Even today, 48 years after Kennedy's visionary statement about landing astronauts on the moon, the goal of reaching Mars and returning our astronauts home safely could not be accomplished within the next decade.

2. *Secondly, the objective must be attainable.* You can have an objective that is realistic. But it may not be attainable in the timeframe that you have proposed. Objectives must be both realistic and attainable in the timeframe you have set. If your objectives do not contain this critical element of attainability, they will probably wind up in the circular file.

3. ***Your objectives must be consistent with your company vision statement, and your company goals.*** A lack of consistency can lead to duplicative effort. Worse yet, you can actually have your company managers working at cross purposes with each other and canceling out the efforts of each other.

4. ***Your objectives must be specific.*** Remember that you are creating a blueprint for action. The objective must be defined sufficiently so that action can be taken based on that objective.

5. ***Your objectives must contain time deadlines for the completion of each element contained in the objective.*** In the example we used of building a house, even if we have the architect's plans, we still need a timetable for the completion of the various tasks involved in completing the house. Obviously, we first need a deadline for obtaining a building permit from the local government. Without this, we can't even begin house construction. Next, we need to do our land grading and prepare the ground for our footers and foundation, etc. There is no way that we can efficiently complete this home without a detailed and sequential timetable. If this is true for building a house, the same is true for the completion of multiple objectives. A sequential timetable is absolutely essential.

6. ***Your objectives must be measurable in terms of the specific actions or tasks that need to be completed according to a time schedule.*** There is no substitute for the element of measurability. If you can't measure an objective, how can you possibly know how far you have progressed towards achieving that objective? Do yourself a favor and build timetables, estimated times for completion, and scheduled completion dates into your objectives, even if you have to use reasonable estimates and update them later on in the process.

7. ***Build a feedback loop into your objectives, to assist you in keeping your objectives aligned with your goals.*** You need to establish guidelines with timetables to ensure that your progress in attaining

your objectives is still in line with your goals. Remember that you are shooting at a moving target! You need to compare your actual results with your expectations. That's why the utilization of the iterative process that we discussed earlier is extremely important in making the required midcourse corrections. And believe me you will have to make corrections many times over! It's all part of the process of adjusting to reality.

8. ***Perform a Post-Completion Analysis.*** After you have completed your project and attained your objective, take the time to analyze what you have learned from that experience. Then, if confronted with a similar project, list the things that you would do differently next time to more efficiently and effectively manage your project. This will assist you by insuring that you don't wind up making the same mistakes in the future.

SUMMARY

The most important part of planning is the process of setting the right objectives that contain all of the elements above. If you accomplish that, you are well on your way to attaining your goals. We are finally ready to develop action plans that will greatly assist us to achieve our objectives. In the next two chapters we will discuss the concept of utilizing Key Result Areas in setting routine objectives and the process of Managing by Objectives.

CHAPTER 17

KEY RESULT AREAS – (KRAs)

KEY RESULT AREAS - WHAT ARE THEY?

You'll read a lot about Key Result Areas (KRAs), in current management literature. A Key Result Area is defined as any important management function where you, as the manager, are primarily responsible for the results of that function. You must be able to measure performance in the Key Result Area, have a basis for comparing the results against some objective standard of performance, and establish a timetable for improvements in the KRA.

HOW CAN I UTILIZE KRAs TO HELP ME MANAGE MY BUSINESS?

Since KRAs, by definition are results oriented, they can be used very effectively to rate the performance of you and your managers. Your manager's duties and responsibilities can be analyzed and segregated into several important Key Result Areas. These are measurable results that are critical to the performance of your managers, and which determine their success or failure as a manager. A grading system should be assigned for each KRA, utilizing scale of one to ten, one being completely unacceptable and 10 being excellent. When you utilize the KRA process to rate performance of your managers, you'll discover that they will focus on their weakest results in order to improve their rating.

HOW DO I MEASURE KRA PERFORMANCE?

Key Result Area performance is usually measured with a key performance indicator (KPI). A Key Performance Indicator is a quantifiable measurement, agreed to beforehand with the manager directly responsible for producing the desired result. KPIs will differ depending on the industry and the type of business organization within that industry.

Past-Due Accounts Receivable as a KRA Example: You have identified past-due Accounts Receivable as a Key Result Area for your controller. Your company has wholesale, retail and governmental customer accounts, but the wholesale and retail accounts are all business customers. Consequently, we can say that your company has primarily business to business sales. Government customers are typically slow pay customers. The wholesale and retail business accounts should pay by statement at the end of the month, and have 10 business days to remit their statement balance. These payment terms are called "Net 10 Prox". It is standard in your industry to rate past due Accounts Receivable according to the following table. Further, assume that your current Accounts Receivable over 60 days old is currently 11%. For purposes of this example, let's say that you and your controller have agreed to the attainment of Key Performance Indicators (KPIs) for Accounts Receivable over 60 days old (A/R > 60) listed below as of January 1st, 2009.

Description	Industry Rating		KPI Rating	Date to Complete
Less than	12% of A/R > 60	Fail	0	
Baseline	**11% of A/R > 60**	**Fail**	**1**	**1/01/09**
Less than	10% of A/R > 60	Poor	2	
	9% of A/R > 60	Poor	3	3/31/09
	8% of A/R > 60	Fair	4	
	7% of A/R > 60	**Fair**	**5**	**6/30/09**
	6% of A/R > 60	Good	6	
	5% of A/R > 60	**Good**	**7**	**9/30/09**
	4% of A/R > 60	Excellent	8	
	3% of A/R > 60	**Excellent**	**9**	**12/31/09**
	2% of A/R > 60	Superb	10	
	1% of A/R > 60	**Superb**	**10+**	**3/31/10**

So what have you accomplished here? Let's sum it up as follows:

1. You have identified an important Key Result Area for your controllership position.
2. You have established that the baseline performance for this KRA is currently unacceptable.
3. This is also an important KRA for your company, as the increased collection of customer receivables has a significant positive effect on cash flow.
4. You have established Key Performance Indicators (KPIs) that will enable you to track the performance of your controller in the pursuit of reducing past due Accounts Receivable to less than 3% over 60 days old in the next 12 months.
5. You have established a schedule of quarterly benchmarks from which to measure performance in the attainment of this goal over the next 12 months.
6. And, more importantly, you have gotten a buy-in from your controller that this KRA is realistic and attainable. You have also gotten a commitment from your controller to achieve this objective over the next year.

TIP - You may want to institute a quarterly A/R bonus program for your controller related to the achievement of these objectives. There is no substitute for a bonus program that rewards legitimate achievement!

SUMMARY

The illustration above is an excellent example of the use of a Key Result Area to achieve a specific objective. KRAs can be utilized to achieve any objective. However, as this example demonstrates, they are best utilized for the attainment of routine objectives that are part of the core competencies of your managers. Also, having monthly or quarterly written reports of the progress of your managers in achieving their KRAs on file is extremely helpful when it comes to conducting their annual performance review.

CHAPTER 18

MANAGING BY OBJECTIVES (MBO)

Management by Objectives is a process that enables management to plan for, implement and attain those objectives that it has previously set for the company to achieve over a defined period of time. Peter Drucker authored his classic book, THE PRACTICE OF MANAGEMENT, in 1954 where he discussed the importance of managing by objectives. Warren Bennis, a management expert, has called Peter Drucker "the most important management thinker of our time". Having read a number of Mr. Drucker's books, I could not agree more.

However, the most critical success determinants of Management by Objectives (MBO) are the objectives themselves. That is why Chapter 16 is devoted to the process of "SETTING OBJECTIVES". There is nothing more important in your planning process than setting the right objectives. Assuming that you have set clear, attainable, specific and realistic goals consistent with your company vision statement that can be measured, you can then identify what objectives are important for your company to attain. Having set your objectives, you are now ready to examine the MBO process, which will show you how to achieve those goals and objectives. Always keep in mind that the MBO process is exactly that, a process. It is simply a management tool used to achieve your objectives, nothing more and nothing less! Now, let's take a look at suggested MBO processes that will help you prioritize, select, implement and attain your objectives.

PRE-IMPLEMENTATION PHASE

Before you begin to evaluate your objectives for implementation, you must review your objectives. Insure that they contain all of the following elements covered in the last chapter that are the necessary prerequisites for you to begin an evaluation. *Your objectives must be realistic, attainable, and consistent with other company goals and objectives. Your objectives must also be specific, measurable in terms of costs and benefits, and must contain time schedules for implementation. They should also contain a process for receiving objective feedback at measured intervals, preferably monthly but at least quarterly at the Board of Directors Meeting. A formal report should be presented at each quarterly Board by your managers updating the progress in achieving the objectives and proposing any necessary mid-course corrections.*

1. **Evaluate Your Objectives** – Take a good look at all of the objectives you have identified. First, you must evaluate each of them in terms of cost, projected benefit, time period to implement, payback period, intangible benefits, and ease or difficulty of implementation. You should assign a number from 1, being the lowest cost and highest projected benefit, to 5 for the highest cost and lowest projected benefit to each Objective Element. Then compute an average rating for all of the objective elements to each objective. This will greatly facilitate your evaluation of each of your objectives.

   A. **Cost** – The total monetary cost of the proposed objective.

   B. **Projected Benefits** – The monetary value of the benefits of implementing the proposed objective by year over the next 5 years.

   C. **Time Period to Implement** – The total estimated time to complete the project, from the project start date to the estimated completion date.

D. **Payback Period** – The period of time it takes for the projected monetary benefits to recoup all costs associated with the implementation of the project.

E. **Intangible Benefits** – Many times there are intangible benefits that are interlinked with the attainment of a tangible objective which can be more easily valued monetarily. Even though some benefits are intangible, such as increasing customer satisfaction and goodwill, try to estimate a monetary value for the intangible benefit, and a cost associated with its implementation. For example, if you increase customer satisfaction, you might reasonably expect some percentage of increased sales as a result. Determine the net income expected from these increased sales estimates as your monetary benefit. Your estimate may not be that accurate, but it's a lot better than having nothing at all to rely on when making your implementation decision.

F. **Ease or Difficulty of Implementation** – The following questions may assist you in evaluating this factor, which by its nature is somewhat subjective because it requires you to make an honest evaluation of the project based on your opinion.

1. How complex is the project?
2. How long will it take to complete the project?
3. How many vendors or third parties will be involved in the project?
4. How much third party assistance in time and dollars will be required from each vendor to complete the project?
5. Will my managers be able to coordinate a project this complex?
6. How much maintenance will be required after the project is completed?

2. **Select the Objectives to Implement** – Based on your evaluation above, select the objectives you would like to

implement. Undoubtedly, there will be other factors involved in addition to the ones described above that you will consider in making your selection.

3. **Plan to Implement a Reasonable Number of Objectives** – Departmentalize the objectives that you have preliminarily selected for implementation. Determine if any department is "loaded up" with too many objectives to implement them all successfully. Conversely, there may be departments that have too few objectives selected for implementation. Initially, you should try to balance these objectives and reasonably distribute the workload. Then, you can then review these objectives with the department managers and rebalance the departmental objectives based on these discussions. Remember that your objective here is to get an early buy-in from your department managers regarding the feasibility of implementing objectives set for their department.

4. **Secure Board Approval** – Once you have selected your objectives for implementation, request approval from your Board of Directors to proceed with the implementation of the objectives you have submitted. If there are any additions, deletions or changes to your list, they should be discussed with the department managers and rebalanced, if necessary, prior to finalization.

THE IMPLEMENTATION PHASE

I have been an ardent supporter of the MBO approach to "getting things done" since I was exposed to it in the United States Air Force as a Captain. In the military, learning objectives range from the lowest level, "*be familiar with*", to the highest level, "*be able to*". Having concrete and easily understandable learning objectives, along with the requisite training, has enabled our military to superbly train millions of recruits from all types of educational and personal backgrounds. In this case the objectives, no matter how well crafted they might be, are useless without the implementation phase which is "*the requisite training*". In our example, we have set our goals, established our objectives, evaluated those objectives, and secured Board approval to achieve those objectives. Now we need a simple blueprint or process that will assist in the implementation of those objectives. I have presented a list of procedures for your consideration below.

1. **Present the Board Approved Objectives to Your Management Team** – Let every manager know what departmental objectives they are responsible for achieving and how their contribution will assist in the attainment of your overall corporate objectives.

2. **Separate Objectives into Their Component Projects** – Each manager should be asked to define and separate the component parts of their objectives into projects. Each project should be further defined with the technical requirements, task schedules, contracted third party schedules and deadlines, and any budgetary considerations that are required by project and phase to attain the objective.

3. **Finalize Your Project Completion Schedules** – You should work with your managers to formally define their project schedules and set deadlines to accomplish their objectives.

4. **Assign Project Completion Bonuses** – Determine, along with your managers, an award or bonus program that will incentivize each manager to complete their projects on time or ahead of their scheduled deadlines.

5. **Performance Review Linkage** - Let your managers know that their performance, or lack thereof, in completing their projects and achieving their objectives, will have a substantial effect on their annual performance reviews.

6. **Project Feedback** – Let your managers know that there will be periodic formal and informal reviews of the progress they have made in achieving their objectives. Also, stress to them that if they encounter any significant problems or impediments to their progress, they are to inform you immediately. That way, the appropriate action can be taken to effectively resolve

these issues before they jeopardize the timely completion of the project.

THE PROJECT EVALUATION PHASE

1. **Define Project Benchmarks and Completion Dates** - You must have defined benchmarks, and phase and project completion dates as part of your detailed objectives.

2. **Create a Standard Project Status Report** - Have your CFO and Information Systems Manager create a Project Status Report that will be utilized for reporting purposes to monitor the progress of a project. The more you can automate the project status details, the easier it will be to report on them.

3. **Project Accountability** - Let each manager know that they will be held responsible and accountable for meeting their scheduled completion dates.

4. **Monthly Project Reporting** - Have each manager report on the status of all their projects at the Monthly Managers Meeting both in writing and orally. You should personally follow up on any project that is notably behind schedule.

5. **Performance Incentives** - A quarterly award or bonus should be presented to all managers who qualify by being on or ahead of schedule with all their projects.

6. **Quarterly Project Reporting** - A more formal written and oral progress report should be presented by you and your managers to the Board of Directors at the quarterly Board Meeting. The report regarding the status of their assigned projects should be in summary form, and emphasize any problems that they have encountered which might affect a timely completion of any project.

7. **Project Re-Evaluation** – In the implementation phase of any substantial and complex project, mid-course corrections are to be expected. Any substantial mid-course correction to a

project should be explained by the manager responsible for the project and a request should be formally presented to the Board of Directors for approval. It's all part of the **iterative process**, whether you are sighting a gun or keeping a project on schedule. Your objective is to have the bullets that you fire hit the target bulls-eye. You aim your gun at the bulls-eye and fire for effect. If you are off the mark, you adjust your gun sights and aim and fire again till you hit the bulls-eye! It's the same for project management.

SUMMARY

The MBO process will not get off the ground without strong support from you, your management team, and your Board of Directors. If it is strongly supported, MBO will encourage and reward better performance from your managers and employees, and together you will be better able to achieve your common goals and objectives.

CHAPTER 19

YOUR BUSINESS PLAN - A ROADMAP TO SUCCESS!

There are two types of business plans. The first one is based upon business fiction. You start with what you want your gross revenues to be and work your way down to the bottom line. Or, you start with what you want to net income to be and work your way back up to gross revenues. It doesn't really matter because, in either case, you are dealing with your wishes and desires and have no detailed plans to achieve any of them. Not only is this type of business planning self delusional, it is also a downright dangerous to the survival of your business. However, it's easy to complete, because you don't have to create any specific realistic plans to accomplish your objectives.

AN ILLUSTRATION OF A FICTITIOUS BUSINESS PLAN WHERE DESIRE OVERCAME REALITY!

In this particular situation, the owner of a small business was convinced by one of his managers that he should invest a substantial amount of money in a piece of equipment that was already becoming obsolete. The investment in equipment and building modifications totaled several hundred thousand dollars. For this business, that was a substantial investment which would require financing. All of the other managers were against making this investment because an analytical forecast suggested that, at best, there would be no return on this investment. The owner, however, did not want to deal with the reality of the projection. He was convinced that he had to make this investment and needed to show the lending bank a substantial rate of return. The CFO could not in good conscience forecast the rate of return needed to convince the bank that this was a good investment.

As a result, the president turned to the wife of the manager who had initiated the project. She dutifully created an Excel spreadsheet that forecasted a rate of return over time that was absolutely fantastic! In fact, after a few years, this investment was projected to dwarf the return of the rest of the department involved. When the CFO finally got a copy of this projection, he was flabbergasted! His first reaction was a big belly laugh at the naïveté this projection displayed. His second reaction, quickly following the first was "Who in the heck created this projection?" You can almost predict the end of this story. The actual equipment usage only produced about 10% of the revenue necessary to justify the cost of the investment, and never even got close to producing a profit.

The second type of business plan is a financial plan based upon the achievement of certain specific objectives over the next one to three years. The sum total of the attainment of these objectives must be incorporated into the financial projections over that same time frame. Although the plan may show the information in summary, it is based upon a detailed analysis of the following items:

GENERAL BUSINESS PLAN INFORMATION

1. A summary description of your business, your industry, your products and services, your competitors, and the market that you currently serve, and your company's mission statement. (In a few sentences, describe how your company intends to serve your market)
2. A statement of your current business goals and objectives.
3. An executive summary of your three-year financial projections, including a summary of your projected Cash Flow Statement.

MARKET INFORMATION

1. A description of the general industry that you serve.
2. What are the trends in your industry?
3. What is your target market?
4. Describe the competition in your target market.

5. What marketing expansion plans have you included in this business plan?

PRODUCT INFORMATION

1. A description of your products and services.
2. Describe any of your proprietary products and services that are not offered by your competitors.
3. Do you anticipate any competition regarding your proprietary products and services over the next three years?
4. Describe your pricing strategy regarding your proprietary products.
5. Describe your overall marketing strategy regarding competitive products.
6. Describe your pricing strategy regarding your competitive products.
7. Describe any competitive advantages you may have in the marketing, distribution, servicing or product warranties regarding all of your products.
8. Perhaps even more important than item 7, describe any competitive disadvantages you may have in the marketing, distribution, servicing or product warranties regarding all of your products.
9. Analyze these areas in conjunction with your specific goals and objectives to strengthen your competitive advantages and improve or eliminate your competitive disadvantages.

FINANCIAL PLANNING REQUIREMENTS

1. Three years of financial projections by quarter to include budgets and forecasts.

2. A general description of the financial projections.

3. **EXTREMELY IMPORTANT: The supporting assumptions underlying the financial projections must be tied to specific and realistic company goals and objectives. Without this underlying foundation in place, your business plan is**

nothing more than fancy paperwork that looks great but signifies nothing!

4. Three years of projected financial statements to include income statements, balance sheets, and cash flow statements. (The more technical term for a cash flow statement is a "Source and Application of Funds Statement")

5. Three years of projected capital expenditures detailing the purchase of all major capital items by the quarter and year of expected purchase.

6. How much it will cost to fund these capital expenditures in total over the three-year period?

7. How much of this funding will be internally generated?

8. How much of this funding will be provided by lenders?

9. A general description of the type and amount of funding to be provided by each lender, along with interest rates, collateral requirements, specific business uses of the funds provided, and any other special loan provisions required by the lender.

DEVELOPING REALISTIC AND ACCURATE PROJECTIONS

Ensure that you have a collaborative process with your management team to establish your budgets and forecasts. The most accurate financial projections that I have been part of were produced at a weekend retreat devoted to budgets and forecasts. Because we were isolated from the office and other distractions, we are able to focus on the tasks at hand. These projections resulted from a collaborative effort between the president, the operations manager, the marketing manager and myself as the CFO. By obtaining differing points of view regarding future revenues and expenses, we were able to combine more optimistic and more pessimistic forecasts. This resulted in a surprisingly accurate projection for the next year.

Tie your projections of increases or decreases in revenue and expenses to specific goals and objectives that have been enumerated in your general business plan information, and specifically detail the underlying assumptions supporting those projections.

AN ILLUSTRATION OF THE IMPORTANCE OF USING REALISTIC ASSUMPTIONS WHEN MAKING FINANCIAL PROJECTIONS

A marketing representative from our major franchisor visited the company regarding their expected sales projections from us for the coming year. He was successful in his demand that we project a 9% increase in our product sales for this franchisor. This was in the year that we were expecting a slowing of demand at best and a recession at worst. The franchise company's own projections for that year showed a significant decrease in projected sales. Even so, we were expected to agree to a projection based upon a 9% increase in sales, when our most optimistic forecast showed no increase at all in revenue for that year. As I said to the marketing representative, you may as well have required us to project a sales increase of 19% instead of 9% because they are both equally unattainable. I also said that I would be happy to trade the fictitious 9% projected sales increase on paper for one specific, realistic and attainable objective that would increase our product sales.

A GOAL SETTING TIP: An interesting phenomenon occurs when goals are set too high without any relationship to reality. I might ask an individual to jump 2 feet high from a standing position. Let's assume there is an agreement with the individual that he can attain this goal. If I set up an incentive program to reward him for his performance at or above that level, he may well jump higher than that. But if I set the goal at 8 feet, a height he knows he cannot reach, and give him a written incentive program based upon that unattainable goal, the incentive program will likely wind up in the circular file. Because this unattainable incentive program will negatively affect the individual's morale, I would have been better off by not offering this person an incentive program at all!

CONGRATULATIONS! You now have a realistic business plan containing company goals and objectives, sales and marketing strategies, and budgets and forecasts. You can use these tools as a roadmap to manage your business in month to month managers meetings, and quarterly board of directors meetings.

SECTION 6

ANALYZING YOUR
FINANCIAL STATEMENTS

CHAPTER 20

FINANCIAL STATEMENTS - YOUR BUSINESS SCORECARD

AN INTRODUCTION TO FINANCIAL STATEMENTS

To many non-financial managers untrained in accounting, financial statements are like a dark jungle, filled with a jumble of unintelligible numbers, but signifying nothing. If you objectively place yourself among those managers, don't feel lonesome. You have some great company, including Roger Smith, a former chairman of General Motors. Smith initiated GM10, a new car program in 1982 which has been called "The biggest catastrophe in American industrial history." The plan was huge in scope, calling for seven plants that would each assemble 250,000 cars, or 21% of the total U.S. car market. GM10 was poorly executed from the start, and was a financial disaster for the company, from which it never recovered. By 1989, GM was losing $2,000 on every car it produced. When asked by Fortune magazine why GM10 was such a catastrophe, Roger Smith replied, "***I don't know. It's a mysterious thing***. *I've said I'll take my share of the blame on all those things. I was part of the team*". Well, if Mr. Smith had paid more attention to his financial statements during that seven-year period, he might have adjusted his goals and objectives to the reality of what his financial statements were telling him, and listened more to his top-level management team. Roger's VP of Finance, F. Alan Smith, stated that the proposed capital expenditures of 35 billion dollars on GM10 could have been spent on purchasing both Toyota and Nissan, resulting in a huge increase in market share overnight. He openly questioned whether these capital expenditures of 35 billion dollars would pay the same dividends as those acquisitions might have produced. Obviously, instead of producing positive results, those expenditures were sucked into a black hole called GM10 and produced a financial disaster for the company. This debacle has resulted in the much diminished GM that we see today, a company that is now emerging from bankruptcy! The purpose of this chapter is to take some of the mystery out of your financial statements and allow you, as a small business owner or manager, to effectively utilize these statements to manage your business to your advantage, and for the betterment of your company.

THE IMPORTANCE OF ACCURATE FINANCIAL STATEMENTS

I have said on more than one occasion that "*financial analysis is like doing a postmortem on dead meat*"! In other words, when you review accurate financial statements, you are engaging in a historical analysis of the past performance of the company. Nothing you can do in the present will change that past performance. If that is true, why waste any of your valuable time engaging in the analysis of your past performance? Obviously, if all you do is analyze your past performance and do not utilize the results of that analysis to implement positive changes, you truly are wasting your time! You must use your financial analysis of past data to modify or change future results. However, most managers do not even take the time to thoroughly review their financial statements, much less engage in the analysis of their financial results. Before you start your analysis of financial statements, you will want to ensure that they are reasonably accurate. Of course, your year-end statements should, at minimum, be reviewed by an independent outside auditor and, if audited, will have an auditor's opinion as to their reliability. However, that review or audit only occurs once each year, and the results are normally not available until 60 days after your year end date. Therefore, for financial guidance as to your progress throughout the year, you will be relying heavily on monthly interim financial statements. Here are some guidelines that will help to ensure that your monthly financial statements are reasonably accurate.

1. Require your controller to reconcile all bank statements prior to the closing and distribution of month-end financials.
2. Insure that your manufacturer accounts payable which you use to acquire sales inventory are posted current and reconciled prior to your month end closing.
3. Post all of your accounts receivable entries and determine what, if any, adjustments must be made to properly reflect the current status of your Accounts Receivable.
4. Have an aged accounts receivable schedule prepared showing 30, 60, 90 and 120 day balances that should agree in total amount with the general ledger accounts receivable balance.
5. Ensure that your vendor account statements are reconciled to your accounts payable detail prior to the month-end close.
6. Have an accounts payable aging schedule prepared showing 30, 60, 90 and 120 day balances that should agree in total with the amount shown in the general ledger accounts payable balance. If you don't have a cash flow problem, there should be no Accounts Payable balances beyond 60 days, unless those balances represent disputed invoices. Pay particular attention to any debit receivable balances from any of your vendors. These debit balances are vendor receivables resulting from overpayments by you or credit invoices from your vendors that have not yet been paid to you.
7. Have your controller prepare a fixed assets schedule that shows the asset description, original cost, current month's depreciation, accumulated depreciation, and the net book balance of each asset.
8. Have your controller prepare a schedule of long-term liabilities showing current and year-to-date payments of principal and interest. The schedule total should agree to the balance shown in general ledger account.
9. Ensure that all payroll tax, sales tax, excise tax if any, and all state, local, and federal income taxes are reconciled from the required tax reports to the general ledger balances. They should be paid current, to include any income tax estimate payments that have to be made to state, local and federal tax collection departments.

I wouldn't propose to tell you exactly how many times I have gone into an organization and looked at their monthly financials which were more representative of accounting fiction, rather than representing an accurate portrayal of their financial position. By demanding that copies of the reports described above be attached to your monthly financial reports, you're insuring that your financial reports, while they may not be perfect, will be accurate enough to be relied upon. Normally, accurate monthly financials can be completed within seven to 14 days after the month end. However, your business may be one where you can't afford to wait that long for preliminary results, I would suggest interim monthly financials be produced within two to three business days after the month-end using actual and estimated balances. Then, more accurate monthly financial closing statements can be produced within 7 to 14 days after month-end. **There is absolutely no substitute for having this work completed timely and with reasonable accuracy each and every month.**

THREE ILLUSTRATIONS OF SERIOUS PROBLEMS CREATED BY INACCURATE FINANCIAL STATEMENT REPORTING

The Startup - I was hired by a start-up company a number of years ago to be their Chief Financial Officer. I had already previewed their monthly financial statements, and they appear to be doing reasonably well financially. After being there for less than a week, I discovered that their bank accounts had not been reconciled for almost 3 years. They had absolutely no idea as to what their correct cash-in-bank ledger balances were! And if you think that it's not a problem to reconcile three years of bank statements to determine corrected opening balance, think again! Of course, that was not the only problem that this company was plagued with. After an analysis of the payroll tax accounts, it became apparent that this company was deficient in its payroll tax payments to the tune of a six figured liability. By the way, there are 100% penalties that the IRS can impose in addition to the unpaid payroll taxes. Any officer or director or manager who has check signing authority can be held responsible for as much as 200%

of the unpaid payroll taxes, jointly or severally. Given the magnitude of this liability, there was no way that I could become an officer and/or a check signer for this company. These problems that I have described were representative of a lack financial accuracy, internal controls and financial analysis. For example, when I arrived the company had no idea as to what it cost them to produce a product. Since its production costs were unknown, the company could not make a direct comparison to the production costs incurred by their competition. When a reasonably accurate estimate of production costs was finally made, it became evident that our production costs were substantially higher than the competition. It was only a matter of time before we would have to declare bankruptcy. Not surprisingly, within 12 months the company was sold to one of its competitors.

The Turnaround - This example involves a management company that was using a cash basis of accounting for book purposes! I know for a fact that a number of small businesses still use a cash basis of accounting for book purposes. This company, when the financial statements were adjusted to an accrual basis of accounting, saw their cash basis profits totally evaporate. In fact, the company had so many unposted obligations to pay that they were technically insolvent. Eventually, I had to arrange for an Informal Consolidation of Creditors to avoid the need for filing bankruptcy. During this orderly process of winding down the company, we were able to transfer our ongoing business to another company that was profitable. The moral of this story is that cash basis accounting does not realistically portray your company's financial position. The ownership of the company in this example had no idea as to their true financial status. Needless to say they were embarrassed to find out that they were insolvent and not able to meet their financial obligations!

The Established Company - More recently, I was hired by this company to be in charge of their financial, administrative, and computer departments. This company had been in business for a few decades before my arrival and was well established. An analysis of the company's monthly financials indicated that the company and its affiliate were profitable. Nothing could have been further from the reality of the situation! The company was hemorrhaging from each and every key control area. Among those were accounts receivable, warranty receivables, inventory control, and cash management. Once we had assessed the damage done to the company's balance sheet, it became evident that we would have to write off well over $200,000 of uncollectible receivables and missing inventory. The affiliate company's financial statements were several months in arrears, and it was impossible to assess their financial position until such time as we had completed the year-end. Because of the fact that no balance sheet accounts were currently reconciled on a monthly basis, the situation required about three months of backbreaking effort to complete the year-end financial statements. By the time the reconciliations were completed and the accounting adjustments made, the expected profit had evaporated and turned into a substantial loss, along with the bonus that I had negotiated for prior to accepting the position. The result was that the financial position of established company had deteriorated so badly that it became a turnaround company.

The lesson of these three examples is a simple one. If your company's financial statements are inaccurate because your financial controls are virtually nonexistent, your company is like a ship without power and without a rudder. You don't know where you are, you don't know where you've been, and you certainly don't know where you're going! And if you don't know where you're going, any errant wave will get you there. However, you may not like the journey and you certainly won't like the destination, when you are dashed against the financial rocks of bankruptcy.

ACHIEVING TIMELINESS AND ACCURACY IN THE PRODUCTION OF YOUR FINANCIAL STATEMENTS

1. Establish a starting date and schedule with your controller to begin key account reconciliation. An estimated time to complete and a completion date should be attached to each key account.

2. Establish a firm date to have the monthly financial statements completed and reviewed.
3. Come to a consensus with your management team as to a firm time and date for a financial statement review that will be scheduled each month without exception.
4. The financial statements must be completed by accounting, reviewed and distributed to management at least three days before the monthly review meeting date.
5. A final copy of financial statements for each department must be given to the department managers at least two days prior to the monthly meeting for their review.

SUMMARY

I can't place enough emphasis on having timely and accurate interim monthly Financial Statements available to you within 1 to 2 weeks after the month-end. **These statements truly are your business scorecard, if you know how to read them!** In our next 3 chapters, we will cover the basic elements of the Income Statement, the Balance Sheet and The Cash Flow Statement that comprise your Financial Statements.

CHAPTER 21

ANALYZING YOUR INCOME STATEMENT

WHAT IS AN INCOME STATEMENT?

An Income Statement measures your financial performance over a specified period of time. It is your financial report that displays sales, cost of sales, expenses, other revenues and expenses, income taxes and net income after tax (The Bottom Line). The Income Statement, also called a Profit and Loss (P&L) Statement is generally produced monthly, although it can be produced on a daily, weekly, monthly, quarterly or yearly basis. Your Income Statement is your operational scorecard for the time period that is being reported on. Therefore, it is critical to your success that you know how to analyze your Income Statement, and take the requisite amount of time to do so. You can report on more than one time period on the same Income Statement. For example, it is quite common to display monthly and year-to-date information on the same Income Statement, along information for the prior year for comparison purposes.

WHAT ARE THE BUILDING BLOCKS OF YOUR INCOME STATEMENT

Your general ledger contains all of your Income Statement and Balance Sheet active account numbers. Generally, your Income Statement will contain the following broad areas of general ledger accounts:
1. **Sales** – All revenues received from the sale of your products.
2. **Cost of Sales** – All product costs directly related to your product sales.

3. **Operating Expenses** – Expenditures such as Selling, General & Administrative Expenses (S, G&A) relating to your primary business activities.
4. **Other Revenues** – Revenues unrelated to your primary business activities such as interest income, rental and royalty income, and gains on fixed asset and security sales.
5. **Other Expenses** – Expenses unrelated to your primary business activities such as weather damage not covered by insurance, certain types of interest expense, and losses on fixed asset and security sales.
6. **Income Tax Expense** – City, County, State and Federal Income taxes.

The general ledger account numbers that make up an income statement are what I call *"collector accounts"*. These P&L accounts collect detailed information for the entire year. As an example, if you look up the balance in your advertising expense account as of March 31st 2009, it will show you the sum of all your first quarter transactions from 1/01/09 through 3/31/09. If you are looking at total advertising expense for the month of March, your computer program automatically subtracts the February 28th balance from the March 31st balance to display the total of March advertising expenses. At the end of each calendar year, all of your revenue and expense accounts are zeroed out and automatically closed to Retained Earnings, which is a Balance Sheet account. Remember that these are your statements! If you want to track an expense, such as inbound freight that is not recorded in a separate account, have your controller set up a general ledger account to track inbound freight expense. If inbound freight is not identified separately on your expanded Income Statement, have your Controller reformat your Income Statement so that it is specifically identified.

HOW CAN I EFFECTIVELY USE MY INCOME STATEMENT TO MANAGE MY BUSINESS?

Your current and future lenders and investors will almost always request current copies of your monthly Income Statement and Balance Sheet to determine your credit worthiness and to establish credit limits. Most lenders will ask for these financials to be sent to them automatically every month. However, the most important benefit of your Income Statement is your utilization of it to analyze current and year-to-date revenues and expenses, determine the operating performance of your business and project future trends from past results. To efficiently analyze your business performance, you need to combine your income statement with a budget for the same period. You can then easily determine which areas of your business are over or under budget. Specific problem areas, such as advertising, office expense and telephone expense can be easily identified by reviewing an expanded Income Statement. You can also track unfavorable trends in sales, product returns or cost of goods sold.

Take the time to examine the Income Statement for XYZ Company below. What useful information can you glean from this Income Statement? What is going on with XYZ Company? What trends are evident and how did you determine this?

EXHIBIT A

XYZ COMPANY INCOME STATEMENT
FOR MARCH 2009 and the 3 MONTHS ENDING 3/31/09

	MARCH 2009	MARCH BUDGET	AMT OVER (UNDER)	% INC/DEC	3 MONTHS MAR 31 09	1st QTR 09 BUDGET	AMT OVER (UNDER)	% INC/DEC
SALES	**$1,000,000**	**$1,100,000**	**-$100,000**	-9.1%	**$3,100,000**	**$3,300,000**	**-$200,000**	-6.1%
LESS COST OF SALES	$820,000	$880,000	-$60,000	-6.8%	$2,500,000	$2,640,000	-$140,000	-5.3%
GROSS PROFIT ON SALES	**$180,000**	**$220,000**	**-$40,000**	-18.2%	**$600,000**	**$660,000**	**-$60,000**	-9.1%
Gross Margin % (Sales/COS)	18.0%	20.0%			19.4%	20.0%		
OPERATING EXPENSES	$160,000	$165,000	-$5,000	-3.0%	$490,000	$495,000	-$5,000	-1.0%
OPERATING INCOME	**$20,000**	**$55,000**	**-$35,000**	-63.6%	**$110,000**	**$165,000**	**-$55,000**	-33.3%
ADD OTHER INCOME	$10,000	$12,000	-$2,000	-16.7%	$32,000	$36,000	-$4,000	-11.1%
DEDUCT OTHER EXPENSES	$5,000	$4,000	$1,000	25.0%	$14,000	$12,000	$2,000	16.7%
NET INCOME BEFORE TAX	**$25,000**	**$63,000**	**-$38,000**	-60.3%	**$128,000**	**$189,000**	**-$61,000**	-32.3%
DEDUCT INCOME TAXES	$4,000	$13,000	-$9,000	-69.2%	$20,000	$38,000	-$18,000	-47.4%
NET INCOME	**$21,000**	**$50,000**	**-$29,000**	-58.0%	**$108,000**	**$151,000**	**-$43,000**	-28.5%

AN ANALYSIS OF THE SUMMARY INCOME STATEMENT IN EXHIBIT A ABOVE

There is a wealth of information contained in the monthly and year-to-date summary income statement for XYZ Company displayed above that will point our detailed analysis in the right direction.

1. First, XYZ's sales volume has decreased by 9.1% from budget in March and our cost of goods sold has only decreased by 6.8%. Our gross margin has declined to 18% from a budgeted 20%. It's costing us more to sell these products than we had forecasted.

2. XYZ's operating expenses have increased from 15% to 16% of sales. This is to be expected because the budgeted percentage of sales was computed based upon a higher sales volume. You have to examine an expanded Income Statement that has all the account information necessary to do a detailed analysis.

3. Other income has decreased $2,000, perhaps because the interest income component may have decreased due to lower interest rates. Again, a detailed analysis is needed to identify the decline.

4. Income tax expense is lower because of lower pre-tax income. Since income tax expense or credit is generally dependent on the amount of pre-tax income or loss, you should pay more attention to pre-tax income than to net income.

5. The quarterly information tells us that XYZ's sales are trending lower, and in the month of March the decline seems to be picking up speed.

6. XYZ's Net Income Before Tax has decreased 32% for the quarter and 60% in the month of March. This is a disturbing trend that, after analyzing the problems and potential solutions, needs to be addressed by swift management action.

7. Was the sales decline caused by lower sales prices to meet the competition, lower product unit sales or both? These questions need a further input of information from monthly and quarterly product sales reports in order to properly answer.

SUMMARY

Although our analysis above was based on a summary Income Statement without much detail available, we were able to use this statement to point us in the right direction for further detailed analysis. ***As I've said on many occasions, the devil (or in this case the answer) is in the details.*** And, analyzing the details involves time and work. That could be the reason that only a few small business owners and managers are proactive about analyzing their financial statements and effectively utilizing this information to help resolve their business problems. But, isn't it better to deal with those problems now when they're small, as opposed to later when they are big enough to eat your breakfast, lunch and dinner?

CHAPTER 22

ANALYZING YOUR BALANCE SHEET

WHAT IS A BALANCE SHEET?

A Balance Sheet, unlike an Income Statement, is a snapshot of the financial position of your company as of the end of the business day on a specific date. That date is usually the last day of the month, since a fair bit of monthly account reconciliation work has to be completed to make the Balance Sheet accurate. However, the Balance Sheet date could be the 15th of the month or any day during the month. A summary Balance Sheet groups certain Asset, Liability and Shareholder's Equity accounts for reporting purposes. A detail Balance Sheet displays the end-of-day balances for all of your balance sheet accounts. This is sometimes called a "Trial Balance". This term goes back to the old green visor and armband days when balance sheets were produced manually and the Trial Balance actually determined whether the Balance Sheet was in balance or not. According to the balance sheet formula, Assets must equal Liabilities plus Shareholders Equity. When you examine your Balance Sheet you will notice that all of your asset categories are displayed on the left and the liabilities and shareholders equity sections are displayed on the right. The total for each side must be identical, or an obvious error has been made.

WHAT ARE THE BUILDING BLOCKS OF YOUR BALANCE SHEET?

1. **Assets** – Assets are physical or intangible things owned by your company that can be valued in monetary terms. Typically, assets are employed in your business to produce and sell products; provide services that can be sold, or for anything

else that enhances the primary business of your company. You also may have investment assets that are held for investment revenue or for sale at a later date. Assets include physical property, such as real estate, plant and equipment, and inventory. Also included are intangible assets that have value such as patents, trademarks, copyrights and goodwill.

2. **Liabilities** – Liabilities consist of short and long term debt, such as accounts payable, payroll and income taxes payable and short and long term loans.

3. **Shareholders' Equity** – Shareholders' Equity is also called equity capital or net worth. It is comprised of the par value of any Capital Stock issuances, Paid-in Capital if any, Treasury Stock offsets to equity, and Retained Earnings.

HOW IS YOUR BALANCE SHEET ORGANIZED?

ASSETS

1. **Current Assets** – Current Assets are cash or other assets that can be quickly converted to cash within the next 12 months. Examples of other Current Assets include Accounts Receivable, Short-term Notes Receivable, Investment Securities which are valued at the market price on the Balance Sheet date, and Inventory which is generally valued at cost.

2. **Fixed Assets** – Fixed Assets are assets which are utilized in your business but that are not available for sale, such as real estate, plant and equipment, vehicles, furniture and fixtures, and other property used in the business.

3. **Intangible Assets** – Intangible Assets are non-current assets and are generally carried on your Balance Sheet at cost less any amortization, and include such items as patents, trademarks, copyrights and goodwill.

4. **Other Assets** – Other Assets are non-current assets held for a term longer than 12 months which can include a variety of

asset types. Other Assets can include utility deposits, insurance prepaid for future years, investments not held for sale, or other non-current assets, like deferred taxes, that do not fit into the asset categories listed above.

LIABILITIES

1. **Current Liabilities** - Current Liabilities are obligations that must be paid within the next twelve months. Examples include Accounts Payable, Accrued Payroll Payable, Short Term Loans, Income Taxes Payable, and Other Accrued Expenses.

2. **Long-term Liabilities** - Long-term Liabilities are obligations or portions of obligations that are payable within 12 months of the Balance Sheet date. Long-term Liabilities can include the Long-term portion of bank loans, real estate mortgage loans, long-term vendor financing and other less defined items such as Deferred Income Taxes Payable over one year away from reversing and having to be paid.

SHAREHOLDERS' EQUITY

Shareholders' Equity - Shareholders' equity is the total book value that the Shareholders' have invested in the business. Shareholders' equity is comprised of the par value of any Capital Stock issuances, Paid-in Capital if any, Treasury Stock offsets to equity, and Retained Earnings. Retained Earnings is the sum of all yearly profits and losses closed to it minus any dividends that have been paid to shareholders. Theoretically, if all assets were sold and all liabilities were paid at their book value as of the Balance Sheet date, there would be cash left in the company in the amount of the Shareholders' Equity at the end of that day.

HOW CAN I USE MY BALANCE SHEET TO ANALYZE MY BUSINESS?

Your Balance Sheet displays a snapshot of your company's assets, liabilities and shareholders' equity as of a specific date. Interim balance sheets do not necessarily make any comparison to other Balance Sheet periods, although audited Balance Sheets will show a side-by-side comparison with the prior year information. If you have a side-by-side Balance Sheet, there is a lot of useful information and ratios that you can develop. However, the Balance Sheet does not report the cash flows into and out of your business during the accounting period. Therefore, you need to examine a Statement of Cash Flows (also called a Cash Flow Statement) to analyze your sources and uses of cash. The Cash Flow Statement is covered in the next chapter.

ANALYZING YOUR BALANCE SHEET

Take the time to examine the Balance Sheet for XYZ Company on the next two pages below. What useful information can you glean from this Balance Sheet? What trends do you see for XYZ Company that might need to be investigated and how did you determine this?

EXHIBIT B

XYZ COMPANY BALANCE SHEET
March 31st, 2009 & March 31st, 2008

	ASSETS 3/31/2009	ASSETS 3/31/2008
CURRENT ASSETS		
CASH	$200,000	$150,000
ACCOUNTS RECEIVABLE	$1,050,000	$950,000
INVENTORY	$500,000	$500,000
FACTORY RECEIVABLES	$50,000	$50,000
TOTAL CURRENT ASSETS	**$1,800,000**	**$1,650,000**
WORKING CAPITAL RATIO	**1.81**	**1.73**
CURRENT ASSETS DIVIDED		
BY CURRENT LIABILITIES		
FIXED ASSETS	$1,650,000	$1,550,000
LESS ACCUM DEPRECIATION	$550,000	$500,000
NET FIXED ASSETS	**$1,100,000**	**$1,050,000**
INTANGIBLE ASSETS		
PATENTS	$50,000	$50,000
GOODWILL	$40,000	$50,000
TOTAL - INTANGIBLE ASSETS	**$90,000**	**$100,000**
OTHER ASSETS		
DEPOSITS	$10,000	$10,000
LONG TERM INVESTMENTS	$150,000	$150,000
TOTAL - OTHER ASSETS	**$160,000**	**$160,000**
TOTAL ASSETS	**$3,150,000**	**$2,960,000**

EXHIBIT B

XYZ COMPANY BALANCE SHEET
March 31st, 2009 & March 31st, 2008

	LIABILITIES 3/31/2009	LIABILITIES 3/31/2008
CURRENT LIABILITIES		
ACCOUNTS PAYABLE	$870,000	$800,000
PAYROLL LIABILITY	$30,000	$40,000
INCOME TAXES PAYABLE	$20,000	$30,000
SHORT-TERM LOANS	$75,000	$85,000
TOTAL CURENT LIABILITIES	**$995,000**	**$955,000**
LONG-TERM DEBT		
LONG TERM BANK LOANS	$500,000	$510,000
LONG TERM LOANS - OTHER	$50,000	$60,000
TOTAL LONG-TERM DEBT	**$550,000**	**$570,000**
SHAREHOLDERS EQUTY		
CAPITAL STOCK	$532,000	$532,000
PAID-IN SURPLUS	$218,000	$218,000
TOTAL CAPITAL	$750,000	$750,000
RETAINED EARNINGS		
RETAINED EARNINGS 3/31/08	$685,000	$685,000
ADD 2008 NET INCOME	$220,000	
DEDUCT DIVIDENDS	$50,000	
TOTAL RETAINED EARNINGS	$855,000	
TOTAL SHAREHOLDERS' EQUITY	**$1,605,000**	**$1,435,000**
TOTAL LIABILITIES & S/H EQUITY	**$3,150,000**	**$2,960,000**

LIQUIDITY RATIOS COMPUTED FROM YOUR BALANCE SHEET INFORMATION

To understand certain liquidity ratios, we first have to define Working Capital. Quite simply, **Working Capital is computed by subtracting Current Liabilities from Current Assets**. If the result is positive you have net working capital and if it is negative you have negative working capital. Negative working capital is not looked upon too kindly by lenders. One of the most important ratios that you compute is your Current or Working Capital Ratio, which is a measurement of your company's liquidity or ability to service its short term obligations. The **Working Capital Ratio is computed by dividing your total Current Assets by your Current Liabilities**. In todays recessionary and credit restricted market, the closer you can bring that ratio into a range of 1.5 to 2 the better off you will be financially. Any Working Capital Ratio less than 1 means you have negative working capital. There is also another measurement of financial liquidity called the Quick or Acid Test Ratio. To compute this ratio you simply add your cash, readily marketable securities, and accounts receivable, and divide that number by your Current Liabilities. Obviously, this is a much more stringent measure of liquidity since it does not include your inventory, and your creditors will not be happy unless your Acid Test ratio is greater than one.

In Exhibit B above, your Working Capital for 3/31/09 is $805,000. The formula is as follows:

Working Capital = Current Assets – Current Liabilities.

I have computed for you the Working Capital (Current) Ratios for the current year of 1.81 and the prior year of 1.73. The current Working Capital ratio is well within our target range and has improved year over year. Now let's compute the Acid Test Ratio from the information in Exhibit B above. The formula is as follows:

Acid Test Ratio = Cash + Accounts Receivable + Marketable Securities/Current Liabilities.

In this case, the ratio in the current year is $1,300,000/$995,000 which results in an Acid Test Ratio of 1.31 compared with 1.20 in the prior year. XYZ's lenders would be happy with these numbers!

OTHER BALANCE SHEET ANALYSES & OBSERVATIONS

1. At XYZ Company, Accounts Receivable have increased $100,000 from the prior year, yet sales were lower than projected last quarter. You will probably want to examine an aged receivables report to determine what has caused this increase.
2. Why has our Accounts Payable balance increased $70,000? An examination of an aged accounts Payable Schedule produced on the same date as the Balance Sheet should help us to analyze this increase.

In our next chapter we will utilize more information from Exhibit B to help us build a Cash Flow Statement. The following Chapter will help you to analyze the sources and uses of cash over the prior year.

CHAPTER 23

UNDERSTANDING YOUR CASH FLOW STATEMENT

WHAT IS A CASH FLOW STATEMENT?

A Cash Flow Statement measures your sources and uses of cash over a specified period of time. The cash flow statement includes only inflows and outflows of cash and cash equivalents and excludes transactions that do not directly affect your cash receipts and expenditures. These noncash transactions can include depreciation, amortization, bad debt expense additions to reserve accounts, and other items that do not involve cash flow. **The Cash Flow Statement is a "Show Me the Money" report** based strictly on the movement of cash and cash equivalents in and out of your company. The Cash Flow Statement reports on the three types of cash flows. They are cash flows generated from operating activities, investing activities, and financing activities. Non-cash operating expenses, such as depreciation, are added back to Net Income and are also reported by the auditors in footnotes to the financial statements.

HOW IS THE CASH FLOW STATEMENT ORGANIZED?

The Cash Flow Statement - The Cash Flow Statement is divided into 3 broad areas. They are funds provided by or utilized by Operating Activities, Investing Activities and Financing Activities. The sum of these three areas should equal the change in Cash & Cash Equivalents for the year being reported on. This change is computed by subtracting the prior year's Working Capital from the current year's Working

Capital. Examples of each of the 3 broad areas of the Cash Flow statement are shown below:

1. **Operating Activities** - You always start this section with the prior years Net Income. You then add back all of the non-cash items that are in your income statement starting with depreciation and amortization which are accounting estimates for the reduction in value of the assets which are being depreciated or amortized over the useful life of those assets. Since depreciation and amortization expense are entries that do not involve the expenditure of cash, they are added back to Net Income. There are other non-cash entries, such as loans or accounts receivable reserve entries, the net change in certain expense accrual entries, and the provision for deferred taxes that do not involve the expenditure of cash, and should be added back to Net Income in this section.

2. **Investing Activities** - Investing Activities include the purchase and sale of plant, property and equipment and other long term assets. It also includes the purchase and sale of long term investments, and corporate loans made to third parties or repayments of those loans.

3. **Financing Activities** - Financing Activities are comprised of a number of finance related items, the most common of which are the issuance, sale or repurchase of Common Stock, the issuance, sale or repurchase of Bonds or debt instruments, new Long-Term Debt or Debt Repayments and Cash Dividends paid to shareholders.

ANALYZING THE EXPANDED BALANCE SHEET AND CASH FLOW STATEMENT

Take the time to examine the expanded Balance Sheet and Cash Flow Statement for XYZ Company on the next three pages. You will notice that I have numerically keyed the year-to-year Balance Sheet Increases or Decreases to the individual items making up the 3/31/09 Cash Flow statement. What information can you glean from this Cash Flow Statement?

EXHIBIT C

Shows the Increase/Decrease for the Year
XYZ COMPANY BALANCE SHEET
March 31st, 2009 & March 31st, 2008

	ASSETS	INC/DEC	ASSETS
	3/31/2009	**3/31/09**	**3/31/2008**
CURRENT ASSETS			
CASH	$200,000	**50,000**	$150,000
ACCOUNTS RECEIVABLE	$1,050,000	**100,000**	$950,000
INVENTORY	$500,000		$500,000
FACTORY RECEIVABLES	$50,000	———	$50,000
TOTAL CURRENT ASSETS	**$1,800,000**	150,000	**$1,650,000**
WORKING CAPITAL* (7)	**$805,000**	110,000	**$695,000**
*CURRENT ASSETS MINUS			
CURRENT LIABILITIES			
FIXED ASSETS (4)	$1,650,000	**100,000**	$1,550,000
LESS ACCUM DEPRECIATION (2)	$550,000	**50,000**	$500,000
NET FIXED ASSETS	**$1,100,000**		**$1,050,000**
INTANGIBLE ASSETS			
PATENTS	$50,000		$50,000
GOODWILL (3)	$40,000	-10,000	$50,000
TOTAL - INTANGIBLE ASSETS	**$90,000**		**$100,000**
OTHER ASSETS			
DEPOSITS	$10,000		$10,000
LONG TERM INVESTMENTS	$150,000		$150,000
TOTAL – OTHER ASSETS	**$160,000**		**$160,000**
TOTAL ASSETS	**$3,150,000**		**$2,960,000**

EXHIBIT C

Shows the Increase/Decrease for the Year
XYZ COMPANY BALANCE SHEET
March 31st, 2009 & March 31st, 2008

	LIABILITIES 3/31/2009	INC/DEC 3/31/09	LIABILITIES 3/31/2008
CURRENT LIABILITIES			
ACCOUNTS PAYABLE	$850,000	**50,000**	$800,000
PAYROLL LIABILITY	$50,000	**10,000**	$40,000
INCOME TAXES PAYABLE	$20,000	**-10,000**	$30,000
SHORT-TERM LOANS	$75,000	**-10,000**	$85,000
TOTAL CURENT LIABILITIES	**$995,000**	**40,000**	**$955,000**
LONG-TERM DEBT			
LONG TERM BANK LOANS	$500,000	**-10,000**	$510,000
LONG TERM LOANS - OTHER	$50,000	**-10,000**	$60,000
TOTAL LONG-TERM DEBT (6)	**$550,000**	**-20,000**	**$570,000**
SHAREHOLDERS EQUTY			
CAPITAL STOCK	$532,000		$532,000
PAID-IN SURPLUS	$218,000		$218,000
TOTAL CAPITAL	$750,000		$750,000
RETAINED EARNINGS			
RETAINED EARNINGS 3/31/08	$685,000		$685,000
ADD 2008 NET INCOME (1)	$220,000	**220,000**	
DEDUCT DIVIDENDS (5)	$50,000	**50,000**	
TOTAL RETAINED EARNINGS	$855,000		
TOTAL SHAREHOLDERS' EQUITY	**$1,605,000**		**$1,435,000**
TOTAL LIABILITIES & S/H EQUITY	**$3,150,000**		**$2,960,000**

EXHIBIT D

XYZ COMPANY CASH FLOW STATEMENT
YEAR ENDED March 31ˢᵗ, 2009

SOURCES AND USES OF CASH		3/31/2009 INC/DEC	Ex C Ref#
NET INCOME		**$220,000**	(1)
ADD NON-CASH ADJUSTMENTS			
DEPRECIATION		$50,000	(2)
AMORTIZATION		$10,000	(3)
NET CASH FROM OPERATIONS		**$280,000**	
ADDITIONS TO FIXED ASSETS		($100,000)	(4)
NET CASH USED FOR INVESTING		**($100,000)**	
DIVIDEND PAYMENTS		($50,000)	(5)
LONG-TERM DEBT REPAYMENTS		($20,000)	(6)
NET CASH USED FOR FINANCING		**($70,000)**	
SUM OF SOURCES & USES OF CASH YE 3/31/09		**$110,000**	
CASH & EQUIVALENTS 3/31/09*	$805,000		(7)
LESS CASH & EQUIVALENTS 3/31/08	$695,000		(7)
NET CHANGE IN CASH & EQUIVALENTS YE 3/31/09		**$110,000**	(7)

*Working Capital for 2009 & 2008

CASH FLOW STATEMENT ANALYSIS

1. In analyzing the expanded Balance Sheet and Cash Flow Statement, you will note the following items that will be of interest to the owner/manager of XYZ Company.

2. Working Capital (7) has increased by $110,000 but not to the extent of the Net Cash provided from Operations of $280,000.

3. $60,000 of non-cash depreciation and amortization expense were add back to Net Income, as those expenses were already included in the calculation of the Net Income.

4. XYZ Company purchased an additional $100,000 of Fixed Assets.

5. XYZ paid a net amount of $20,000 to reduce Long-Term Debt.

6. $50,000 in Dividends was paid to XYZ shareholders.

7. As already indicated, Accounts Receivable have increased by $100,000. This should be investigated.

SUMMARY

We have reviewed all of the major Financial Statements, comprised of the Income Statement, the Balance Sheet and the Cash Flow Statement. You should now have a better understanding of these financial reports. The Shareholders' Equity Statement for small businesses is relatively simple with yearly changes usually occurring only in the addition of profits and losses to Retained Earnings and the payment of shareholder dividends, if any. Therefore, I have elected not to cover this Statement, as it duplicates what we have already covered in the comparative Balance Sheet.

SECTION 7

INCREASING SALES AND IMPROVING GROSS MARGINS

CHAPTER 24

MAXIMIZING SALES REVENUES

SALES – THE WELLSPRING OF INCOME

Let's face it squarely, without revenue or sales there is no income! Maintaining and increasing sales is absolutely critical to the survival of your business. Therefore, you need to spend the requisite amount of time that it takes to analyze your sales and revenue sources by product or service, and by government, contract, wholesale and retail customers within that line of business. You should list your various types of customers by descending sales volume, high to low, along with the individual customer's pricing structure. Don't overlook those customers with low sales volume. They may be prime candidates for a personal sales call from the sales manager to find out the reasons that the customers may have reduced their purchases with your company. Once you have this information on your desk, you are ready to analyze your sales with the objective of increasing your sales and income.

STRATEGIES FOR INCREASING SALES AND GROSS PROFIT

There are endless ways to increase sales and sales gross profit, limited only by your creativity. I have listed below some of the more important strategies that are generally applicable to most businesses. You will notice that I have listed these strategies from ones that are short-term and easily implemented to longer-term strategies that are more difficult to implement. I will cover each of these strategies in more depth after this summary, in future chapters.

1. **Pricing Strategies** – In the short term, this strategy is one of the most important and least understood tools in your arsenal. Pricing is also one of the most misused strategies by small businesses. This results because they have not done their homework, and established the market and customer information it takes to make effective pricing decisions. Do you have an overall company pricing strategy? If you do, is it working for or against you?

2. **Products and Services** – How are your products and services selling? How do they stack up with the competition? What do you need to do to improve your products? Do you need to add to existing product lines, delete others, or add entirely new products? What do your customers think that you need to do? What is your competition planning to do in the way of new product offerings? Some of these product-related strategies can be implemented in the short term. Others are intermediate to long term strategies.

3. **Availability** – This is a key strategy that directly affects your customer's buying decision, and your pricing strategy. Your customer is calling in or is at your location and is ready to buy your product. The customer is probably willing to pay an additional amount for the convenience of having the product available for purchase. The question is "Do you have that product on hand?" And if you don't, what is the reason for the out of stock condition, and how long will it take to get the product to the customer?

4. **Selection** – Although selection is highly related to product availability, you have got to examine the product line that you are stocking. Do you have a full line of the product, including all types, sizes and colors? Or are you stocking only the best sellers in that product line?

5. **Advertising and Promotion** – What kinds of advertising programs are you currently supporting? Please include on your list any yellow page advertising that you do. How effective is your advertising? How do you know? Is the effectiveness

of your advertising measureable? If not, how do you modify your advertising programs to make them measureable?

6. **Quality** – Are your products and services tested for quality? Do you get feedback from your customers as to the quality and durability of your products? If not, why not?

7. **Product Guarantees or Warranties** – Do you or your vendors guarantee or warranty your products? Are extended warranties available from your company or third parties. Are those third party warranties properly serviced by the provider? Are your customers happy with the warranty service that you provide or sell?

8. **Customer Service** – Do you service the products that you sell? If so, have you measured customer satisfaction with your service department?   How do you typically handle customer complaints? What is your return policy regarding customer purchase returns? Is this policy properly communicated to the customer on your invoice at the time of purchase? Do you give your customers the benefit of the doubt when addressing their problems?

9. **Reputation** – What is your reputation within the business community? With your customers? With your vendors? With your competition? If you don't know, you should find out by taking the appropriate action to develop this information on a regular basis.

10. **Convenience** – There is far more to convenience than simply location. For example, do you make deliveries to your customers, and on what terms? Is your store or location conveniently designed for your customer base? Is there sufficient parking available? Are your products easily identified, priced and labeled. Are there enough knowledgeable salespersons and cashiers to properly service your customers without encountering inordinate waiting times? Is it easy for the customer to request a special order, establish credit, check

out and pay by credit card, and arrange for a customer pick-up or delivery of a product?

11. **Location** – Perhaps it's not the best time to think about it because of your lease commitments, but is your location helping you or holding you back? Is your current location too small or too big? Is it attractive or an eyesore? Do you need to relocate nearer to your customer base? Do you need to consider a new satellite location, closing an existing one, or both? Are there substantial financial advantages to any of these options? How does your current location and your relocation options reconcile with your customer convenience requirements above?

SUMMARY

All of these factors are critical to increasing your sales and gross margins. We will cover each of these strategies designed to increase sales and gross margin in more detail in following chapters.

CHAPTER 25

SALES PRICING STRATEGIES

Implementing rational pricing strategies is your quickest way to achieve both higher sales and increased gross margin. First, you must analyze your business in terms of what your customers purchase from you and why they choose to purchase from your company. What is your mix of proprietary and competitive products and services? Without a doubt, you have much greater flexibility in setting prices for proprietary products. Secondly, you have to analyze your customer purchases by type. Obviously, there is nothing that can be done about contract (fixed) pricing until the contract is up for renewal. Government sales generally fall into this category. However, you probably have considerable leeway in setting retail and wholesale pricing strategies. There are several broad areas where the establishment of a fair and consistent pricing strategy can generate a lot of extra profit. And remember that if you generate increased gross margin from implementing more profitable pricing strategies, that same amount will add to your net income before tax on a dollar for dollar basis. Listed below are several pricing strategies that can, individually or in combination, significantly increase your gross profit on sales and your net income.

1. **Retail and Wholesale Customer Purchase Volume Pricing -** Analyze your retail and wholesale customers for the frequency and total amount of annual purchases. Are your customer's pricing structures in line with their purchase amounts? Many companies simply give their best pricing to large companies without analyzing their purchase volume. As an example, you may have IBM as a customer. However, to better service their customers, they are only purchasing a small amount of product from you that they don't already carry in their inventory. In

this case, if you have IBM set up with a discount pricing matrix, change that matrix to list price as soon as possible! They probably won't argue with the price increase, given the small amount of their purchases. And, your sales won't decline since they are only purchasing from you what they absolutely need to better service their business. Take the time, along with your sales manager, to analyze all of your accounts for volume based pricing. You may be amazed at what you find! Once you have analyzed your wholesale and retail accounts, you should assign them new price codes based on their purchase volumes. Then, you should implement those price matrix changes that you have agreed on. Expect to identify a few customers that, because of their volume, should actually be given a lower price matrix. Use that information to meet with them and offer them a better discount if they agree to purchase even more of your product!

2. **Proprietary Products Pricing** – This is also called captive products pricing, where you are the only one in your territory selling the product. Since you are "the only game in town", you can, within reasonable limits, set your own price. Obviously, if you get too greedy on pricing, your customers can and will go out of town to buy that product. However, in the short term, within reasonable price limits the product supply/demand curve may be relatively inelastic. In other words, customer purchases of the product will not change significantly in a range between product give-away prices and a price that has a substantial profit built in to it. So, why give it away? Your proprietary product price matrix sales prices should average 15% to 20% higher than your competitive products. Take the time to analyze this information, and set your proprietary products price matrixes accordingly. Assuming that you have not already increased your proprietary product pricing, you will be able to increase sales, gross margins and generate a ton of profit to your bottom line when you start.

3. **Low Cost Product Pricing** – It will generally cost you as much to sell a 50 cent item as it does to sell a $50.00 item, from the standpoint of stocking, selling, invoicing and sales processing

costs. Since that is obviously true, why not systematically add an extra mark-up to your low cost products. The extra gross margin will help to offset your selling expenses, which are a much larger percentage of your low cost product sales prices. You are simply trying to achieve a reasonable return on low cost product sales. Let's say you are selling a 50 cent product, and your normal markup over cost is 100%. Your sales price would be $1.00 and your 50 cent gross margin on sale would probably not cover the direct and indirect costs of the transaction. However, if your low cost price markup is 400% of cost, you have now sold the product for $2.00 and your gross margin is now $1.50! The incremental price difference to your customer is only a dollar. However, when you total up all your low priced product sales, it will make a significant difference to your company's bottom line. It's up to you and your computer whiz to input your own low cost product price matrix parameters and start making more money!

4. **Slow-moving Product Pricing** – Let's assume that you have made a favorable decision to have a full line of products on hand to service your customers needs. Some of those products will be slow movers. You have made a good decision, but you shouldn't have to pay for all of the extra costs of stocking slow moving products. Set up your price matrix to charge an additional 10% to 15% on slow moving parts. If you define a slow moving part as one that sells from 1 to 4 times a year, you will have to pay additional inventory holding costs and the product will be taking up space in your warehouse for a longer period of time. Why not recoup these extra expenses by incorporating a slow moving product surcharge into your pricing matrix? It's only a reasonable return to you, and your customers will be so happy about having the product available for purchase that they probably won't complain about the additional mark-up! So why wait? Pay your computer whiz a little overtime to input a slow moving product pricing matrix and start making a lot more money!

5. **Core Returns** – If your business sells products or parts that allow a credit for the return of the used product or part as

a "Core Return", tune into this. If you are not marking up the cost of the core to your customer by at least 20%, you are losing money on your core returns. Keep in mind that your customers receive a full "core credit" if they return an undamaged core. Therefore, only the customers who didn't return their cores are charged the additional markup. This additional charge helps to offset the cost of core handling, tracking, shipping, and in some instances, partial or full denial of the core credit by the manufacturer.

6. **Two Money Making Ideas Regarding Core Returns** – I was hired as a CFO for a company that was not marking up core sales to their customer. They were selling cores at their cost. However, because of the attendant expenses relating to core returns, they were actually losing money on every core they sold! I instituted a core pricing policy that eventually marked up cores at 60% over cost. If the customer did not return the core, we also contracted with companies that specialized in core returns to purchase cores from them at 50% of the core cost. This core price included the freight expense to ship the core to the manufacturer from the core return company's core inventory. The company also guaranteed that we would receive a 100% core credit from the manufacturer. After instituting this procedure, when the customer didn't return a core, our company made a gross profit of 110%. This was comprised of the 60% customer mark-up plus the 50% manufacturer credit of the original core cost. How sweet it is to make a 110% profit on customer cores not returned, while our competitors were losing money on the same transactions!

An Example of the Importance of Pricing Strategies – Some time ago, I visited a small grocery store that a friend of mine owned in a medium sized city in California. He was not as profitable as he should have been, and was wondering what he could do to improve his bottom line. I offered to do an analysis of his business and made the following observations and suggestions regarding his product pricing.

A. His customers lived in the neighborhood, and a number of them were walk-ins.

B. He offered delivery service to a number of his regular customers.

C. His store pricing was very competitive on commonly purchased grocery items such as milk, bread, soft drinks, chips, beer and other fast moving items.

D. He was trying to be equally competitive on other grocery items.

My friend really had 2 stores in one! On the one hand, he was a grocery store selling staples at a competitive price. On the other hand, he was a specialty convenience store offering other grocery items and delivery services to his customers at the same competitive price. The solution I recommended for him was to mark up his non-staple grocery items substantially over his current mark-up. He would not lose any significant volume because his walk-in and delivery customers were effectively captive customers. His other customers were attracted by his competitive pricing on food staples, but were not going to go to another store just to purchase a can of green beans or asparagus! Once he realized he could utilize a two tiered pricing structure and implemented it, his profitability soared!

SUMMARY

You can utilize pricing strategies in various ways to actually increase your total sales and gross margin. The higher your gross margin, everything else being equal, the higher your gross sales even though your unit sales may not have increased at all. And almost all of the increase in gross margin will add to your net income before tax!

CHAPTER 26

SALES PRODUCT AND SERVICE INNOVATIONS AND IMPROVEMENTS

I used the word "improvement" to illustrate that you need to take a broad gauge view of product and service innovation. You can't hit home runs with every innovation, but you can hit singles, doubles, the occasional triple and even walk to first base. And, not every change is intrinsic to the product itself. The change may be in the packaging. As a great example, look at the Coors cold activated bottle. Its not the bottle, it's the thermo-chromic ink in the label that turns the mountains blue when the beer is cold enough to drink, and vice-versa when the beer warms up! What a great advertising idea, which only required changing the label at minimal cost. Even though the beer and the bottle were the same, the perceived value of the product in the mind of the consumer increased substantially! So, as you're thinking about "product innovation", don't be constrained by the conventional definition of what a product innovation is. Be a maverick and think outside the box! Consider the product, the service and anything that has to do with the product or service, such as packaging, labeling, product display, discounts, coupons, contests, game pieces, and delivery options, to name a few. Let your imagination run wild. Who knows, you may be more of a "product innovator" than you thought! With that thought in mind, I would suggest the following more conventional approaches to the development of unconventional ideas.

1. **For all the products you sell, attend all of the product conventions, seminars, factory tours and trade shows that you are able to schedule** – Of course the closer the trade show is to your location the better, as it saves you a lot of

time and expense. If you can't attend personally, perhaps one of your employees can. As part of their attendance, they can collect the product literature and debrief you about what they learned when they return. This has the added advantage of focusing their attention while they attend the trade show, and improving their presentation skills when they debrief you. If none of your personnel can attend, arrange with someone you know who is attending the seminar or trade show to collect as much product literature as they can and mail it to you. Upon receiving and reviewing the product information you can then call the individual, personally thank him for his efforts, and pick his brain about any general or specific things that he has observed.

2. **Take a customer to lunch!** – Plan regular lunches and visits with a cross-section of your customers, both large and small. Before visiting with them, review any customer surveys they have completed to avoid being caught flat-footed. Among other things, find out what they would like to see in your product or service lines that you don't currently offer. Also ask them about any product changes or modifications they would like to see you make. Ask them how you stack up against the competition. Also ask them how you can improve their perception of you, your company and your products.

3. **Contact your outside Board members and other owner/ managers in affiliated businesses that you can trust to get their opinion of your business and products** – This information, along with the information you have already developed, can help you complete a strengths and weaknesses (SWOT) analysis for your business. However, don't be as simplistic as one franchisor I know of who required a SWOT survey. You had only two choices, to identify a survey item as either a strength or a weakness. Believe it or not, there were no other choices! This proves again that sometimes incomplete information is worse than no information at all! Can you imagine filling out a mandatory survey about a product related item, i.e. packaging that is neither a competitive strength nor a weakness, and having

to flip a coin to answer the question, knowing that either answer is wrong! **You need at least 5 levels for your SWOT analysis.** They include a substantial strength, a moderate strength, neither a strength nor a weakness, a moderate weakness, or a serious weakness. This will allow you to properly sort, categorize, and report on your competitive data.

4. **Set aside one hour each month at the end of your monthly managers meeting as a creative product innovation hour** – Insure that you and your managers prepare for this hour by writing down all the ideas that come to mind regarding how your company can innovate, update or modify your existing products to increase sales and profits.

5. **Armed with the information generated above, take a long and unbiased look at your existing products and services with regard to the feasibility of implementing any of the ideas you have developed** – If an idea is feasible and passes a cost/benefit analysis, start planning for its implementation!

6. **Have your implementation project managers report on the progress that has been made to implement these ideas during your monthly managers meeting before the creative hour begins** – You will be amazed at how much power and punch your project implementation reporting will generate for your creative hour. Your creative hour will be the psychic beneficiary of the positive reporting on other creative ideas that are turning into reality. Your staff will know that many of the product innovation ideas for implementation sprang from the creative hour. If that doesn't light a fire under the creative juices of your staff, get a new staff!

SUMMARY

The area of product innovation and improvement is a place where you can allow the collective imaginations of you and your management team to run wild! The actions outlined above will provide you with information for creative sessions that will generate new ideas. These ideas will lead to the implementation of improved products and services for your company to market. Be patient with the process because in all the clutter of ideas that you generate, there will be a few golden nuggets!

CHAPTER 27

SALES PRODUCT
AVAILABILITY AND SELECTION

We sometimes called this "the big A", as product availability is that critical in achieving your sales goals. When you don't have a product on hand, unless it's proprietary and the customer doesn't have an alternate vendor, you can't sell it. Therefore, if the product is competitive, lack of product availability will generally result in a "lost sale". This is one of the key indicators of your ability to service your customer's needs. Of course, to track a key indicator, you have to have some method of measuring it. To provide accurate information regarding lost sales, you must enter the following information into your computer system daily at the point of sale.

1. The Employee Code or Name reporting the Lost Sale
2. Department Code or Name
3. Date of Lost Sale
4. The number of individual products, and Product Codes of the Lost Sale items
5. If you don't have product codes because the requested product is not in your computer database, provide a product description and an estimated sales price.
6. Reasons or Reason Codes for your Lost Sales
7. Customer # or Name
8. Sales Loss, in dollars (If you have a customer number and product code, this can be computer generated)

The responsibility for entering lost sales information could be assigned to the cashier, the floor sales assistant, or the salesperson inputting the information to determine whether the product is in stock. In most automated sales and inventory tracking systems, this information will be stored for past and future reporting automatically. Your inventory demand will also be updated for future purchase requirements, but this only occurs when the "lost sales" data is entered into your computer system. In all too many cases, the "lost sale" information is not entered properly, if at all. Therefore, this valuable information is lost. The point here is that you have to insure that you are getting accurate "lost sales" information entered into the computer system daily by the responsible employees.

Assuming that you now have accurate "lost sales" information, what do you do with it? First, you need to generate regular Lost Sales Reports by the day, week or month as you feel is appropriate for your business needs. You will want to have this sorted by product, item and customer. You may also want to have a sort based upon the dollar value of lost product sales in descending dollar value so that you can review the high dollar lost sales first. If you have not done a review of "lost sales" before due to a lack of information, you may be unpleasantly surprised at the results! You can now use the lost sales information to adjust your inventory levels, increase your sales revenue, and reduce those lost sales! By the way, lost sales will never go to zero, as there are lost sale items that you won't want to stock. However, with the proper input, reporting, review and inventory follow-up, you can reduce the number of lost sales to an acceptable level.

SUMMARY

You may be surprised at the amount of lost sales that you are experiencing, but you will never get this information unless you have a procedure to enter the lost sales data into your computer system. You can then generate meaningful lost sales management reports on a regular basis that will allow you to reduce those lost sales to an acceptable level, based on the inventory you are willing to stock.

CHAPTER 28

SALES ADVERTISING
AND PROMOTION

Almost every company advertises and promotes its business, products and services. However, do you advertise intelligently and get the most out of your advertising dollars? Intelligent advertising means that your advertising dollars are spent in ways that produce positive and measurable results. Results are measured by increased customer calls and other responses, new customers and increased sales. But, before we proceed, let's briefly discuss your yellow pages advertising. This is an arena where scams are rampant. Beware of advertising in unknown or little known yellow pages. You will certainly get a bill that will far exceed any measurable benefit your company may receive from a "no name" yellow page ad. Assuming that you are paying some amount for your legitimate yellow page advertising, is it really doing anything for you? For some companies, effective yellow page advertising is absolutely essential, but for others the least expensive way to utilize the yellow pages may be to simply pay for a **bold** listing for each of your company's classifications. This costs very little and makes your company name stand out from other company names that are not in bold.

How do you intelligently advertise your company, products and services and then measure your advertising effectiveness? There are several methods that can be utilized to develop and measure this elusive but important aspect of your business.

1. **An Advertising & Promotions Game Plan** - Advertising is expensive and you don't want to waste those advertising dollars on ineffective advertising! Advertising and promotions can

only be implemented effectively if you have an overall plan and budget for your corporate advertising. If you don't have an advertising plan, here are a few ideas for your consideration to assist you in developing a plan.

A. *Product Marketing Analysis* – Spend a little money to have a product/service marketing analysis done by a professional. Reasonably accurate market information is needed prior to setting your advertising goals.

B. *Your Advertising Goals* - The goals of your advertising plan must relate to your type of business and industry, your overall corporate goals, your marketing analysis, your business plan, and the amount of funds that you have available in your budget for advertising and promotion.

C. *Your Advertising Plan Contents* – Your advertising plan should be fairly comprehensive and include the following information:

1. Your target markets
2. Summary marketing information for each of the target markets
3. Your advertising message for each of these markets
4. The advertising media that you will employ to reach these markets
5. A media plan and budget
6. Person or persons responsible for implementing the advertising plan
7. A proven method or procedure for tracking the effectiveness of your advertising

2. Your Company Name – There's a lot of symbolism in a company name. Does your corporate name truly reflect what your company does? You corporate name can be one of your best advertisements. Of course, we have conglomerates that are into so many different businesses that it would literally be impossible to summarize these activities with only one name. We also have names, like Wendy's, that are so well known that everyone knows what they sell. Assuming you don't fall into either category, your corporate name should reflect what you do. Take as an example the A1 Lock & Key Company. The A1 portion of the name was not chosen by accident. Not only does it get "near the top" listings in the yellow pages, but there is a subliminal representation of quality work i.e. A-One! In particular, if you are a new, start-up, or turn-around company, you need to take the time to select a corporate name that really identifies and brands your business.

3. **Your Company Slogan** - This slogan should be the theme of your advertising campaign. If you have a good slogan, you can even incorporate this in your stationery, envelopes, business cards, invoices, statements and all of your materials that go out to the public such as promotional pens, etc. We'll use Wendy's again for their "Where's the beef" slogan. They started that campaign in 1984, and most people who have seen their ads still remember it. Take the time to develop a great company slogan. You won't regret it!

4. **Your Company Brochure** – You definitely need a company brochure if you or your staff meet regularly with other companies, whether they are your customers, vendors, banks or others. A well done brochure says something about the quality and professionalism of your company. A brochure also gives you the opportunity to advertise your company and its management, products and services by providing a visual image of what your company is all about. Also, a brochure has time value that lasts well beyond your presentation. Therefore, the recipients can browse through your company information at their leisure. If you don't already have a company brochure, you can start the design process by creating text to include your logo, slogan, mission statement, key owner/manager information, and company history. You can also collect visual material such as pictures of your building, operations, products, and staff. **However, when it comes to brochure design and printing, it's time to get a professional involved to help you create a great looking brochure!**

A Money Saving Idea – When you print a typical 11" by 17" sheet size, it doesn't matter whether you utilize only the front cover page or all 4 pages it contains. Use a high quality cover and print both sides to utilize all four 8.5" by 11" pages. You can use the first interior cover page to incorporate your company slogan and mission statement, along with your company's history. You might add a tab or pocket on the interior of the last cover page to hold key employee biographical information and other advertising information. The back page of the cover could be utilized to give the company name, main office address, telephone and fax numbers, and web site address. Also consider a main office picture and location map, and information on your other locations, if any. A well done company brochure is relatively expensive, so make those unused cover pages work hard for you! The additional cost of utilizing these pages is minimal, and will save you substantial expense by reducing the overall size of your brochure. A lesser weight of paper should be utilized for the interior pages. Keep in mind that you are working with sheet sizes that will give you 4 regular sized pages, front and back. Therefore, 2 large interior sheets will give you 8 pages and 3 sheets will give you 12 pages. I wouldn't recommend that you go past 12 or 16 pages. You are producing an easy to read brochure, not a book. Use separate 8.5" by 11" sheets for any staff biographies (bio's) you wish to include. These can be inserted or removed at any time. If you incorporate the staff bio's directly into the body of your brochure, you will have to redesign and reprint your brochure every time you change a key staff position. It's so much easier and cheaper to simply pull one of your 8.5" by 11" bio's and replace it with another one!

5. **Your Company Sales Staff** - Do your sales and marketing staffs properly represent your business? Your outside salespersons must first sell themselves, then the business, and then the product. Are they equipped to do any or all of these things? You shouldn't have to guess about something as important as that! You or your sales manager should plan to accompany your salespeople on selected sales calls. The stated objective of these calls is to review the advertising materials they present to the prospective customer rate their

performance. I'll bet that when you review your company advertising materials that are presented to the customer, you will probably want to change or modify a few things. After reviewing the performance of your salespersons, they will generally fall into four categories as follows:

A. This salesperson is a real professional and represents himself and the company very well.
B. This salesperson does a good job but needs some training or mentoring in a few areas.
C. This salesperson is currently at a mediocre performance level, but you believe that, with the proper training and mentoring, she has the ability and the personality to become an excellent salesperson.
D. This salesperson's contribution to our sales effort is so negative that we need to terminate him as soon as possible. We also need to review our hiring and training procedures so as to eliminate future hiring mistakes like this one!

Your salespeople are the front line of advertising for your company. If one of your salespersons turns off a potential customer, you may never get your foot in that door again! With that in mind, make the investment in sales training, mentoring, and product education a high priority in your company. Your investment of time and money in sales training and development will pay huge dividends in terms of future sales and positive customer relationships.

6. **Controlling and Measuring the Performance of Your Outside Salespeople** – This isn't as tough as you might think! There are several things you can do to measure and control the productivity of your outside sales staff. The following are performance measurement ideas for your consideration.

A. Have all of your outside salespersons present a weekly customer contact plan to your sales manager on Thursday for the coming week.
B. Instruct your sales manager to have the customer contact plans approved by Friday.

C. On Monday, have the outside salespersons turn in a simplified one page report on each of their customer sales contacts during the previous week. No excuses are acceptable. They have the weekend to complete the reports, if necessary. Actually, these one page reports should be completed by the outside sales staff daily upon completing each sales call.

D. The sales manager should review the sales call reports on Tuesday and plan to meet with the outside sales staff on Thursday.

E. The sales manager should make it known that they will be following up at random with the customers listed on the sales call reports to assess and verify the sales calls. As soon as this follow up procedure becomes widely known, any fabrication of sales call reports by your outside sales force will be minimal. Any falsification of sales call reports should result in disciplinary action. The first offense should result in a written warning and the second offense should result in the termination of that salesperson.

F. If you provide vehicles to your outside sales staff, equip all of them with a GPS vehicle tracking and recording system. The knowledge of this will keep your outside salespeople working for you rather than having mid-day dalliances with spouses or friends, taking an afternoon nap, running errands for their wives or husbands, or even working at another job! Believe me, this kind of behavior and worse occurs frequently with outside salespeople that are not made responsible for their performance. You need to control your outside salespeople by holding them accountable for their actions.

7. **Yellow Page Ads** - If you have a separate yellow page ad, consider offering a discount when the customer mentions the ad. Alternatively, your ad can feature a coupon that the customers must present at purchase to receive the discount. If you don't have or want a separate yellow page ad, at least **have your company name stand out in bold face type in the yellow pages** as previously mentioned.

8. **Advertising Flyers** - If you mail or hand out advertising flyers, have them printed up with a sequential number located inside of a coupon to be used for a promotional discount. This way, you can track each advertising campaign where those flyers are used, and you can even track the areas where they were mailed out or distributed. This will also control multiple uses of the same coupon. The additional printing cost for the numbered coupon is negligible.

Another Money Saving Idea - Consider sending advertising flyers to your customers with their monthly statement or other regular customer mailings. It is particularly important to address these flyers to the appropriate manager in your customer's organization who is responsible for purchasing your products or services. This will insure that your flyer is routed to the right person and will substantially increase your response rate. This advertising is very cost effective, because all you pay for is the cost of printing the flyers. No additional postage expense is required.

9. **Major Media Advertising** - What kind of print or broadcast media ads most effectively advertise your business? Newspaper advertising on a one-time basis usually produces nothing of value for the modest ads that are generally run by small businesses. TV advertising is more expensive, but even more ephemeral and less productive than newspaper ads on a one-time basis. Of course, if you are an auto dealer, you will most likely be running a TV, radio and newspaper ad campaign on a regular basis. However, even the experts agree that major media advertising is the most inefficient and least productive way to spend your advertising dollars. This is particularly true for most small businesses, where name recognition for your business is probably minimal. It is also very difficult to track and measure the effectiveness of TV and radio advertising.

10. **Trade Publication Advertising** - If you are not planning a newspaper or TV ad campaign, consider placing an effective ad in trade publications that cover your industry. **An effective print media ad grabs your attention, communicates**

your message, and rewards a potential customer who responds to your ad. The customer response should be directed to a specific person in your company who is trained to professionally handle these responses. The ad response should also be measurable. Your measurability can be assured by rewarding the responder with a free gift, a coupon special, or a one time discount for purchasing an item based upon their response to your ad. I'm sure you can come up with many other rewards to entice a potential customer response. The effectiveness of trade publication advertising is greatly enhanced because you are reaching out to a target audience that is much more likely to respond to your ad. And, there is much more time value to a trade publication advertisement, as it may be read by the recipient or others even several months after it is received.

A Money Making Idea – Consider writing an article for a trade publication in which you currently advertise. You can also ask them to do a feature story about your company. When you make that request, provide them with the photos and story line to help them compose the article. Make it easy for them to say yes, and feature your company in their publication!

11. **Classified Advertising** – This is the one type of print media advertising where potential customers will look for your ad. If you have the type of product that can be sold using classified ads, don't be shy about using them. For example, auto dealers account for a majority of the used car classified ads in most cities. They wouldn't use these ads if they didn't sell used cars with them. They know that the cost of using classified ads is relatively low and the success rate is relatively high. Also, the effectiveness of these ads is easy to measure. Include in your ad an identifying product number and your website address.

12. **Signs** – Signs are, without question, your most effective and least expensive way to advertise your business. Signs advertise your business to the mobile public 24 hours a day, 365 days a year and they never call in sick or take a vacation. Three of the most important elements of commercial site selection are

visibility, accessibility and sufficient parking space. Your on-premises signage is the most critical component of visibility. Therefore a well designed pole mounted sign having at least a 6' by 8' minimum size which is visible from the street can increase your business sales 5% to 10%, according to a recent SBA study. The same study says that if you already have a street sign, an additional on premises sign can increase sales by another 5%. However, don't waste your hard-earned money on unproductive signage. Your premises sign should contain the following elements to be effective:

A. **Street Visibility** – Your sign must be visible from the street that fronts your location.

B. **Legibility** – Potential customers should be able to read your sign from their cars as they are traveling past your location.

C. **The Sign Must Be Conspicuous** – The sign must draw the attention of passing traffic. It must stand out from other signage competing for your attention.

D. **The Sign Must Communicate a Message** – Your name, your address or directions, and your fame (what are you known for?) should be on your sign. An example might be as follows:

BOB'S BURGER BISTRO
WORLD FAMOUS BURGERS
TURN RIGHT HERE ---->

An Unproductive "Monument to Ego" Sign Story - One family-owned business I know of decided to place a large lighted pole sign at the back of their property which was only visible from a 6 lane high-speed highway below and behind their location. The cost, not including the cost to operate the sign, was an $87,000 lease payment each year for 7 years. This payment did not create any ownership interest in the sign because it was a pure operating lease! As you were traveling down the highway, you had about 10 seconds of time to see and read the sign if you knew where it was and were looking for it. Unless that was your sole purpose, you probably didn't even notice the sign, much less read the messages that were flying by. To summarize this snafu, by the time you included the operating costs of about $20,000 per year, this sign cost over $750,000 in seven years and produced only negligible results. But, look on the bright side. It did have the family name on it!

13. **Successful Internet Advertising** - There have been many books written about internet advertising. My purpose is not to replicate the contents of these books in this short space, but to give you a few basic pointers about successful advertising on the "net".

   A. If you're in business today, you have to be listed on the Internet with a Website address. Many of our younger generation and other computer literate folks use the net browser as classified Yellow Pages to look up the products and services they have an interest in.

   B. Your Internet Website address should be simple, related to your business name and easy to remember.

   C. Include your business name, address, telephone numbers, website address and e-mail address on the top of every website page.

   D. Your Website should be easy to navigate.

   E. You should have a Website page devoted to soliciting a response from the viewer back to your business. The response should include the viewer's name, their business name, address, telephone number, cell number, fax number, e-mail address and summary information regarding the response request.

F. Have links established to your franchiser product information, your internet classified ads and other internet information you deem appropriate.

G. Request reciprocal links from the companies you have established links with. There is nothing like mutually beneficial two way traffic on the net!

H. Submit your website address to the following business directories: franchisers, vendors, trade associations, general business directories and other businesses you can think of that make sense.

I. Have your Website and e-mail addresses printed on all of your business cards, stationery, advertising materials and just about anything that you distribute to the public.

J. Incorporate a "freebie" into your Website design. Think in terms of a contest entry for a product prize, a discount or a free promotional item in exchange for the viewer's contact information.

K. Utilize the Website contact information you have developed to send direct mail advertising over the net to your potential customers.

L. **Last but not least, if you don't have a productive Website established, contract with an experienced website design company to design and maintain your site. If you have a Website that you designed internally, have your Website professionally analyzed for improvements. If you don't have the internal expertise needed to design a first class Website, this function is too important to the advertising success of your company to place in the hands of amateurs!**

14. **Evaluating the Effectiveness of Your Website Advertising and Internet Sales** – It is easy to determine how many sales are attributed to your Website advertising and site presence.

The more difficult aspect of internet selling is to determine the effectiveness of your Website in promoting the sales of your products and services. Here are some items to consider when making this analysis.

A. What goals have you established for your web site?
B. List these goals in terms of monetary value, high to low.
C. Have you been successful in achieving these goals?
D. What is the overall cost to set up and maintain your Website?
E. How much money have you made or lost on your internet sales, after deducting your cost of sales, your Website expenses, and a realistic estimate for overhead?
F. There are independent companies who can assist you in evaluating the effectiveness of your internet Website, if you are not achieving your Website goals and objectives

SUMMARY

Without any advertising, your small business will slowly die as existing customers move on. It's virtually impossible to sell your products to potential customers who don't know anything about you or your products. Therefore effective business and product advertising is a key critical part of increasing your customer base and your sales. You need a game plan to effectively budget and allocate your advertising dollars to competing media in a way that makes the most sense for your business. You also need ways to measure the results of your advertising campaign, and if necessary, reallocate your advertising budget to more effective media outlets. **Although we are in recessionary times, don't make the mistake of reducing effective product advertising. Your advertising may become even more effective for you as your competitors reduce or eliminate theirs.**

CHAPTER 29

SALES PRODUCT QUALITY, GUARANTEES, AND WARRANTIES

WHY CONCERN YOURSELF WITH QUALITY CONTROL?

The mental images that a quality product invokes in the mind of the customer are multivalued. Here are a few of the things to consider when you think about a quality product.

1. **Functionality** – The product is easy to use, and the instructions are easy to understand.
2. **Performance** – The product does what it is advertised to do.
3. **Appearance** – The product "looks" like a quality product, with no exterior flaws or blemishes.
4. **Maintainability** – The product is easy to service and maintain.
5. **Durability** – The product lasts its life cycle without major repairs or scrappage,
6. **Service** – During the product life cycle, quality product parts, service and repairs will be available at a reasonable cost.
7. **Upgradability** – This element is not universally applicable to all products. However, in computer software and the internal software in computer hardware, upgrade availability is an absolutely essential component of a quality product.
8. **Warranty** – the product is backed by the manufacturer or supplier with a no nonsense guarantee of quality throughout the period of the warranty.
9. **Reputation** – The reputation of the manufacturer and the seller are intertwined with the elements of quality listed above.

Because of a company's reputation for quality, the customer will expect quality products and services from that vendor.

If you can deliver a quality product, it will cost you less to manufacture, fabricate, or assemble that product. Additionally, your company will spend less on sales and marketing because you have built a reputation for quality. You will receive a high percentage of repeat business from customers who have confidence in your company and your products. Additionally, your customers will pay a slightly higher price for quality and reputation. A recent British survey indicated that customers were willing to pay a price more than 5% higher than the competition, to purchase a product from a company with a high reputation for quality. The increase in sales price, reduction in manufacturing costs, and reduction in sales and marketing expense you will achieve by providing your customers with quality products over time, will more than offset the added investment in the cost of inaugurating and maintaining a quality control function. Unfortunately, most small companies don't make the initial and ongoing investment in quality, and that is the principal reason that they stay small companies.

1. **Planning For Quality Control** - If you assemble or manufacture a product, do you have a system of quality control built into the process? This would necessitate, at minimum, a quality inspection station at the end of the assembly line that would thoroughly inspect the product. To be effective, the inspections should be completed at the end of each assembly or sub-assembly. If you want to institute a system of Quality Control you need to ask yourself the following questions:

    A. What things do you need to measure to improve the quality of your products?
    B. Where (at what checkpoints) in the manufacturing, fabrication, processing or shipping process are you going to measure quality?
    C. How are you going to measure quality at those checkpoints? You need a quality checklist for each checkpoint.
    D. If you fail an item at a quality checkpoint, what do you do with it? Do you send it back through the line or scrap it?

E. Who is going to do the quality control inspections? Who will the quality control inspectors report to? Who will follow up on quality control problems?

F. How do you record quality control checkpoint failures? Do you keep enough failure information so that it can be used to analyze and improve the manufacturing or assembly process?

G. You must utilize any process errors that your quality control process identifies to modify and improve your overall manufacturing process. By consistently analyzing your product failures and implementing the indicated process corrections, your product failure rates will be minimized, and your product quality will improve substantially. Additionally, your scrappage and rework costs will be substantially reduced, and may more than offset the additional cost of your quality control program.

2. **Customer Quality Control Surveys** – Do you mail or e-mail customer quality control surveys that measure customer satisfaction with your products and services? These surveys should be brief, easy to fill out, and limited to five or six questions. You may want to include the following customer satisfaction questions in your survey:

A. Product or service performance

B. Product quality, reliability and durability

C. Customer understanding of your product or service guarantees, if any and the availability of extended product warranty at the point of purchase.

D. Delivery options and timeliness of delivery

E. Did the product or service fill the needs of the customer? If not, why not?

F. Space for any other comments (Always include this in any survey you request!)

These brief quality control surveys can be extremely important tools in evaluating your product and service performance, and pinpoint problems that you can address before they become major obstacles.

A Better Idea – Why not include in, on, or with your product or service a pre-stamped, self- addressed card with the survey information imprinted on it, and space for customer contact information (Name, company name, address, telephone, cell, and e-mail address). Advertise on the survey card that you will send out a little gift (you name it) to all survey respondents to thank them for their participation!

3. **Product Guarantees** – These are guarantees that come with or are attached to the product at the point of sale. These guarantees may be backed by the product supplier or manufacturer, or the guarantees may be supported by your company. In a number of instances the guarantee may be backed by both you and the manufacturer. Some product guarantees are effective advertising for the quality of your products, and others may in fact contribute to a negative opinion of your business in the opinion of your customers. I have listed a number of factors below that should help you evaluate the value of your product guarantees.

   A. Does your product contain clear, easy to read, step-by-step instructions about what your customer has to do in the event of a product failure?
   B. Is the product guarantee serviced at your location or does the product have to be shipped to the manufacturer's guarantee service center?
   C. Does the product have to be shipped back to the manufacturer or returned to your location in the original packaging?
   D. Is the original purchase receipt required?
   E. If the product has to be returned under the guaranty, is a Returned Merchandise Authorization (RMA) required?
   F. If the product has to be shipped, who pays the shipping charge to and from the customer?
   G. How strictly are the guarantee requirements enforced, or does common sense prevail?

Obviously, the more difficult you, your manufacturers or your vendors make it for your customers to return a product that is "guaranteed", the fewer product guarantees will be honored and the more dissatisfied customers you will have.

4. **Service Guarantees** - You might think that because you operate a service business, you don't have to offer any specific guarantees other than the usual "to your satisfaction" or "we will credit your account for the unacceptable service". These types of guarantees are pretty standard stuff in the pest control business. Well, consider a company that will guarantee your building to be pest free, and if you detect a pest, you will be paid several thousand dollars. And, if your business has to be closed for a time to eliminate the pests, they will insure you up to $1,000,000 for the interruption of your business. There is a commercial pest control company in Florida guaranteeing this and more. If this company is so convinced of the effectiveness of their pest control service that they are willing to purchase business interruption insurance and other insurance coverage on behalf of their customers, that tells me a lot about how they value their customers and their reputation!

A Great Idea for Service Differentiation – Examine your service guarantees, and compare all aspects of them to what your competition currently offers. Then, get a little wild and crazy, and brainstorm ideas to substantially improve your customer guarantees and give you a competitive advantage. You may want to have specific guarantees fully insured, or you can retain some or all of the risk yourself, depending on the amount of coverage, the average claim and the expected frequency of the claims. Of course, you can only afford to implement this guarantee if you are providing a quality service in the first place. All the performance guarantees in the world will not make up for shoddy service!

5. **Processing Product Guarantees for Your Customers** – As stated above, the more difficult you or your manufacturers make it for your customers to return a product that is "guaranteed", the more dissatisfied customers you will have. If you can manage it, the best arrangement for the customer is an agreement with your suppliers and manufacturers to have

their warranty honored at your location. This way, you can confirm the customer date of purchase to check guarantee applicability, reprint a copy of the customer invoice if needed by the manufacturer, and exchange the product or arrange for the return shipment of the damaged product all at the same time. This method will result in a minimum of hassle for your customers, and substantially increase your customer satisfaction with the process.

6. **Product Extended Warranties** – The sale of extended product warranties at the point of purchase can significantly boost your in-store revenues and gross margins. Your mark-up over the cost of an extended warranty can exceed 100%. While these sales are a sweetener to your bottom line, since you get to keep about 50% of the warranty sales price. You should also insure that your warranty is a good deal for your customer. Most third party extended warranties are really bad deals for the customer because:

A. Some extended warranty companies are nothing more than rip-off artists. They have no intention of honoring a warranty claim if they can possibly avoid it.

B. The warranty requirements are so tightly drawn that very few customers can qualify to qualify for them. The warranty rip-off companies love to write these! Read paragraph 3 above to review potential burdensome requirements.

C. Some products are covered by the manufacturer's guaranty for time periods of a year or more after the customer purchases the product, so that very little coverage is provided by the extended warranty company.

D. Most products don't fail within the effective extended-warranty period of two or three years after the expiry of the manufacturer's guaranty.

E. When a product does fail, the cost of repair may be less than the cost of the extended warranty.

F. If most products are going to fail, they usually do so within the manufacturer's initial guaranty period.

Extended Warranties provided by the manufacturer, and sold by your company, are probably the best and safest bet for your customer. You can give your sales assistants some price flexibility to help sell these extended warranties to the customer at the point of purchase.

A Money Making Idea Regarding Extended Warranty Sales Since, as indicated above, almost everything is working in your favor, you can become your own Extended Warranty Provider! You will collect the entire extended warranty premium in advance, to cover a relatively low failure rate for most electronic equipment and appliances. Further, your liability for product repair or replacement will only begin after the manufacturer's warranty ends, usually in 90 days to 1 year after the date of purchase. Believe it or not, the failure rate for regular sized TVs from 25" to 36" is only 6% to 8% in the first 3 to 4 years, according to a Consumer Reports National Research Center 2006 Product Reliability Survey. In the case of most of the products you sell, your failure reserve requirement would only be about 20% of your extended warranty sales. This allows you to take 80% of your extended warranty sales to your gross margin! You would also be doing your customers a favor by dealing with them directly on extended warranty claims. This will allow them to avoid the hassles of dealing with a third party extended warranty rip-off company. You could end up making more money on the sale of your own extended product warranties than you make on the sale of the products themselves, and create greater customer satisfaction in the process.

Recommendation: To further bolster your product warranty reserve, I would recommend that you deposit your reserve requirement in an interest bearing FDIC insured bank account. Have the interest earned on this account added to your warranty reserve balance to provide an additional margin for your reserve calculation, if needed.

SUMMARY

There is no doubt about it! Customers associate quality with reputation, and are willing to pay a higher sales price to purchase from a company that has a high reputation for quality and service. Customers like the security of an extended warranty and are willing to pay a relatively high price for it. These extended product warranties are very profitable for the third party companies who offer them. However, in many cases the third party warranty providers make it difficult for your customers to collect on a valid claim. If your company can offer the extended warranties for sale to your customers and properly service them, you can greatly enhance your profitability while creating considerable customer goodwill at the same time. It's another win/win situation!

CHAPTER 30

SALES - YOUR COMPANY'S REPUTATION AND CUSTOMER SERVICE

Your company's reputation and customer service are joined together like a hand in a glove. Recently, I read an article in Wal-Mart Watch about "Wal-Mart's poor customer service damaging the Company's reputation." "Wal-Mart's customer service is notoriously bad: chronic understaffing, low wages, high turnover and ever-shifting work schedules mean employees are unhappy and unlikely to perform well. So it's no surprise that Wal-Mart winds up "among the worst" on AOL's list of favorite grocery stores." As Wal-Mart should know well, it is impossible to separate reputation from customer service. Your company's reputation will be damaged in short order if your customer service is substantially below average. It takes about six to twelve months to change your company's perceived reputation in the minds of the public, one way or the other. If you previously had great customer service and you have substantially reduced your commitment to it, the downgrading of your reputation with your customer is a lagging indicator. Unfortunately, reputation is also a lagging indicator if you are striving to upgrade your reputation by increasing the quality of your customer service. I have listed below a few ways you can greatly increase your customer satisfaction without spending a lot of money.

1. **Clean and maintain your premises** – There is no bigger turn-off for most customers than a dirty and unkempt facility. It almost shouts out that you don't care about your customers or their business. Unfortunately for you, the inference is that your products or services are also sub-standard.

2. **Make it easy for call-in customers to get operator assistance** – It infuriates customers who call your company and get lost in a voice-mail maze! Let your customers and others know immediately that they can talk to a trained operator by simply entering the number "0".

3. **Train all of your operators, receptionists, sales staff and others who deal with the public to properly service incoming phone calls** – Some managers assume that employees answering phones automatically come to the company with this information hard-wired into their heads at birth! This is definitely not the case. I worked for one company where there was no training in telephone call procedures. Nor was there any agreement by the ownership as to how calls should be answered. This was a no-win situation for the employees, and the company customers, vendors and others who were calling in. The owners never did settle on a policy for answering calls, and without a policy how can you conduct effective training. Therefore, the employees were always tenuous about answering calls because there was no set policy to guide them

4. **Have only personnel fluent in English (and Spanish, if you have an initial telephone answering selection for either language) answer your phone calls!** This may not be popular with the "everybody's equal" affirmative action crowd but it's your business, not theirs. As you have undoubtedly already observed, it is extremely disturbing for you to try to communicate with any person who can't speak and communicate in English, which is our primary business language here in the United States. The same is true for any of your customers, vendors or others who are calling you. They want to be able to easily communicate with your employee who is answering the phone, and have their calls quickly and efficiently routed to one of your staff who can assist them. *If a fair percentage of your customers primarily speak Spanish or any other language, accord them the same courtesy and direct their calls to one of your staff who is bilingual and fluent in Spanish or another language that you service, and English.* To avoid any potential problems with the EEOC,

make sure that English language fluency is a job requirement for any of your staffers who will regularly answer your telephones.

TIP – Don't outsource your telephone answering service! You will wind up having your calls answered by people from any number of foreign countries, who are not fluent enough in American English to properly communicate with your callers. Don't be swayed by the prospect of lower costs into making a critical mistake that you will regret later on. Believe me, even large companies have tried this kind of customer service outsourcing, and realized later on that it was a big mistake!

AN EXAMPLE OF AN OUTSOURCING FAILURE

A large service company that was one of our vendors had recently outsourced their customer service operation to an Indian subsidiary company to decrease their customer service costs. After encountering significant start-up and training costs, they began to integrate the Indian call center into their customer service network. The customer service from the Indian operation was unbelievably bad for several reasons:

1) Even though the Indian service representatives (reps) spoke passable English, there was still a communications problem regarding accent, grammar, syntax, idioms, common expressions in American English that are not commonly used in India, and other voice communications problems.

2) The typical U.S. computer service reps had substantially more than 5 years of experience in their jobs. The Indian reps had less than 5 months experience in a training mode.

3) The Indian service reps soon became nothing more than order takers. They never actually resolved problems, and simply passed on those problems to their U.S. counterparts.

4) The U.S. service reps had to call the customer and start from scratch because they either did not get all the information from their Indian counterpart or, worse yet, they received incorrect information concerning the nature of the problem.

5) Indian call center reps, supposedly working from home, began to outsource their own call center responsibilities to friends, relatives and others! You might ask how they were able to do that. Well, doesn't everyone work from home these days without any management control or oversight?

6) As the Indian call center efficiency and effectiveness dropped further, customers either stopped using them, or used them when there was no other alternative.

7) You may have already guessed that this downward spiral had to end soon. Within a few years after it opened, the Indian call center was shut down, at some considerable expense to the computer service company involved!

The moral of this story is "DON'T EXPERIMENT WITH YOUR CUSTOMER SERVICE"

5. **Greet your customer coming through the door with a "Good morning ma'am or sir, how can I help you?** – Then insure that your staff is ready, willing and trained to help your customer or prospect.

6. **Have enough trained and dedicated sales staff to service your customers** – Even if you have several of your store personnel multi-tasking in stocking, delivery, cashiering, and customer sales, insure that you are staffed with knowledgeable and courteous sales people. Your direct customer interface at the point of sale is your opportunity to impress your customer with the best possible service that you can provide.

7. **Follow up with your customers to assess their satisfaction with your company and your products and services -** Keep in mind that in your business there are many interfaces with customers that we can measure at the point of contact. These contact points could be product point of sale, customer call-ins, company web-site usage satisfaction, guaranty or warranty servicing, product returns and exchanges, credit processing and more. If it's possible, these transactions can be measured at the points of interface with the customer by a short survey form. For example, you might have a short half-page survey about your customer product return experience given to every 100th customer to fill out. You could offer the customer a small reward to complete the survey, such as 5% off of their next purchase or an inexpensive gift. The survey form should be simple to fill out and contain no more than 4 or 5 questions.

8. **Customer Satisfaction Surveys** – Do you mail or e-mail comprehensive customer surveys regarding customer satisfaction with your products and services? These surveys should be brief, easy to fill out, and limited to about 10 questions. You may want to include the following customer satisfaction questions in your survey:

   A. Overall satisfaction with your business
   B. Product or service performance
   C. Product quality and durability
   D. Evaluation of product or service guarantees, if any
   E. Availability of extended product warranty at the point of purchase
   F. Delivery options and timeliness of delivery
   G. Evaluation of your customer service representatives and their performance
   H. Satisfaction with any customer returns or exchanges
   I. Evaluation of your location in terms of accessibility, visibility, parking and premises layout.

    K. Does the customer have needs that are not being met? Do you need new products or services, or do you need to expand existing product lines?

    L. Space for any other comments

SUMMARY

All of these customer service suggestions and quality control surveys are extremely important tools in evaluating your customer satisfaction. They measure your need to improve, modify or change some underlying aspects of your overall customer relationships. Improvements in customer satisfaction resulting from the implementation of any of these suggestions should boost your company's reputation and increase your sales accordingly. And don't forget to take your customers to lunch periodically. What you learn from them about how they perceive your business will more than pay for the lunch!

CHAPTER 31

SALES – YOUR LOCATION
AND CUSTOMER CONVENIENCE

Look at your business from your customer's point of view. What aspects of your business are customer friendly, and what aspects present difficulties for your customers or could be improved? You want to concentrate on improving any of the customer interfaces that make it difficult for your customers to do business with you. Keep in mind that the more convenient you make it for your customers, the more purchases they will make from you! While it is impossible to tell you specifically what you need to improve upon, the following factors are areas of customer interface that you can evaluate for your business:

1. **Location** – Is your location convenient to your customer base and does it provide adequate space for current needs and future expansion requirements?

2. **Signage** – Are your signs visible and easily read from the street fronting your location? Is your on-premises sign clearly visible and your entrance clearly marked?

3. **Parking** – Is the parking adequate, and is it conveniently located near your entrance with sufficient handicapped parking. This is particularly important if you have an older customer base.

4. **Location Interior** – Is your location clean and attractive? Do you provide baskets or carts to facilitate your customers shopping? Do you provide motorized carts for handicapped shoppers? This might be a critical difference if you are selling medical supplies for the handicapped. Are the traffic flows into

your location designed for the convenience of your customers, so that they can quickly and easily find the products they want to purchase? Are your products displayed in an orderly way, and clearly marked with an easily read product description and price?

5. **In-store Customer Assistance** – Are your sales assistants knowledgeable, courteous, trained in assisting your customers, and available?

6. **Checking out** – Do you have enough checkout stations and cashiers? Is your computer pricing current? Do you have a lot of price checks at the checkout counter? Are your cashiers trained to deal with customer problems during checkout, and empowered to make the minor corrections that are necessary to resolve the problem? Do you provide customer assistance for older or infirm customers from checkout to their vehicle, if needed?

7. **Delivery** – Does your company make deliveries of your products to your customers? Do your customers have delivery options to choose from? Is it easy for your customer to pick up product purchases at your location?

8. **Returns and Exchanges** – There is nothing more disturbing to a customer than a product return policy so tightly controlled that it makes returning a product almost impossible. Return and Exchange restrictions cover almost everything, but here are a few of the most common ones for an in-store return or exchange.

    A. Do you allow for returns or exchanges of any or all of your products?
    B. Do you require a store receipt to authorize a return or exchange?
    C. Must the return be completely intact, including the product and packaging, along with all written information such as warranties, guarantees, and instruction, owners, and operating manuals enclosed in the packaging?

    D. What are your time limits from the date of purchase for allowing product returns or exchanges?

    E. Do you have the customers fill out and sign a form for a Return or for an Exchange?

    F. Is the return form simplified or complex?

    G. How do you handle the return or exchange of gifts, where the customer may or may not have the attendant paperwork?

9. **Internet Sales Returns and Exchanges** – In addition to all of the above requirements, the return or exchange of online merchandise may have additional requirements such as:

    a. Is a return material authorization number (RMA) required?

    b. Who pays for return shipping of the product? Who pays for the shipping cost of the exchange item back to the customer?

    c. Do you charge a restocking fee on the return, and if so, is it reasonable?

    d. Do you communicate the status of the return to the customer online and in a timely manner?

    e. Do you explain to the customer by phone or online why the return has not been authorized, and what the customer must do to get an RMA approved by your company?

You need to evaluate your return and exchange procedures with regard to the convenience and opinion of the customer. **Look at your procedures from the customer's standpoint, and apply some "common sense" and logic with regard to changing your procedures and making them more customer-friendly.** Whatever additional expense you encounter will be more that offset by increased customer satisfaction and business!

10. **Evaluating the Convenience and Customer Friendliness of Your Website** - You can evaluate the sales performance of your Website as follows:

1) Are you selling the right products on your Website?
2) Is your Website user friendly in assisting new customer purchases?
3) Does it welcome back repeat customers and remember prior customer purchases?
4) Is your Website design clean, simple and easy to navigate?
5) Is your Website attractive to potential customers?
6) Does your Website capture the attention of the viewer? Keep the interest of the Viewer? Motivate the viewer to consider a product purchase? Facilitate the necessary action by the viewer to purchase your product?
7) How do you process your customer internet inquiries?
8) How quickly do you respond to your customer inquiries?
9) **Do you have an internet help desk staffed with a real live human being? If you don't, you will loose customers to one of your competitors who consider this an important aspect of their customer service.** Having done a lot of shopping online, I rate the ability talk to an informed person about internet product purchases highly enough that, without that ability, I would seriously consider not shopping at that Website again.
10) Do you have an internet survey form for viewers and purchasers to complete? Do you reward them with a discount or a promotional item for completing the survey? You may want to include the following questions in your survey.

   a. What products did prospective buyers purchase quickly?
   b. If they procrastinated, what caused the delay?
   c. What information did they browse or request about the products?
   d. Why did they purchase your product instead of your competitor's?
   e. How do they rate their shopping experience at your Website?
   f. Would they recommend your products to others?
   g. Would they recommend your Website to others?

    h.   What would they change about your Website?

    i.   What was the best part of their shopping experience with you?

    j.   What was the worst part of their shopping experience with you?

    k.   Would they purchase products again from your Website?

    l.   If they purchased from one of your competitors, what was the main factor that influenced their purchasing decision?

11) Do you systematically implement customer or viewer suggestions that are worthy of consideration?

12) Do you contact your customers to inform them about suggestions they have made and that your company has implemented? From my own observations, very few companies take the time to "blow their own horn" about the fact that they not only listen to their customers, but act upon what they hear. It's great publicity for your company. Don't pass up the opportunity to capitalize on your positive response to your customer's suggestions!

13) There are independent companies who can assist you in evaluating the effectiveness of your internet Website, if you are not achieving your Website goals and objectives.

If your internet business is large enough, you might consider the latest internet management tool from Oracle named "Oracle Real User Experience Insight". This package contains comprehensive Website management software released in 2008.

SUMMARY

It's all about making your location and your Web site more convenient and easy for your customers to use. The more customer friendly you are, the more you will grow your customer base. You will also increase the number of visits and sales from your existing customers. You should utilize the feedback from your customer satisfaction surveys to implement suggested improvements, and make shopping at your location an even better experience for your customers!

CHAPTER 32

COST OF SALES REDUCTION IDEAS

HOW TO REDUCE YOUR PRODUCT COSTS

There is an old adage, "Buy low and sell high". You can add one more item to that "Buy low, sell high and sell more!" However, in this chapter we will concentrate on ways to buy your products at a lower price, and manufacture your products at a lower cost.

LOWERING YOUR PRODUCT ACQUISITION COSTS

First, we will address the savings that can be found in the product purchasing process. The following list of suggestions regarding vendor analysis is equally applicable to the purchase of your manufacturing, assembly or fabrication components, and should be helpful to you in either case.

1. **Vendor/Supplier Analysis** – Whether you are buying parts, components, or the products themselves, you should have a Vendor Analysis listed alphabetically and in descending order of total purchases to assist you in your analysis. Your expanded Vendor Analysis should contain the following information:

   A. Vendor Name, Address & Main Office Telephone Number.
   B. Primary Vendor Contact Person, with Title, Location, Phone & Cell Numbers.
   C. Date Business Relationship (Purchasing) Started.
   D. Products, Parts and Components that you purchase from that Vendor, with current prices, sub-totals for each item and a grand total.

E. Overall Discounts that you have negotiated with that Vendor, if any.
F. Special Product Related Discounts.
G. Other Discounts, such as a Prompt Payment Discount.
H. Vendor Payment Terms.
I. Special Delivery Arrangements and Shipping Charges.
J. Vendor Special Product Programs, such as Seasonal Discount Programs and others.
K. Vendor Quality Control Program Information.
L. Vendor Product Guaranties and Warranties.
M. Vendor Insurance Information – Workman's Compensation, General Business Liability Insurance, Umbrella Insurance and Product Liability Insurance with Designated Insurance Carriers and Policy Limits.
N. D&B or Other Third Party Rating of the Vendor's Financial Strength.
O. Is This Vendor a Designated Business Partner?
P. Any Other Information You Deem Important.

Once you have this information in hand, unless you have done a similar vendor analysis recently, you will undoubtedly make a few interesting observations that you will want to address such as:

1. Why am I paying this vendor more than I should for this part, component, or product when I could buy it for less from another vendor?
2. Why am I dealing with a vendor that is underinsured?
3. Why am I choosing to buy from a primary vendor who is a candidate for a bankruptcy filing?
4. Why am I paying to have this product shipped in, when I could buy it for the same price or less one block away? Given the trend toward higher shipping charges, the total cost savings could be substantial.
5. Why am I buying parts or products from a vendor who has little or no product quality control?
6. Why am I not receiving a discount from my primary product vendor?
7. Why am I not taking advantage of special vendor programs?

8. Why am I purchasing from vendors who do not sufficiently warranty their products?
9. Why am I purchasing the same products from so many vendors?
10. Why have I not made my primary vendors my business partners?

2. **Vendor Business Partners, It's a Win/Win Situation -** Business in these technologically complex and fast changing times has become more collaborative than ever. New developments in technology, particularly computer related technology, require a company to form operating partnerships with its key vendors and suppliers. There are many ways that this collaboration can be achieved to the benefit of your company and your vendors. Listed below are a few of those ways:

A. Review your vendor analysis to determine the suitability of that vendor to be considered a business partner.

1) Is the vendor an important supplier of product to your company?
2) Has the vendor been in business for at least several years?
3) What is the financial strength of the vendor? (Get an expanded D&B report on the vendor, public financial information if the vendor is a publicly traded company, or financial information directly from the vendor)
4) How long have you known and done business with this vendor?
5) Has the vendor worked well with you in the past?
6) Can you trust this vendor with proprietary information?
7) Will the vendor sign a non-disclosure document?
8) Does the vendor have the technical expertise you need to assist you in product development?

B. Utilize your components vendor as a "design partner" in the design phase of a new product.

C. Utilize your vendor partners to analyze components in your existing products for upgrades or replacements.
D. Ask your vendor partners if they can upgrade any products or components that they currently sell to your company.
E. Utilize your vendor partners to direct ship product from your inventory stored at their location to your customers.
F. Ask your vendor partners to assist you in identifying customers for the market ready products that you purchase from them.
G. Solicit innovative product ideas from you vendors about how to improve your products or the product components that you purchase from them. Since they build it, they know more about that product or component than anyone else does.

HOW YOU CAN ACHIEVE OTHER REDUCTIONS IN YOUR MANUFACTURING COSTS

Secondly, we will address the savings that can be found in the manufacturing, assembly or fabrication process. The following list of suggestions may be helpful to you in that regard.

3. **Insist on Product Design Efficiency** – It is not well known, but studies have shown that product design and development determines 70% to 80% of the cost of the finished product! Also, product cost is very difficult to reduce once you have started production. With that fact firmly in mind, you must design cost savings into the product in the development stage well before you have even completed a prototype product.

4. **Don't Reinvent the Wheel** – Use off-the-shelf parts and sub-assemblies that can be purchased in bulk at a discount from a reliable supplier who has implemented a reliable and effective quality control function. This should insure that your outsourced products are readily available and of the highest quality.

5. **Component Redesign and Replacement** - Moore's law is an observation of a long-term trend in the development

of computer processors since 1958. Basically, it states that computer processing power has doubled about every two years! From everything I've read, this trend will continue well into the next decade. Since recent history supports this incredible rate of technological advancement, when is the last time you have reviewed the computer processor related components contained in your existing products? Chances are that you can purchase components with superior performance, better quality, and greater longevity at a lower price. You might even be able to have the new component perform the tasks of 2 or 3 existing components, thus saving you considerable manufacturing expense. If your company doesn't have the in-house capability to do the design analysis required, there are a number of design and engineering companies that offer this service.

6. **Standardize Your Product Components** – You should design your products to use standardized parts and sub-assemblies across your product lines. This can only be accomplished if one of the primary objectives of your product design phase is standardization. As part of standardizing your list of components, you should again review purchasing off-the-shelf components.

7. **Product Standardization Facilitates Automation** – If you are utilizing standard components, it is much easier to facilitate robot machining, fabrication, and assembly. You will already have everything you need to know about the design, dimensions, installation and assembly, and other requirements for your standardized components. You can immediately program this information into a Computer Aided Design and Manufacturing CAD/CAM program designed to automate your manufacturing process. Chances are if the component is standard, you may have already input this information into your design program!

8. **Standardization Facilitates Contemporaneous Machine Tooling** – Machine tooling refers to the fixtures and work-holding devices which aid in the machining or fabrication of

parts. Since you already know all the dimensions and details of your standard parts and components, it is possible to design your machine tooling requirements along with your product design. This considerably shortens the lead time necessary to begin the manufacturing phase and bring your product to market. You will also have prototype machine tools available when you are ready to test manufacture your prototype product.

9. **Standardization Reduces Component Costs** – Because you will purchase larger quantities of standard components utilized by several of your products, you will be able to negotiate better deals with your vendors. By negotiating a quantity discount on each standard component, this can reduce your purchase cost by 5% to 20%.

10. **Standardization Will Substantially Reduce Your Components Inventory** – Not only will you have a much smaller components inventory, but you will reduce the amount of obsolete inventory related to special order parts that you have stocked in the past. You will also reduce the minimum on-hand quantity that you have to carry by at least 20% to 30%, as most of this inventory requirement will be stocked by your suppliers. In addition, you will be able to dramatically reduce the warehouse and production factory floor space that was required by the larger, less efficient non-standard inventory.

A Cost Saving Idea – You can negotiate larger purchases of standard components with your suppliers by having them store a portion of your purchases at their warehouse. You can then draw down on this stock as required by your production schedule.

11. **Determine Your Manufactured Products Actual Factory Overhead** – To quote an old proverb, "The devil is in the details". In other words, if you are looking at the forest, the health of the individual tree is impossible to determine. If you have a manufacturing cost system that is robust, the factory overhead information by product will be available. However, if you are like most small businesses, your factory

overhead will be aggregated for all of your manufactured products and will be allocated out to all of them based on a popular allocation method using direct labor hours. While this simplifies the overall process of allocating factory overhead, actual overhead costs by product, like the trees in the forest, are lost in the "big picture". In order to analyze your products bottom line performance, you must have a close estimate of the actual cost of manufacturing that specific product. Therefore, your factory overhead costs must be allocated and expensed by product. Additionally, you need to have a rational basis for allocating selling, general and administrative costs by product. You also should include a reasonable estimate of profit in your individual product analysis. Once you have this information by product, your decisions about what products to keep and emphasize, and what products to eliminate or outsource will become readily apparent.

12. **Product Rationalization** – The Pareto Principle, named for an Italian economist, simply states that 80% of the outputs, (in this case, product sales revenues), are created by 20% of the inputs (products). In more recent studies, this initial observation of percentages by Pareto has been updated in a 2001 paper by Micheaux and Gayet. They state that "In practice, the 80:20 rule is more often found to be a "15:35:50" rule, where the top 15 percent [of customers] generate 50 per cent of revenue, the next 35 percent generate 35 percent of the revenue, and the remaining 50 percent contribute 15 percent of revenue or less". Although the exact percentages may be disputed, there is no doubt about the fact that you will have unproductive products in your finished goods inventory in terms of low sales volume, high overhead, low or no profitability, and little or no prospects for profitability improvement. In fact, some "legacy products" may actually be costing you money to produce and sell. Obviously, it will pay you big dividends to analyze your products and product lines to determine which ones are the best candidates for elimination. If you absolutely need to stock and sell a legacy product, consider outsourcing it and marking up the cost of the product 30% to 50%. After all, some of your customers need this product, and are probably willing to

pay a premium to have it available for purchase. By the time you have eliminated unprofitable and marginally profitable products and outsourced others, you will have removed at least 20% of your product line. This reduction will not happen overnight, as you have product catalog advertising and customer notification requirements to consider. However, that should not deter you from starting the product rationalization process.

13. **Contract Manufacturing** – If you have legacy products or other unprofitable products that you must stock to support your customers, and you can't outsource the products, consider contract manufacturing. There are a number of reputable vendors who are familiar with your industry and will happily provide you with quality contract manufacturing at a reasonable price. Here again, if your customers have a need for this product, they should be willing to pay the contract manufacturing cost plus a 30% to 50% mark-up for it.

A Money Making Idea – You should add a product availability surcharge on any products that you stock and sell after the average product life cycle has expired. For example, if your product life cycle is 3 years, you could increase the sales price of replacement parts by 30% in year four, 60% in year five, 100% in year six, and discontinue sales of replacement parts in year seven. This surcharge pricing over and above your normal mark-up based upon product life will also increase demand for your new products, as it will not be worth the additional expense for your customer to maintain and repair your old products.

14. **Inbound Freight Costs** – Controlling the cost of inbound freight is a bit of an "orphan" area in a small business in that not much attention is paid to it. However, there are several simple things that can be done to control inbound freight costs and save money.

   A. Negotiate freight costs with product vendors. Your vendors may agree to deliver to you free of freight charge, depending on the size of the order. At minimum, they may agree to absorb some of the freight cost.

B. Negotiate inbound freight costs with customers who are purchasing special orders. Your customers may agree to pay for all of the inbound freight charges if you arrange to drop ship their orders directly to them.

C. Reduce the number of freight carriers that you utilize, and contract with them to reduce freight costs and your costs of traffic administration.

D. Utilize freight management software to control and reduce freight costs.

E. Contract with a freight management company to outsource your inbound and outbound freight requirements to achieve a savings on freight costs, administrative costs and demurrage expense.

15. **Waste Disposal Expense Reduction** – Your opportunities to reduce waste disposal costs and save money will vary by industry and location. For example, up to 80% of construction job site waste is recyclable. Here are a few ideas for your consideration.

A. Use waste oil to heat your building.
B. Sell your waste oil to a legitimate recycler.
C. If you are an auto dealer or service facility, crush your used oil filters and sell them for scrap.
D. Sell your scrap copper, aluminum and steel for cash to a recycler.
E. Recycle and sell your waste paper, cardboard, scrap wood and pallets.
F. Recycle and sell your spent batteries.
G. Replace hazardous parts solvent cleaning equipment with steam cleaning equipment, using environmentally friendly non-hazardous soaps and solvents.

H. Buy remanufactured toner cartridges and turn in spent toner cartridges for credit.

I. If you have a lot of wood waste, sell your waste product to a wood waste recycler.

J. If you produce a lot of food related waste, arrange with a local farmer to haul away your waste product to be used as animal feed or fertilizer.

K. Consider engaging a waste management consultant to help you control your waste reduction and removal costs.

SUMMARY

There are certainly many other areas where product fabrication and manufacturing costs can be reduced in your company. Some of them may be specific to your industry. However, I have tried to cover some of the topics that might result in substantial savings to your company, whether you are a retailer, wholesaler, manufacturer or a fabricator.

SECTION 8

CONTROLLING AND REDUCING EXPENSES

CHAPTER 33

EXPENSE REDUCTION STRATEGIES

NO NONSENSE EXPENSE REDUCTION AND CONTROL

There are many systems of cost containment. Some are so bureaucratic and cumbersome to administer that they would overload your small business with administrative cost, with very little expense reduction to show for your efforts. You have to concentrate your efforts in Key Result Areas (KRAs) to achieve substantial expense reductions. To illustrate this point, here is an example from my own experience.

An Example of Anal Retentive Expense Control – When I started work for this company, I soon found out that it was hemorrhaging from every key control area imaginable. However, the previous Controller had instituted a system of charging out copies made to each individual department! What a waste of precious time, while the company was sinking into the financial abyss like a lead boat anchor going over a cliff! Obviously, I put a stop to that nonsense immediately and concentrated my efforts on the almost non-existent control of inventory, customer and warranty receivables, cash management and control, accounts payable reconciliation, major expense reductions, improvement of gross profit margins and other key critical areas that would amply reward my time and efforts. Within a year I had stabilized the company's finances, and by the end of the second year we were making money!

The following expense areas are fertile ground for major expense reductions. We will cover them in summary here, but each area will be covered in a separate chapter of its own.

1. **Computer-related IT Cost Reduction** – Computer-related costs are not just measured by the cost of your Information Technology (IT) department, provided that you are large enough to have one. The intelligent use of current computer technology is even more critical to your employees' productivity and your company's success. A significant problem for a small business is that you can't afford the expense of hiring a full time IT employee to manage, maintain and oversee your IT function. In many cases, the IT function is usually farmed out to the Controller or another computer literate manager who is willing to take on the IT function as an additional duty. Therefore, in companies where IT is a stepchild, not enough time is spent on planning and budgeting for the IT function. Obviously, if you don't plan to spend money maintaining and upgrading your computer systems, over time the performance and reliability of your computers and networks will decline. This costs you money every day as your employees are wasting time working with slow, obsolete computers and networks. Obsolete equipment also puts your business at risk operationally if a critical computer or server should fail. As a result, your IT function becomes distributed to the operating departments, and tends to grow without any centralized control in a haphazard fashion that makes it even more difficult to manage. Fortunately, there are some basic things that a part-time IT manager can do to effectively manage the costs of the IT function and you don't have to be a computer geek to do it.

    A. **Standardize your computers, accessories and software**
       You should be purchasing the same kind of desktop or laptop PC utilizing the same operating system. If you are purchasing a Hewlett Packard PC with an Intel processor and a Windows Vista Home Premium operating system, stay with that. Try not to mix manufacturers, processors and operating systems if you can. You know that even though hardware capability changes every 3 to 6 months, Microsoft's Vista operating system will be supported by Microsoft for several more years. Also, stage

your computer purchases so that you don't have to replace all of your computers at the same time

B. Periodically replace your computer hardware - I guarantee that your computer hardware will not last forever. Normally, you can expect about 5 years of regular usage from your computer before it fails. However, you can expect your computer to be technologically obsolete at about the 3 year mark. This may explain why most manufacturers only sell a maximum of 3 year maintenance contracts. Therefore, I recommend that you consider regular replacement of your computers after about four years of use. This is one year after the time that your extended warranty has expired but one year before your average failure time of five years.

C. Purchase your computers, software and related equipment at a discount - You can easily go online to a Website like **www.TigerDirect.com** and purchase computer equipment at a substantial discount from retail pricing. You can compare software pricing by doing a Google search on the software name to find discounts.

D. If a software or hardware item has substantially more capability for a slightly higher price, buy it - In some cases there is very little difference between the price of a basic edition of equipment or software and the more robust version. Is there any doubt as to which version you should buy?

E. If the hardware price is about the same, go with the quality brand – You can insure that you are buying reliable and well tested equipment by staying with a quality brand. You can also be confident that your warranty will be honored by a company well known for quality and customer service, and that the manufacturer will still be in business to honor the warranty.

F. Add the cost of an extended warranty to your advertised price when making your cost comparison – All else being the same, buy the computer or related equipment that offers a 3 year warranty compared with a 90 day warranty. Don't consider the separate purchase of a warranty that would extend beyond 3 years. You will probably end up replacing the computer after 3 to 4 years in any event because of technological obsolescence.

G. Consider engaging an IT professional – Your IT professional should be able to provide you with the planning, budgeting for purchases and maintenance, problem resolution, and the future direction that your IT function requires. Insure that your IT consulting company is a Microsoft Gold Certified Partner, has completed Microsoft competency certifications relating to your systems requirements, and has experience in your industry. If you engage a Microsoft Gold Certified Partner, they can also integrate a multivendor solution for your IT systems requirements covering hardware, software, and networking products from other vendors. This is critically important because very few IT consultants will produce an overall comprehensive solution for your IT system needs. Even though there is a cost for this consulting engagement, the pay-back of having a planned approach to your IT function should far exceed your fees.

For more information, see my Chapter on "THE EFFECTIVE USE OF COMPUTERS".

2. Telecommunications Cost Reductions - The face of the telecommunications industry has changed significantly over the last several years. You have voice-mail systems that are very flexible, to include receiving faxes directly from the sender to your computer through your digital phone system. You have telephone companies providing not only regular desk and cellular phone service, but also internet services through T-1s and fractional T-1s that can combine your telephone and internet services through

VOIP (Voice over Internet Protocol). You can also take advantage of DID (Direct Inward Dialing) and WAN (Wide Area Access) handsets that act much like a cellular phone over a 25 mile distance from your office in any direction. There are old and new ways to reduce your telecom costs. Here are a few of them for your consideration.

A. **Control cell phone usage** - Stop handing out cell phones to relatives and employees as if they were candy canes at Christmas! Expenses for individual cell phones can exceed $100.00 per month, that's $1,200 per year, because of cell phone add-on charges for additional minutes, roaming charges, long-distance and international calling, text messaging, and picture and other downloading services. The only persons that should have a company sponsored cell phone are your employees who absolutely need one to perform their job functions.

B. **Have your cell phone company aggregate minutes** – Select a cell phone provider who will aggregate all of your minutes of usage for billing purposes. This should save you substantial individual overcharges on your monthly cell phone bills.

C. **Get 2 or 3 Quotes from cellular providers** - Have cell phone providers bid for your business by providing you with the best comprehensive quotes they can offer to secure your cell phone business.

D. **No long term contracts** – Try to keep your commitment term to one year, unless there is a significant concession by the cellular provider. In any event, don't sign up for more than 2 years of service. At the end of the term, they will make significant concessions to keep you as a customer, and the cellular service will be less expensive by then.

E. **Investigate Voice over the Internet (VoIP) lines** – If your phones are digital and VoIP capable, you can consider switching to this dual purpose communication channel. You can then have a number of features such as direct inward dialing (DID) and wide area network (WAN) mobile phones that can replace some of your cellular phones, and other digital phone VoIP based applications.

F. Reduce or Eliminate Long Distance calling expense – If you are negotiating for VoIP service, you can generally get at least 200 to 500 free long distance minutes with your contract. This will substantially reduce or eliminate your long distance calling expense.

With the increasing complexity and choice of options, you may want to seek the assistance of a telecommunications consultant in order to maximize the value of your telecom expenditures. Please take the time to read my Chapter on "TELECOMMUNICATIONS, THE GREAT GREY AREA"

3. **Reduce the Cost of Employee Health Insurance Plans** – To reduce the cost of employee dental, health, vision and disability insurance plans, start by instructing your general agent/broker to shop your policy with other health care providers. Let your broker know that you are looking for a company that is "aggressively buying business" and is willing to offer you the very best rates for comparable coverage. Ideally, you will be receiving at least 3 to 5 competitive bids. After reviewing these bids with your broker to compare price and coverage, you can then make an informed decision as to which health insurer is the best for you. The following items should be considered as part of the negotiating and decision making process. (Yes, you can negotiate a better deal with an Insurance Company that is "buying business".)

A. You can negotiate the best premium rates with your insurance carrier for single person, employee and spouse, and family coverage.
B. You can negotiate with your insurance brokers to reduce their commission, resulting in lower health insurance premiums.
C. You can negotiate a longer fixed term for the initial premium rates to stay in effect. The standard is 12 months; however it is possible to negotiate up to 24 months or even longer,

depending upon how much the insurance carrier wants your business.

D. If you currently offer an employer paid vision plan to your employees, consider self-funding this plan. As my own experience has proven, you can save over 80% of the premium cost if you have a simplified self-funded vision plan with low coverage limits.

You can employ other cost-saving measures that will directly affect your employee's amount, type and cost of coverage. The following ideas represent several ways for your company to reduce its overall cost of health insurance by reducing benefits and/or increasing the employee contribution to their health care premium costs.

A. You can negotiate different levels of individual deductibles and the overall policy limits with your health insurance carrier. Most insurance companies have already packaged policies with different levels of deductibles. If you elect to change employee deductibles and limits, you must communicate this to your employees in writing before the effective date of the change.

B. You can increase the amount that employees must contribute to their health coverage plans.

C. If you determine that this is not acceptable to your existing employees, you can increase the amount that new employees will contribute to their health coverage plans without affecting your existing employees.

By increasing the amount of the employee contributions to their health plans as suggested in items B and C above, both you and your employees may be able to save a portion of their contribution increase. If you have a Cafeteria Plan in place, the employer and the employees benefit by eliminating social security taxes and employee income taxes on the increased employee premium contributions that are deducted as part of the Cafeteria Plan. Please read the paragraph below on Section 125 Cafeteria Plans. Also read my Chapter on "THE INSURANCE GAME" for more information.

4. **Section 125 Cafeteria Plan Savings** – Cafeteria Plans are a win/win situation for you as the employer and for your employees. Your employees save the 7.65% FICA tax and federal, state and city income taxes on any contributions they make to the Cafeteria Plan and you, as the employer, do not have to pay the matching 7.65% FICA tax on the employee contributions to the plan. I would advise that you set up a simplified Cafeteria Plan containing only Health, Dental, Vision, and Disability Insurances. This will keep your administrative costs to a minimum. And, as an employer you don't even have to contribute to any of these insurance plans to receive the 7.65% FICA reduction! If you don't already have a Cafeteria Plan, don't hesitate to inaugurate one and start saving payroll taxes courtesy of Uncle Sam! See my Chapter on "CAFETERIA PLANS" for more information.

5. **401k Plan Advantages** – I have included 401k plans in this section because even though having a 401k plan does not result in an expense reduction for your company, there is a considerable benefit to all employees who participate in the plan. In 2009, your employees can contribute up to $16,500 to their 401k plan. If they are 50 years old in 2009, the allowable plan contribution is $22,000 of pre-tax earnings. And remember that your company does not have to match any of the employee's contributions. Therefore, the cost to the company would be minimal, probably not exceeding several thousand dollars each year including administrative costs. See my Chapter on "401k PLANS" for more information.

   A Cash Saving Idea for Your 401k Plan – We live in a period of financial turmoil, credit restrictions, foreclosures, bankruptcies and generally tough economic times making it even more difficult for small businesses to make a profit. If find yourself in a cash crunch, consider reducing or eliminating your company 401k match. It won't be a popular decision, but it's a lot better than having to lay off employees who are contributing to your business. I am assuming that any employees who were marginal have already been terminated or laid off.

6. **Group Life Insurance Advantages** - This tax-free insurance benefit of up to $50,000 is permitted courtesy of Section 79 of the IRS code book. Thanks again, Uncle Sam! It's a great benefit for your employees as many of them don't have sufficient personal life insurance coverage outside of work. Also, it's totally flexible in terms of the amount of individual coverage you choose to obtain up to the tax-free limit of $50,000. For example, you could initiate your group life plan with $10,000 of employee life insurance coverage and $2,000 of spouse or dependent life coverage. You can also tier your life insurance, and give your managers $25,000 of coverage, and cover your officers and directors to the maximum tax-free limit of $50,000. **However, my strong recommendation is that you do not allow the plan to exceed the $50,000 employee limit or the $2,000 spouse or dependent limit. Also, do not allow the employees to pay for coverage in excess of the coverage that you provide as the employer. The payroll administrative burdens for a small business of not "keeping it simple" are substantial.** See my Chapter on "GROUP LIFE INSURANCE" for more information.

7. **Workers Compensation Insurance Cost Reduction** – Yes, in some states there are ways to save a substantial amount of your Workers Compensation Insurance Premium up front. However, you can achieve savings in all states by doing the following things:

   A. Insure that your employees are properly classified at the lowest Workers Compensation rate possible for their occupation and job description.

   B. Follow up on all of your Workers Compensation Insurance claimants to insure that their claims are valid.

   C. Contest any claims that you believe are without merit. Even though you may not win, by contesting the claim, your employees will know that you are not going to be a pushover regarding contestable Workers Compensation claims.

D. Offer any employees currently collecting Workers Compensation Insurance temporary light duty positions not involving excessive stretching, bending or heavy lifting. This will not only reduce your Workers Compensation Insurance claims payments, but it also discourages employees from malingering at home and taking further advantage of the system!

E. Analyze your Workers Compensation Insurance claims and implement preventative measures to reduce repetitive claims to an absolute minimum.

Finally, if you are in a state that allows partially self-funded groups to insure for Workers Compensation, investigate what they can offer your company in the way of premium cost reduction, preventative services, and claims control. For more information, see my Chapter on "WORKERS COMPENSATION INSURANCE".

8. **Payroll Processing Costs** – If you are a small business, your payroll administration costs will be greater if you process your payroll in-house. Not only do you have the personnel costs to consider, but also the administrative costs of payroll forms, payroll check costs, payroll setup, payroll bank account reconciliations, internal control problems, maintaining payroll software, and insuring that payroll taxes are paid accurately and timely. The following are my recommendations for reducing your payroll processing costs:

A. Schedule your payroll for semi-monthly processing if possible. You only pay for 2 payrolls a month, as compared with 4 or 5 payrolls when you pay weekly. You also eliminate the need to post monthly payroll expense accruals, since one of your semi-monthly payrolls always falls at the end of the month.

B. Hire a known and trusted outside payroll service, like Paychex who specialize in small business payrolls, to process your payroll. You'll be miles ahead compared to processing your payroll in-house, and the cost is reasonable for a small business.

C. Inaugurate a Section 125 Cafeteria Plan to save on payroll taxes for your employees and your company. For more details, see my Chapter on "PAYROLL".

9. **Legal Expense Cost Control** – Legal costs have a way of becoming astronomical if they are not controlled. In summary, here are a number of ways to save money on your legal and compliance costs.

   A. **Choosing an Attorney** – This is the most important decision you will make in terms controlling your legal costs and having a successful relationship with your attorneys, whether they are specialists or corporate counsel. The following are several important factors you may want to consider.

      1. Industry Experience
      2. Communication Ability
      3. References
      4. Fee Costs
      5. Do You Actually Require an Attorney Specialist
      6. Will Your Attorney be a "team member"

Read my Chapter on "CHOOSING YOUR CORPORATE ATTORNEY" for more information. **If you skip this critical step, you can wind up with unbelievably high legal fees for shoddy performance delivered late or not at all.**

   B. **Ask Questions** – Don't be shy about asking questions about items that may have legal implications.

   C. **Utilize Standard Business Contracts** - Have your corporate attorney create or review any standard contracts for you that are specific to your business. Negotiate a fixed price for this service.

D. **Negotiate Fixed Project Fees** – Always get a fixed contract price (No ups- No extras) in writing from several attorney firms before making a decision to go forward.

E. **Settle Disputes Without Litigation** – If at all possible, avoid expensive and time consuming litigation by settling the matter. This keeps you out of the courtroom, and allows you to put your full attention to making money for your business.

F. **Utilize Standard Legal forms for Common Legal Problems** - Have your standard legal forms reviewed by your attorney, revised if necessary and downloaded to your controller in an M/S Word format.

G. **Prepare an Internal Draft Document for Your Attorney.** You will save substantial legal costs if you provide your attorney with a draft copy of your document to simply review, as opposed to creating the document from scratch. Read my Chapter on "CONTAINING AND REDUCING LEGAL COSTS" for more information.

10. **Office Supplies and Other Consumables Expense Control** – There are a number of things that you can do to control supplies expense as follows:

A. **Consolidate Vendors** - If the supply items are readily available from a number of vendors, consolidate your purchases with one or two vendors to receive discounts, special terms, free delivery, off site storage or other considerations.

B. **Buy Generic Products** – If generic products are available buy them, not the brand names which cost more.

C. **Get Banded Volume Discount Quotes From Your Vendors** – This will allow you to determine price breaks based on volume and calculate an "Economic Order Quantity" (EOQ).

D. **Buy in Quantity** – Buy up to a six months supply of a product to receive volume discounts of at least 10%.

E. **Ask for Vendor Storage Assistance** – Storing forms, supplies and other consumables at your vendors location allows you to store other supply items at your location where space may be at a premium.

F. **Ask for Special Payment Terms** – You can probably get 60 to 120 day payment terms with some of your vendors and suppliers. This creates additional working capital to help you get through tight credit times like the one we're currently in.

G. **Control Supplies Theft** – Have your supplies inventory kept in a locked room or cabinet with controlled access to these areas.

To get more information about supplies expense reduction and control, read my chapter titled "SUPPLIES INVENTORY – A BASKET OF SAVINGS".

11. **Records Storage Management Costs** – This is an area that you don't give much thought to until you need to retrieve critical records. Then it hits you like a ton of bricks! You have no records management system in place, and either you can't locate the necessary records or, worse yet, they've been thrown out with the trash. I will give you some ideas concerning the control and management of records and, in my opinion, the best ways for your small business to minimize the costs of storing your records.

Reducing the Costs of Storing Your Records – There are several ways that you can reduce the cost of records storage and still have all of the benefits of a managed records retention program.

A. **Keep the last 4 years of records on site**. It shouldn't take up too much space, and most everything you need to access will be at your fingertips.

B. **Utilize a recognized records storage management company for your permanent records storage requirements** – This will be relatively inexpensive, since most of the records you send to storage will be stored permanently.

C. After the 4 year cycle, destroy all records that have a 4 year retention requirement or less – Do this **before** you send the remaining records to your records storage company. Then send the records that have a five year or greater retention requirement to your records storage company. This should be done once a year immediately after you have completed your year-end financial statements. This saves you all of the acquisition, storage and destruction charges on records with a temporary records retention requirement of 4 year or less.

D. Use the Records Destruct Listing sent by your storage company to order the destruction of records beyond their retention cycle – Periodically, at minimum once a year, your records storage company should send you a suggested listing of records past their retention cycle. I said they should send the destruct listing, because sometimes they don't. It's up to you to insure they do! Use this listing to mark for destruction all of the records you no longer have to keep. This will keep your records growth to a minimum.

12. **Utility Costs** – Utility costs are the largest facilities-related expense item in your budget, according to a number of researchers. And because of the substantial planned increases in utility costs, your utility expense will only grow, unless you become proactive about inaugurating effective energy cost reduction programs. A company wide strategy to implement utility cost reductions can reduce your company's energy expense by at least 10% to as much as 30% or more. And in these tough times a penny saved is the proverbial dollar earned! See my chapter on "Controlling Utility Costs" for more information concerning the development of an effective energy efficiency policy, and the identification of cost effective energy usage reduction projects.

13. **Waste Disposal Expense Control** – Your opportunities to reduce the cost of waste disposal and save money will vary by

industry and location. For example, up to 80% of construction industry job site waste is recyclable. Here are a few ideas for your consideration.

A. Use waste oil to heat your building.
B. Sell your waste oil to a legitimate recycler.
C. Crush your used oil filters and sell them for scrap.
D. Sell your scrap copper, aluminum and steel for cash to a recycler.
E. Recycle and sell your waste paper, cardboard, and pallets.
F. Recycle and sell your spent battery cores.
G. Replace hazardous parts solvent cleaning equipment with steam cleaning equipment, using environmentally friendly non-hazardous soaps and solvents.
H. Buy remanufactured toner cartridges and turn in spent toner cartridges for credit.
I. If you have a lot of wood waste, sell your waste product to a wood waste recycler.
J. If you produce a lot of food related waste, arrange with a local farmer to haul away that waste product to be used as animal feed or fertilizer.
K. If you produce a large amount of waste, consider engaging a waste management consultant to help you control your waste reduction and removal costs.

14. **Travel and Entertainment (T&E) Expenses** – There are always meetings requiring travel that you absolutely have to attend. However, to reduce your T&E costs to a minimum, here are a few ideas that will save you money.

   A. **Don't travel!** – This sounds like an oxymoron, but do you really have to make that trip if other avenues are available to you?

   B. **Consider Web Conferencing** – Take a good look at Web Conferencing as an alternative to travel.

    C. **Consider an open-ended phone call** – Perhaps all you really need is an open-ended phone call with your customer or vendor.

    D. Schedule your meetings to coincide with client or vendor planned visits at or near to your location.

    E. Schedule your meetings with clients, vendors, or others to coincide with other planned visits near their offices

    F. Designate one of your employees as your Travel Director.

    G. Control the costs of approved travel.

    H. Institute a written Travel Policy.

    I. Have Employees use Hotel Shuttles, not Taxis.

    J. Have Employees File a Standard T&E Form for Travel.

15. **Repair & Maintenance Expenses** – There are a number of ways to control Repair & Maintenance Expenses. I have listed them below in a timeline sequence starting with asset purchase selection followed by the periodic maintenance requirements of the asset purchased, and ending with asset disposition criteria.

    A. Asset Selection – Choose a manufacturer known for their quality products. This is the best way to insure that your product will probably last through its normal life cycle.

    B Select the manufacturer with the longest product guarantee period.

    C. Negotiate the cost of any extended warranties.

    D. Create a Periodic Preventative Maintenance (PM) schedule recommended by the manufacturer for each asset requiring maintenance. This schedule should be attached to the asset in a protective plastic folder, along with a copy of the manufacturer guarantee and extended warranty, if any. A copy should be given to the employee who has been assigned to insure that the PM has been scheduled and completed.

E. Insure that you have received an authorization from the manufacturer or warranty provider to complete any warranty repairs.

F. Insure that you file a claim for all repairs and replacements covered under the manufacturer guarantees or any extended warranty.

G. If the asset no longer has any warranty coverage, compare the cost of needed repairs with the market value of the asset. If the repair cost equals or exceeds the market value of the asset, consider a guaranteed remanufactured or a new asset purchase.

H. In the case of company maintained roads and parking lots, consider using an asphalt sealer to extend the life of your roads and lots. This will defer the prospect of having to make major expenditures for substantial repairs.

16. **Building and Equipment Lease and Rental Expenses** – There are many different types of assets that you can rent or lease rather than purchase. Currently there are many desperate vendors and property owners who would love the opportunity to rent or lease to your company. Today, you are definitely in the driver's seat regarding any lease or rental negotiations. The following list will give you some negotiating points you may not have thought about that will save you money now and potentially make you money in the future.

   REAL ESTATE LEASES – There are many points of negotiation a Landlord will consider in today's very soft real estate market that definitely favor you as the Lessee. Here are some of the more important deal points to negotiate.

1. First and foremost, negotiate the best monthly lease rate possible for the longest term that you can negotiate including renewal provisions, based on "usable" (the amount you actually occupy) square footage. Do this part of the negotiation first, without giving up any other covenants. Your Common Area Maintenance (CAM) charges, if any, should be based on your actual square footage.

2. If the building is under construction or construction has not yet begun, you may be able to negotiate custom design features at little or no cost. Also, you can negotiate to have the landlord provide and pay for tenant improvements that would normally be paid for by the tenant, even if the building is older. These concessions can amount to a considerable amount of up-front money that you don't have to cough up!

3. Don't be shy about asking for several months of "free rent" as part of the lease provisions. This will help pay for part or all of your relocation expenses and more!

4. Tell the landlord that a Consumer Price Index (CPI) increase provision will not be part of this lease!

5. Make sure that you have clear and easily met Assignment and Subletting provisions inserted into your lease. This will give you maximum flexibility in case you have to downsize or vacate the lease premises.

6. If possible, have a lease purchase option at a favorable price inserted into the lease document. When commercial real estate recovers, this purchase option could become extremely valuable to you and literally pay for all of your rent and more. If you can't get the landlord to agree to this, at least have a "right of first refusal" provision incorporated into the document.

7. Negotiate a first and second period lease renewal provision at a fixed rate.

8. Always let your prospective landlord know at the start of negotiations that nothing will be signed until your attorney has completed a review of the lease document.

EQUIPMENT LEASES – These leases are much less negotiable because there is usually a third party financing company involved. You are probably not going to be able to negotiate an effective interest rate below the third party finance cost, but there are several areas you can negotiate.

1) First, always negotiate the lowest price for the equipment as if you were going to make an outright purchase. This will give you a good baseline from which to determine the actual finance cost of the lease.

2) Negotiate a reasonable residual purchase cost value of the lease when the equipment is turned in. Be realistic about the value that is being assigned to the equipment, particularly cars and trucks.

3) Negotiate realistic mileage requirements on auto or truck lease turn-ins, as they are generally tilted in favor of the dealership. Pardon the pun, but now you are in the driver's seat regarding these lease negotiations, not the dealership.

4) Negotiate your actual finance cost of the lease as close as you can to the finance company's cost to the dealer.

5) Negotiate for a reasonable "early termination" clause in the lease document.

6) Always let your prospective vendor or lessor know at the start of negotiations that nothing will be signed until your attorney has completed a review of the lease document. Armed with this information and assisted by your attorney, you should be able to negotiate very favorable lease terms!

17. Company Vehicle Management and Cost Control – When you have employees using vehicles for company business there are always opportunities to control usage and costs. Here are a few suggestions that will save you some money.

    A. Consider replacing a company provided vehicle with a car allowance – A car allowance works well if the employee is not using a vehicle full time for business purposes. Employees like it because they see it as additional and usually non-taxable income. Employers like it because they know that they can substantially reduce the costs of providing a vehicle to the employee. These costs include interest, depreciation, fuel, licensing, insurance, and maintenance. The average monthly car allowance is about half of the true cost of operating the vehicle. Also, there is no long term commitment with a car allowance. If the employee is terminated or laid off, their car allowance terminates that month!

    B. Consider purchasing low-mileage used company vehicles – Let's say that you are operating 3 delivery pick-up trucks in your business. Further, your operations are demanding and you log 60,000 miles a year on each vehicle. Does it make sense to buy new vehicles when 3 or 4 years from now, they will be sold to a wholesaler at about 15% of your purchase price. Consider buying a two to three year old pick-up truck still in warranty with less than 35,000 miles on it and save the 25% to 30% that you lose when you drive a new truck off the dealer's lot.

    C. Establish a regular Preventative Maintenance (PM) Schedule – Have a regular PM schedule recommended by the manufacturer set up for each vehicle. This schedule should be taped to the glove box inside the vehicle and scheduled by an employee who has been assigned to insure that company vehicles are properly maintained. I would recommend the Accounts Payable person be assigned this responsibility, as they will be checking the PM invoices for each company vehicle.

D. Add your company vehicles to your master business P&C policy – It's much less expensive to insure all your business use vehicles through your master business liability policy than to insure each vehicle individually.

E. Provide a listing of all employees eligible to drive company vehicles to your insurance company – Insure that your employees have current valid driver's licenses and have complied with the requirements of your drug testing program.

18. **Property and Casualty Insurance** – Believe it or not, you can negotiate with your Property and Casualty Insurance Company to reduce your premium as follows:

    A. Your first objective should be a reduction in the quoted cost of your P&C insurance as compared with your prior year. Don't let the fact that your current P&C insurance company has already given you a current quote deter you from asking them for a better, more competitive quote. Let them decide whether they want to keep your business or not!

    B. Examine your deductibles. If you have a low deductible on certain coverages that are highly unlikely to result in a claim, have that area of the policy quoted again with a higher deductible.

    C. Review all of your physical damage coverage. There may be segments of your policy where you could save considerable premium cost by self-insuring those assets.

    D. Review of all of your required bond coverage. There may be bonds that you are being charged premiums for that are no longer necessary. These bonds should be deleted from your policy.

    E. Review all of your real property coverage to ensure that it is accurate. Any real property no longer owned or occupied by your company should be removed from the P&C policy.

F. Review your business interruption insurance. Make sure that the coverage is a realistic estimate of your business interruption costs plus 10%. If it is substantially in excess of that amount, consider reducing the coverage.

7. Review all of your insurance coverages with your broker each policy year for potential savings.

See my Chapter on "PROPERTY & CASUALTY INSURANCE" for more information.

19. Controlling Freight Costs – Controlling the cost of inbound freight is an "orphan" area in a small business in that not much attention is paid to it. However, there are several simple things that can be done to control inbound and outbound freight costs.

A. Negotiate freight costs with product vendors – Your vendors may agree to deliver to you free of freight charge, depending on the size of the order. At minimum, they may agree to absorb some of the freight cost.

B. Negotiate inbound freight costs with customers who are purchasing special orders. Your customers may agree to pay for all of the inbound freight charges if you arrange to drop ship their orders directly to them.

C. Negotiate outbound freight costs with customers who are not currently paying all of their freight costs. Your customers may agree to pay for all of the freight charges on smaller orders. At minimum, they may agree to absorb some of the freight cost. You will never know until you ask!

D. Reduce the number of freight carriers that you utilize, and contract with them to reduce freight costs.

E. Utilize freight management software to control freight costs and administrative expense.

F. Contract with a freight management company to outsource your inbound and outbound freight requirements with them to achieve a savings on freight costs, administrative costs and demurrage expense.

See my Chapter on "COST OF SALES REDUCTION STRATEGIES" for further information on reducing costs of production and other sales related costs.

SUMMARY

Once again, I'm sure that there are other expense areas where costs can be reduced in your company. Some of those areas may be specific to your company or industry. I don't propose this to be a comprehensive list of all possible expense reductions for your specific company. However, I have tried to cover most of the topics that would yield substantial savings to your company, whether you are a retailer, a wholesaler, a manufacturer or a fabricator.

CHAPTER 34

THE EFFICIENT AND EFFECTIVE
USE OF COMPUTERS

INTRODUCTION

No matter what anyone thinks, computers are here to stay! In fact, as we advance into the 21st Century, the use of computers will broaden both horizontally and vertically. In other words, we will find ourselves performing new tasks with computers, and there will be more companies utilizing computers to perform existing tasks. The rate of change in technological advancements at this time seems to have no practical limitations. If you purchase new computer hardware today, it may be superseded by cheaper and better equipment in three to four months. Keeping pace with the advancements in computer technology would present a challenge to a corporate information technology executive in a large corporation who has access to significant resources. If that's the case, how much more difficult is it for a small business to keep abreast of new technology developments? Yet, no one would disagree that advances in computerization have created many new opportunities for small businesses. By utilizing computer technology efficiently and effectively, a small business can expand its goals, accomplish more objectives, and gain a competitive advantage without the need to increase staff or substantially increase expenditures. Businesses that are not flexible and adept at utilizing computer technology will soon find themselves at a competitive disadvantage. Therefore, the small businesses that are willing to make a planned and structured investment in new computer technology will substantially increase their chances for overall success in managing their business profitably.

EXTERNALLY GENERATED TECHNOLOGY CHALLENGES

Small businesses face unique challenges in light of expanding requirements for more computerization thrust upon them by external sources. In many cases, the small business is sandwiched in between the requirements of their customers, vendors, governmental authorities and, in a number of cases, their franchisors and others. For example, let's say than previously one of your largest vendors has been sending you paper invoices and statements. Now, the vendor has informed you that they will not be mailing out paper invoices or statements to you in the future. You will, however, be able to go online through the Internet at their website, and download your invoices and statements. However, the invoices will only be available on line for 45 days, and statements will only be available for 90 days. You would be well advised to print copies of your invoices and statements to back up your check requisition requests and to provide you with some historical hardcopy documentation. Alternatively, you could have a procedure to copy this information to a disk drive, or a removable disk medium. If you choose this alternative, you then create another problem relating to how you secure this information, catalog it and save it for future reference and records keeping requirements. There is no doubt that the elimination of the cost of producing and mailing paper invoices and statements is a considerable advantage for your vendor. But as a small business, your vendor's cost-saving changes end up costing you a fair bit of time and money regardless of whether you choose to print the available copies, or store them on magnetic media. The trend is quite clear. More and more businesses and governmental agencies will transfer part of their costs to the small business owner who is least able to absorb these costs.

Another challenge for the small business owner is the staffing necessary to cope with the new tasks created when the increased computerization requirements of customers, vendors, governmental agencies and others require your company's participation. Let's say that you have a large customer who wants to pay your invoices by electronic funds transfer (EFT). At first glance, this sounds like a great idea because you just might get paid on time. However, you will now have to post each individual EFT to your bank account. You'll probably need to arrange with your bank to receive trailer information regarding these EFT receipts. You will also need to receive an e-mail from your customer detailing the invoices that are being paid on each EFT. Imagine the extra work for the accounts receivable person if all of your customers were paying by EFT! You would have to record each EFT payment transaction separately, whereas today most of your payments are currently paid in cash, credit card or by check, and the posting of your total bank deposit is done in one batch. And, of course, adopting any of these changes will mean more work for your IT staff. This makes for an interesting scenario if your IT staff consists of your controller, who is performing this function as an additional duty.

Additionally, governmental and regulatory bodies are now requiring many of their forms and reports to be filed online. This certainly makes it easier to input the data, but now we have some additional problems to consider as follows:

1. Who is responsible for filing the report online?
2. What kind of signature authority does the report require?
3. Has the report been reviewed by signing authority?
4. Has a copy of the report been printed, distributed and filed correctly?
5. Will there be any paper notification of additional reports that need to be filed?
6. Will the notification of additional reporting requirements be sent on line and to whom?
7. Is there a procedure in place to change this reporting responsibility when employees are promoted to another position or leave the company?

Believe me, once you move away from hardcopy reporting, it's very easy for any of these procedures to fall through the cracks, even if you implement specific controls to prevent this from happening.

INTERNALLY GENERATED INFORMATION TECHNOLOGY (IT) OPPORTUNITIES

In order to develop computer related opportunities, you must first analyze your company's current status regarding your IT capabilities versus your IT requirements. To accomplish that, you should start by creating a listing of your computer related hardware and software. You would be amazed at how many small businesses don't even know how much IT equipment and software that they currently lease or own. You should then assess in general terms how long your existing hardware and software will be capable of supporting your current IT requirements. As an example, if you are currently using Windows 2000 as an operating system, it's important that you know that Microsoft will no longer support Windows 2000 after July 11, 2010. You should develop the following information regarding all of your hardware and software.

DEVELOP A CURRENT COMPUTER SYSTEMS HARDWARE AND SOFTWARE CAPABILITY ASSESSMENT

Existing Hardware

1. What is the name, model, serial number, cost and date of purchase of the hardware item.
2. Is the hardware still being supported by the manufacturer? If so, how long will the manufacturer continue to support the hardware? This can usually be determined online at the manufacturer's website.
3. Do you have a maintenance contract on the hardware?
4. What does it cost each year for maintenance, and when does the contract expire?
5. Can the maintenance contract be renewed?
6. Has the hardware been made obsolete by changes in technology?
7. Can the hardware be upgraded and, if so, what is the cost of the upgrade?

8. In the opinion of you and your staff, is the existing hardware capable of supporting your computer systems requirements for the next year or two?

9. If this hardware has to be upgraded or replaced, establish a priority for this action.

10. What is the cost of new OEM equipment that is a reliable replacement for the existing hardware and will it provide a performance enhancement?

11. What is the term of the guarantee or warranty on the new equipment, and what is the term and cost of a follow-on maintenance contract?

12. Will the new hardware be compatible with your existing hardware and software?

Existing Software

1. What is the name and version, cost and date of purchase of the software item?

2. Is the software still being supported by the developer? This can usually be determined online at the developer's website.

3. Do you have a maintenance contract on the software?

4. What does it cost each year for maintenance, and when does your maintenance contract expire?

5. Can the maintenance contract be renewed?

6. Has the software been made obsolete by upgrades and newer competing software?

7. Can the software package be upgraded and, if so, what is the cost of the upgrade?

8. In the opinion of you and your staff, is the existing software package capable of supporting your computer systems requirements now and in the immediate future?

9. If this software is to be upgraded or replaced, establish a priority for this action.

10. What is the cost of a new software package that is a reliable and proven replacement for the existing software and will it provide more capability and flexibility?

11. What is the initial term of developer support for the new software, and what is the term and cost of a follow-on support contract?

12. Will the new software package be compatible with your existing hardware and other software packages?

CONDUCT A CURRENT AND FUTURE COMPUTER SYSTEMS REQUIREMENTS SURVEY WITH THE ASSISTANCE OF YOUR MANAGEMENT TEAM

1. Based upon your current computer systems hardware and software capability assessment, are there any items of hardware and software that are currently in need of updating or replacement?

2. These items should be listed in order of priority by company and for each department, but no action should be taken until this survey is completed. You may well discover increased capability and flexibility requirements for your hardware and software as a result of this survey.

3. In your next managers meeting, define the elements of your computer systems requirements survey. Explain why the thoughtful completion of this survey is critical to the long-term success of your information technology strategy.

4. Give a copy of the current computer systems hardware and software capability assessment to each manager. They should also be given a copy of the current company and departmental priority listing.

5. Explain that this is the hardware and software currently in use companywide. The managers can use this information as a starting point for the creation of a future needs assessment.

6. The future needs assessment should not exceed three years. This period is close to the projected life of your computer hardware equipment before it becomes obsolete, is out of warranty, and is subject to replacement. Therefore, for small businesses, it makes little sense to forecast future computer systems requirements past three years, unless there is a significant reason to do so.

7. Projected future computer systems requirements should be based upon forecasts that are as specific as possible. At minimum, they should contain the following information:

A. Any new company offices that are projected to open over the next three years, and the location, departments and staffing, new products or services, computer hardware and software requirements, and any items worthy of special consideration.

B. Any additional increase of square footage in existing company offices, with projections for staff or capability increases.

C. A projection showing the forecasted increase or decrease in transactions and staff requiring a computer or workstation over the next three years.

D. Any new products, product lines or services that the company will be undertaking over the next three years. Also, include any products or services that will be curtailed or eliminated during that period.

E. Have your managers solicit assistance from your IT department, or the individual who is designated in charge of IT for your company, and your computer systems vendors in order to evaluate the cost and feasibility of the increased hardware and software necessary to support this projection.

F. Have your managers assign a priority, using a scale of one to five, for each hardware and software item.

   a. Number one would indicate a high priority item that should be implemented as soon as possible.

   b. Number two would indicate a moderately high priority item that is important to the department's performance but does not have to be implemented immediately.

    c.   Number three would indicate a medium priority item that can be deferred at least a year.

    d.   Number four would indicate a moderately low priority, which could be implemented over the next two years.

    e.   Number five would indicate a low priority item that could be eliminated, depending upon other relevant factors.

It is important to take the time to develop these priority ratings, as they will significantly affect the next step in this process.

PRIORITIZE THE IMPLEMENTATION OF YOUR CURRENT AND FUTURE SYSTEMS REQUIREMENTS

You need to simplify the process of prioritizing the implementation of your computer systems requirements. I have outlined the steps of a method that I have used which should assist you in this process.

1.   List all of your overall company and department manager's priorities by company and department in order of the priorities assigned (1-5) in EXCEL spreadsheet form.

2.   Have your IT manager or the person who is acting in this capacity along with your IT vendors, assign a difficulty factor using a scale of one to five for the implementation of each item listed above. Then enter the difficulty factor into the spreadsheet mentioned above.

    a.   Number one would indicate an item easy to implement that could be done in the few months.

    b.   Number two would indicate an item that is fairly easy to implement and could be accomplished in next six months.

    c.   Number three would indicate a medium difficulty item that can be implemented in the next year.

   d. Number four would indicate a moderately difficult item, which could be implemented over the next two years.

   e. Number five would indicate a high difficulty item that could possibly exceed a three-year time frame. Depending upon other relevant factors, this project might not be worth implementing at all.

3. Have your CFO or controller evaluate the cash flow requirements of each of these items and assign an ease of funding factor, using a scale of one to five, for the funding of each item listed in Step 1 above.

   a. Number one would indicate an item not requiring much in the way of funding and could be implemented by the company at any time.

   b. Number two would indicate an item requiring some advance planning, but could be funded by the company over the next few months.

   c. Number three would indicate a moderate funding requirement that would involve vendor financing to be paid back over the next two or three years.

   d. Number four would indicate a moderately difficult funding requirement which would require the approval of your bank or another lender, and be implemented and paid back over the next three to five years.

   e. Number five would indicate a high difficulty funding item that would possibly exceed a five-year financing time frame and, depending upon other relevant factors, might not be currently achievable.

4. Now we finally get to the fun part. Sort all of the requirement items that are designated number one in terms of high priority, ease of implementation, and are easy to fund. Believe it or not, you have just completed a cost/benefit analysis that

justifies your implementation of these items over the next several months, without much more work required for further analysis!

5. First, analyze all requirement items that are designated with a number one or number two in terms of priority, funding, and implementation. All of these items are worthy of consideration for implementation over the next 12 months.

6. Remove from consideration all items that are designated as number five in all three categories.

7. Scrutinize requirement items that contain numbers four and five in all three categories to determine whether they are really important enough to be considered for implementation.

8. Now list at all the items with a top implementation priority of one, but a difficulty in implementation or funding factor of numbers three or four. Then, select from this list the items you would like to implement. Obviously, there is a practical limit to the number of items or projects that you can commit to undertake in any given time period, so be selective.

SCHEDULING THE IMPLEMENTATION OF YOUR CURRENT AND FUTURE SYSTEM REQUIREMENTS

Initially, you must determine how many of these items you can afford to implement from the standpoint of staffing, affordability, funding requirements, training and the overall ability of your company to manage change. Obviously, there is a practical limit to the number of items or projects that you can commit to undertake and successfully implement in any given time period. However, by using the methodology described above, you have put yourself in a position to identify and select the highest priority computer related projects that have the least difficulty and cost associated with them for implementation!

1. Determine overall which of these projects will be implemented, which projects will be removed from consideration, and which projects will be deferred for consideration to a later date.
2. Communicate the results of your implementation decisions to all of your managers.
3. Schedule a management meeting to discuss an orderly and rational schedule for the implementation of the priorities, and have your managers agree that the schedule is attainable.
4. Input the results of your project scheduling meeting into your spreadsheet. The additional information should contain the expected costs of the project to be implemented, the manager in charge of the implementation, and the expected completion date of the project.
5. This information should be communicated in writing to all of your managers. One copy should be initialed by them and returned to you, with another copy for their work file.
6. Progress reports regarding this implementation schedule should be presented by each manager at a monthly managers meeting. Any major problems encountered in meeting the schedule should be duly noted and, if necessary the estimated completion date should be adjusted accordingly.

COMPUTER HARDWARE AND SOFTWARE LIFE CYCLES

It is important to remember that all items of computer hardware and software have life cycles. Unfortunately, particularly in the case of software, the purchasers are the final beta test site. That's why we often see massive software updates by software developers within several months of the inauguration of the product. However hardware, unlike software, is generally well tested before release to the public. Hardware updates are usually confined to the internal software. Both computer-related products have a definitive life. That life is determined in large part by the obsolescence factor, and the length of time that the hardware manufacturer or the software developer continues to support the product.

Recommendation: Don't buy software when it is first released to the public. Why volunteer to be a beta test site for the software developer without pay! Wait for at least three to six months, while the software is being debugged by the developer and the general public. If there is still bad news about the performance of the software product after six months, either wait longer until the software problems have been corrected, or consider the purchase of another similar product that has successfully gone through the development process. The same would be true for any hardware product that has been released to the public and has had performance problems. There is an old saying among computer professionals. **"Don't be on the bleeding edge of technology"**. If that makes sense for the big boys, it makes even more sense for small companies who do not have the time to cope with the problems that improperly tested software and hardware can create.

There is a corollary to the front-end developmental problems on the back-end of the life cycle of computer-related equipment. Beware of purchasing any software or equipment that has passed the midpoint of its lifecycle. These days this would probably include any equipment over two years old, measured from the date of its release to the public. There are two reasons for this. The first is that the equipment will probably be technologically obsolete in the next two years. The second reason relates to the date of termination of maintenance and/or support by the equipment manufacturer. If you purchase discounted equipment that is too far along in its lifecycle, it is no bargain! You will be replacing the equipment much sooner than you think.

A TIP that will save you substantial equipment replacement costs in the future: When you replace or upgrade computer equipment, don't base your equipment purchase decisions on equipment that will simply allow you to service your current computer system requirements. Have your equipment vendor quote you several levels of upgrades for the hardware item you are replacing. If there isn't much difference in relative cost, choose the equipment with more capability and flexibility than you currently need or will need in the immediate future. This will protect you in the event that you have underestimated your equipment needs. And in this rapidly changing technological environment, underestimation of computer systems requirements is commonplace.

AN ILLUSTRATION OF A PROCESS FOR IDENTIFYING, EVALUATING, PRIORITIZING, AND SCHEDULING COMPUTER SYSTEMS PROJECTS

A few years ago, a computer systems service company specializing in the automobile and truck dealership business realized that they would have to change their approach to revamping the software that their customers were using. At the time, their software development was a few years behind their competition. This resulted in potential sales opportunities that were lost to their competitors. They began to directly involve their customers in the process of developing new software and improving the design of existing software. Every year, at least four months prior to the customer's annual seminar, the company would send surveys to each customer. The accompanying letter asked the customer to list at least 10 improvements that they would like to see in the company's software for each software module that the company offered. The customer was also asked to numerically prioritize those improvements from one to ten, one being the highest priority. When the company received the surveys, they would sort the responses by item and priority. Then they would send the summarized listing to their best programmers, who would numerically rate each item for ease of implementation from one to five, one being the easiest to implement. They then instructed their programmers to implement those changes which had a priority and an implementation rating of one or two. These changes were then loaded on a CD program update disc. The company then distributed those CDs to their customers at an annual seminar and reviewed with them all of the programming changes that had been requested and implemented. Can you imagine the impact that this process had on their customers? Participation in the survey doubled after the first year and in three or four years had doubled again. After five years of engaging in this process, the company's software was three or four years in advance of the competition! Believe me, this process can work minor miracles in a relatively short period of time!

CONTROLLING COMPUTER RELATED IT COSTS

Computer related costs are not just measured in the cost of your IT (Information Technology) department, if you are big enough to have one. The intelligent use of current computer technology is ever more critical to your employees' productivity and your company's success. A significant problem for a small business is that you can't afford the expense of hiring a full time IT employee to manage, maintain and oversee your IT function. In this case, the IT function is usually farmed out to the Controller or another computer literate manager who is willing to take on the IT function as an additional duty. Therefore, because it's a stepchild, not much planning and budgeting is done for the IT function. Obviously, if you don't plan to spend money for computer maintenance and upgrading, over time the performance and reliability of your computers and networks will decline. This costs you money every day as your employees are wasting time working with slow, obsolete computers and networks. It also puts your business at risk operationally if a critical computer or server should fail. Your utilization of the IT function also becomes distributed out to the operating departments, and tends to grow without any centralized control in a haphazard fashion that makes it even more difficult to manage. Fortunately, there are some basic things that a part-time IT manager can do to effectively manage the costs of the IT function, and you don't have to be a computer geek to do it.

A. **Standardize your computers, accessories and software** – You should be purchasing the same kind of desktop PC, or laptop PC utilizing the same operating system. If you are purchasing a Hewlett Packard PC with an AMD Quad-core 6600mh processor equipped with a 640 gigabyte drive, and having a Windows Vista Home Premium operating system, stay with that manufacturer (HP), the AMD processor and the Vista operating system. Try not to mix manufacturers, processors and operating systems if you can avoid it, as standardization of your equipment and software should allow for better systems integration and functional operability. Also, you know that even though hardware capability changes every 3 to 6 months, Microsoft's Vista operating system will be supported for another 6 or 7 years. Additionally, stage your computer purchases so that you buy in batches and don't have to replace most of your computers at the same time.

B. **Periodically replace your computer hardware** – I guarantee that your computer hardware will not last forever. One company I was with had an old K-Pro computer that lasted about 15 years before we trashed it. The computer was still operating, but its tape drive was inoperable and could not be replaced. We were lucky, because this computer should have been replaced 10 years beforehand. Normally, you can probably expect about 5 years of regular usage from your computer before it fails. However, expect your computer to be technologically obsolete at about the 3 year mark. I guess this is why the manufacturers only sell a maximum of 3 year maintenance contracts. Moore's law is an excellent observation of a long-term trend in the development of computer processors since 1958. Basically, it states that computer processing power has doubled about every two years! From everything I have read, this trend will continue for at least the next decade! Since recent history supports this incredible rate of technological advancement, when is the last time you have reviewed your computer related equipment for obsolescence? Chances are that you can purchase new computer hardware with superior performance, better quality, and greater longevity at a lower price than your old, obsolete computer equipment cost you. Therefore I recommend that you consider regular replacement of your computers after 3 and 4 years of use. This is not long after your extended warranty has expired but before your average failure time of about five years.

C. **Purchase your computers, software and related equipment at a discount** - You can easily go online to a Website like **www.TigerDirect.com** and purchase computer equipment at a substantial discount from retail pricing. You can find discount software pricing by doing a Google search on the software name.

D. If a software or hardware item has substantially more capability for a slightly higher price, buy it - In some cases there is very little difference between the basic version of the software and the professional version. I just looked up the lowest price of $125 on Vista Home Basic (not recommended) and $190 on Vista Ultimate (highly recommended). There is only a $65 difference for a more robust version of Vista with a lot more capability. Is there any doubt as to which version you should buy?

E. If the hardware price is about the same, go with the quality brand – You can insure that you are buying reliable and well tested equipment by purchasing a quality brand name. You can also be confident that your warranty will be honored by a company well known for quality and customer service, and who will still be in business.

F. Add the cost of an extended warranty to your advertised price when making your cost comparison – All else being the same, buy the computer or related equipment that offers a 3 year warranty compared with a 90 day warranty. Don't consider the purchase of a warranty that would extend beyond 3 years. You will probably end up replacing the computer after 3 to 4 years in any event because of technological obsolescence.

G. Consider engaging an IT professional – Your IT professional should be able to provide you with the planning, budgeting for purchases and maintenance, problem resolution, and the future direction that your IT function needs. Insure that your IT consulting company is a Microsoft Gold Certified Partner, has completed Microsoft competency certifications relating to your systems problems, and has experience in your industry. If you engage a Microsoft Gold Certified Partner, they can also integrate a multivendor system solution for your IT systems requirements covering hardware, software, and networking products from other vendors. This overall approach is critically important for a small business because very few IT consultants will produce a comprehensive solution for your IT system needs.

COMPUTER SYSTEMS MAINTENANCE AND SECURITY ISSUES

A. **Configure your Windows operating system (O/S) software programs for automatic updates** – Make sure you have turned on automatic updates from Microsoft to keep your Operating System (O/S) current. In many cases, particularly when the software is first released, the software updates will automatically correct the minor glitches that you are experiencing with the product.

B. **Order or install standard anti-virus software on all of your new computers before releasing them to users** – Don't forget to turn on the auto-update function in your anti-virus software set-up.

C. **If you have your computers networked, insure that you have Firewall software installed with the auto-updating feature turned on** – You can also turn on your Windows Vista firewall to provide your network with some security, if you don't have a firewall program.

D. **Assign an employee Log-In Identifier (I.D.) and Password to all of your computer users** – Typically, I would use the employee's last name as their I.D. If there is a conflict, i.e. 2 Smiths, use the first letter of the first name and the last name. Also, assign a password that is simple for the user to remember and for you to keep track of. An example would be the first initials of the user's first and last name and the last 4 digits of the user's SSN.

An Example of Non-Existent Control of Passwords – When I went to work for this company, there were no individual passwords or user profiles set up in the company's computer software. You simply logged into your computer using the department name. If you were in the accounting department, your log-in and password were "accounting". This was just a little bit better than no control at all! However, we had instances of employees who were unauthorized, logging into critical software modules and tampering with set-up information. As soon as possible, I assigned user I.D.s and passwords to all computers and computer users. Once having the user log-ins and passwords under control, I then created a specific user profile for each position. This became the platform for the establishment of computer security throughout the company.

An Example of Passwords Embedded in the Operating System I did some overall turn-around consulting for a company that owned an IBM AS-400 mid-range computer system. I told the management that I could log into their computer without being set up as a legitimate computer user in their system. They couldn't believe that I was able to do just that in two minutes, using one of two default passwords that were embedded in the operating system software! You had to enter the system administrative module and change the default passwords to have any real security.

E. **Limit employee computer access to only that portion of the software programs necessary to perform their job functions** – Unauthorized personnel should be blocked from loading new software, or trying to access control features in existing software that they are not authorized to access.

F. **Limit your employee's access to the internet** – The "net" can be a productive and useful tool. More and more, most of your job position descriptions must be able to access the internet for legitimate business purposes. It is also one of the biggest employee time wasters that have ever been created! In many companies, unauthorized use of the internet exceeds authorized usage by a substantial percentage. Fortunately, there are a few ways to control unauthorized internet access.

1) Block access to the internet for those who don't need to have access.
2) For those employees who have net access, limit their access to the business sites that they need to visit to perform their job functions.
3) Consider disciplinary action for those employees who abuse their internet access privileges.

G. **Create a computer user policy guide for distribution to your employees** - Let your employees know what you expect from them regarding their usage of your business computers. You should include the items in the 3 paragraphs above in your policy guide.

H. **Consider engaging an IT professional to audit your computer security** – Your IT audit professional should be able to provide you with audit services that will examine the following sensitive areas:
   1. Physical security of equipment, programs and data storage.
   2. Network security.
   3. Internet traffic control inbound and outbound with allowed internet sites.
   4. User accessibility and positive control with IDs and Passwords.
   5. Identification of unauthorized users.
   6. Identification of unauthorized programs.
   7. Review of network activity logs.
   8. Is sensitive data encrypted for transmission?
   9. Are other systems having access to the same network reasonably secure?

You may question the need for a specialized audit of this type. However, it is at least two decades since computer systems were only used only for internal purposes and did not communicate externally. Recent technological advances have opened the door to potential abuse from both internal and external sources. Therefore I would recommend that you ask your CPA whether they provide this service. If not, they can probably recommend a firm who does.

SUMMARY

A small business has one substantial advantage over a larger business, and that is flexibility. You don't have to go through a mountain of red tape and several layers of bureaucracy to make a decision and implement it. By being able to implement computer technology quickly, efficiently and effectively, a small business can gain a competitive advantage over its larger rivals without the need to greatly increase staff or substantially increase expenditures. Businesses that are not flexible and adept at adopting and utilizing innovative computer technology will soon find themselves at a competitive disadvantage. Therefore, small businesses that are willing to make a planned and structured investment in new computer technology and successfully implement their plan will substantially increase their chances for survival in the tough economic times that we are facing today.

CHAPTER 35

TELECOMMUNICATIONS – THE GREAT GREY AREA

The area of telecommunications (telecom) services has become exceedingly murky, and apparently it is not in the best interest of the companies that service this industry to bring any light to the subject. It is difficult to get any technical information from many of these companies, even though telecom issues have become exceedingly technical and complex. At times, it is also difficult to have your contracts honored by the carrier, who is predisposed to interpret those contracts to their own benefit. This means that your company will have to do some of its own research on any proposals that you receive from telecom company providers. I would recommend that you solicit at least three quotes along with technical information regarding any telecom services that you are currently considering, or on existing contracts that are due to expire. The following are a few simple recommendations designed to control your telephone costs that you can implement quickly.

CELLULAR PHONES – ONE OF YOUR LARGEST TELEPHONE EXPENDITURES

Your cell phone bills are probably the largest single item in your telecommunications budget! I can remember that several years ago your telephone carrier long distance bill used to be the largest item of telephone expense. Now, everyone in or out of your company has to have a cell phone. It's become the new-age status symbol! I have seen employees sitting next to a land line, making calls on their cell phone on numerous occasions. However, there are several no-nonsense ways to reduce this major expense.

1. Stop handing out cell phones to relatives and employees as if they were candy canes at Christmas! Expenses for individual cell phones can exceed $100.00 per month. That's $1,200 per year! Your baseline billing increases substantially because of add-on charges for additional minutes, roaming charges, long-distance and international calling, text messaging, picture downloading and other services. The only persons that should have a company sponsored cell phone are you and your employees who absolutely need to have one. Examples of these types of employees would be outside salespersons, mobile employees such as delivery drivers, service technicians, and officers and managers who need the availability of a cell phone to perform their executive functions.

2. Have your employees who are occasional users of cell phones sign up for a cell phone contract under their name (They probably have one). You can choose to reimburse a set amount of the monthly cell phone cost, or simply reimburse the business portion of their cell phone usage.

3. You can also place employees who are occasional cell phone users on a prepaid cellular plan. Cell phone companies like TracFone will provide your employees with a free camera phone and up to 800 minutes of airtime and 16 months of service for $99.00, no ups, no extras and no commitments of any kind.

4. If you issue a company cell phone to an employee, you can then have the employee identify the personal calls made on that cell phone for reimbursement back to the company. This procedure will have the additional benefit of substantially reducing the amount of personal calls made from company cell phones by employees who are taking advantage of the "free" cell phone privilege and "stealing your time".

5. Choose a cell phone provider who will aggregate all of your company's minutes of usage for billing purposes. This should save you substantial individual overcharges on your monthly cell bills. Have cell phone providers bid for your business by

providing you with the best comprehensive quotes they can offer to secure your cell phone business.

6. If you either currently have or plan to have VoIP service with direct inward dialing (DID), look into having wide area network (WAN) mobile phones incorporated into your telephone system. These mobile phones are a true extension of your phone system and have the same features and capability as your desk phone. With direct inward dialing (DID), you can even assign a unique and separate telephone number to each mobile phone in addition to an extension. The range of the wide area network (WAN) phones is a radius of about 25 miles from the central office location, giving you a circle of coverage with a diameter of 50 miles. With this wide transmission coverage, you may be able to eliminate a substantial number of your company cellular phones at very little additional cost.

An Example of Cellular Phone Problem Contracts – A few years ago we renegotiated our cell contract with a major carrier. Since we didn't require new cell phones, we were able to negotiate a billing credit of over $12,000, to be applied to our monthly bills. The credit was not forthcoming, and it was virtually impossible to find a carrier employee who had the authority to resolve the problem. Finally, six months later and after a certified letter to the president of this company threatening suit, we were assigned a person who resolved the problem and we began to receive our $12,000 credit. However, this is not the end of the story. After numerous other problems with this company which required major efforts on our part to resolve, we decided to change carriers at the end of our 2 year contract. The problem here related to the fact that the carrier updated our contract date by six months to the date that they had resolved our credit problem! We had to jump through a number of hoops to get the contract date corrected. Again, almost none of the carrier's employees were empowered to resolve customer problems, and our prior contact had left the company. Needless to say, my respect for this company quickly slipped into negative territory, and we couldn't wait to stop doing business with them. The moral of the story is to make sure you get any commitments from any telecom vendor in writing, reviewed by a telecom expert, and signed by an individual with the authority to enter into an agreement. Unfortunately, as this story shows, even with a written agreement, you may have a fight on your hands.

LONG DISTANCE CALLS

Although long distance charges on landlines have steadily reduced in cost, there may be an even better way for you to save on long distance calls. **How would you like a ZERO COST for your long distance calls?** Many carriers are offering bundled VoIP packages which include 200 to more than 1,000 long distance minutes free of charge. Just make sure you negotiate this as part of your bundled package of services.

VOIP JOINT INTERNET AND PHONE SERVICE

Practical usage of **V**oice **o**ver **I**nternet **P**rotocol (**VoIP**) is a relatively recent development in telecommunications facilitated by larger bandwidth availability and advancing communications hardware and software development. VoIP services can convert voice transmissions into digital signals that travel over the Internet. If you are calling a regular phone number, the signal is converted to an analog telephone signal before it reaches the destination. VoIP can allow you to make a call directly from a computer, a special VoIP phone, or a traditional phone connected to a special adapter. In addition, internet sites at locations such as airports, hotels, and internet cafes allow you to connect to the Internet and may enable you to use VoIP service wirelessly. Unfortunately, there are a few technical terms you will have to become familiar with in order to understand your telecom representative and negotiate your best deal. I'll do my best to keep it simple.

1. **What is a T-1 line?** A regular ISDN T-1 line is either a fiber optic or copper line that the phone company provides which can carry 24 digitized voice channels, or it can carry data at a rate of 1.544 megabits per second. If the T-1 line is being used

only for telephone, it connects to your phone system. If the T-1 is used for data transmission, it connects to your network router.

2. **What is a PRI type of T-1 line?** - A Primary Rate Interface (PRI) type of ISDN line consists of 24 channels divided into 23 B channels and one D channel. It operates over the same physical interface as T-1. The big difference between an ISDN T-1 and an ISDN PRI is the D channel. You can use the D channel as a traffic manager to determine all of your signaling and call control requirements and have the remaining 23 channels available for any mix of voice and data you require. The PRI type of T-1 enables VoIP to be utilized for voice or data.

3. **Quality of Service (QoS) Issues** – Quality of Service (QoS) issues are of paramount importance when considering a PRI ISDN connection with a Voice and Data (VoIP) network. If you have not properly addressed these QoS issues, you can experience voice packet delays where the voice transmission stops midstream, then restarts. You will also experience dropped calls inbound and outbound, squeals, reverberations, echoes and voice-overs. These problems result from the fact that your system is not assigning the highest priority to your voice packet transmissions. You must have several items in place for the voice portion to be assigned the highest priority and function properly. These are as follows:

   A. Your physical phones must be digital and must be technically certified and approved for VoIP transmissions. If you don't have digital VoIP phones, you will have to replace your whole phone system, and you may not be ready for that kind of expense just yet!

   B. You have to have a router that is VoIP capable, and can deliver quality telephone voice service by assigning the highest priority to voice traffic.

C. Your VoIP service provider must properly program your equipment to handle QoS issues by assigning the highest priority to voice packets.

D. Hire a qualified telecom consultant with an NCE or an NTE certification from iNARTE and who is a member of The Society of Telecommunications Consultants to assist you in creating your telecom plan, acquiring software and hardware, designing training, implementing your plan, and performing post-implementation follow-up.

E. If the hardware is QoS compliant and properly programmed to give the highest priority to your voice packets, you shouldn't experience any problems with your voice transmissions. Unfortunately, as the following true story indicates, you can't expect much help from the "so-called" experts. As my dad has said many times, "You know, son, a self-proclaimed expert is nothing but a damn fool away from home (Where nobody knows what a damn fool he is)!"

An Example of a Botched PRI ISDN Installation - A few years ago, we decided to update our phone system with what we thought was a VoIP compliant phone system (The Vendor who sold us the system will remain incognito for obvious reasons!). A few months later we changed our telecom carrier and inaugurated VoIP lines. We then began to experience quality of service (QoS) problems that were so disruptive that we had to reinstall the old telephone system. We worked for months with our telecom carrier, our telephone equipment vendor, and with networking vendors to isolate the problem. We correctly identified the QoS issue as a problem in assigning the highest priority to voice traffic. Finally, after about 8 months of having to utilize our old phone system, our new phones were sent back to the manufacturer for testing and diagnosis. After another month, we found out that our problem related to the fact that these supposedly VoIP compliant phones did not have the capability to assign a high priority to voice packets! We were then promised that these phones would be operational after some modifications. After waiting another six weeks, the phones arrived and were reinstalled. They still didn't work! Finally, the phone equipment vendor stepped up to the plate and replaced those phones with VoIP certified phones from another manufacturer. We were able to assign a high priority to our voice packets, the replacement phones gave us the Quality of Service that we needed, and the 15 month nightmare came to an end!

SUMMARY

Telecom today is a real minefield for the unwashed and uninitiated! You have telecom cellular plans, even the ones that are provided by some large companies, which are about as close to rip-offs as you would want to get, and still be legal! You have VoIP plans that are not technically supported by the companies that sell them. In many cases, the so called telecom consulting firms do not have the technical expertise that they advertise. You also have telecom equipment vendors who don't really know the technical aspects of the products they sell, and are not technically qualified to service and maintain those products. All this uncertainty also has as a backdrop the continued integration and advancement of telecom and computer hardware and software. However, very few telecom companies seem to have the technical capability to effectively integrate your telecom and computer requirements. It's a grey and murky area for a small business to have to successfully navigate in. Therefore, if you are considering changes affecting your telecom system, you may want to hire a certified telecom consultant to assist you in developing and implementing an all-encompassing telecom plan for your company.

CHAPTER 36

PAYROLL RELATED EXPENSE REDUCTIONS

PAYROLL SAVINGS

1. **Cut Staff** – This is an excellent time to trim the fat and lay off or terminate marginally productive employees. With mandatory and voluntary benefits included, you will save about 130% of the salary of every full time employee that you terminate.

2. **Eliminate Your Overtime Expense** – Except for special circumstances, all overtime hours should be eliminated. Those special circumstances involve true emergency situations, and small amounts of planned overtime that will eliminate the need to hire another employee. Remember that overtime hours, assuming a 150% hourly cost, add up to nearly 200% of your employee's hourly rate with benefits added in.

3. **Lay Off Your Payroll Person and Outsource Your Payroll Processing** – I have recommended this action for small businesses because you win two ways. First, you reduce the direct costs of processing the payroll. Secondly, you substantially reduce the administrative costs associated with the payroll. See my chapter on "PAYROLL PROCESSING COST REDUCTIONS" for more information.

4. **Reduce the Hours That You Are Open for Business** – With less business, do you really need to be open all those hours? If you operate a retail enterprise, analyze the amount of business you generate by the day and by the hour during each day.

Seek to eliminate unproductive days or hours that you are currently open for business. An example would be a Monday where only 4% of your business is being generated. Obviously, you need to be closed on that day. This will save you employee costs, utility bills and other associated expenses.

5. **Declare a 5% to 10% Salary Reduction** – Reduce your employees' salary and hourly rate by 5% to 10% depending on the severity of your financial distress. This will save you an additional 20% of the wages you have saved in mandated employee benefits such as FICA, Unemployment Insurance and Workers Compensation Insurance in addition to any employer provided benefits tied to compensation.

6. **Reduce Vacation Time** – If you have an overly generous vacation policy allowing as much as 3 or 4 weeks, consider the financial effect of reducing the vacation period to 2 weeks maximum. It may or may not be worth the effort, depending on the number of your employees receiving 3 to 4 weeks of vacation.

7. **Eliminate Voluntary Sick Pay Benefits** – If you provide voluntary sick pay benefits, which are generally used by employees as additional vacation or time off, eliminate this benefit entirely.

8. **Reduce or Eliminate the 401k Employer Match** – Now is not the time to be supporting a rich benefit package, when you are fighting for the survival of your business. Change the paragraph in your 401k plan document and reduce or eliminate the 401k employer match percentage (Not a big deal to do from a paperwork standpoint). Then communicate this change in writing to your employees and implement the change as of your next payroll.

9. **Reduce or Eliminate Employer Provided Employee Benefits** - These are tough times. It would be better for you and your employees if you reduced or eliminated some or all

of your discretionary benefits, rather than having to reduce staff that you really need to operate your business.

10. **Start a Cafeteria Plan** – If you don't have a Section 125 Cafeteria Plan, get one started effective next month to start saving on payroll taxes for your company and your employees! This will also help you with any discretionary benefits that you have decided to reduce or eliminate, since the employees will be contributing an increased amount to these plans through the Cafeteria Plan.

11. **Hire Independent Contractors** - By hiring independent contractors, you will save the employer's share of all the mandated employee costs such as Social Security and Medicare taxes, state and federal unemployment taxes, and Workers Compensation Insurance plus all of the voluntary benefits you pay on behalf of your full time employees. However, have your corporate attorney insure that your independent contractors don't qualify as employees. If they do, you won't want to deal with the back taxes, penalties and fines that you will have to pay, so be careful with this one!

SUMMARY

In challenging times like these, the going is tough and tough managers have to make some hard decisions consistent with being in a survival mode. No owner or manager wants to think about having to reduce employee staff, pay and benefits. However, when the alternative is bankruptcy or voluntarily going out of business, your best decision is to reduce your payroll costs and survive!

CHAPTER 37

THE INSURANCE GAME-
EMPLOYEE BENEFITS INSURANCE

THE HEALTH INSURANCE GAME

The Insurance Game has been playing since I became involved in the management of small to medium sized companies in 1971, and has most likely been played a long time before that. The essence of the game is this. Insurance Companies are either adding to their book of business, (buying business), or reducing business, (shedding existing customers). When they reduce their book of business, they accomplish this by increasing their premium! It really doesn't matter what your claims experience or loss ratio has been. Good, bad or indifferent, your premium will increase substantially if the company is reducing its business. If, however, the Insurance Company is increasing its book of business, they will discount their premium, and even take on risks that were less than acceptable beforehand. It doesn't matter whether you are purchasing Property & Casualty Insurance or Health Insurance, the game is the same. Taking advantage of the game can save you and your employees hundreds of thousands of dollars over several years without sacrificing the scope of your coverage or the quality of the product.

HEALTH INSURANCE - PREPARING TO PLAY THE GAME

If you are in the market to purchase Health Insurance you will have to start this process at least 60 days in advance of your policy expiration with your insurance broker. In order to receive quotes from other companies, you will need a copy of your health claims history for the last three to five years. If you are currently being insured by a Health Maintenance Organization (HMO), you may not be able to get this information. If you don't have a broker who is a general agent, (an agent who can represent multiple insurers), I would suggest you find one. If you are currently purchasing your insurance from a captive agent, (an agent who is employed by only one company), have him quote the policy also. The agent will know that you are shopping the policy because you have requested your health claims experience reports. Instruct your agent to have the company sharpen their pencil and give you their best quote. He should be able to get a renewal quote from your existing carrier about 45 to 60 days from your policy expiration date. You then need to instruct your broker to shop your policy with other health care providers. Let your broker know that you are looking for a company that is aggressively buying business, and is willing to offer you the very best rates for comparable coverage. Ideally, you will be receiving at least 3 to 5 competitive bids to choose from.

HEALTH INSURANCE - PLAYING THE GAME TO WIN

After reviewing these bids with your broker to compare price and coverage, you can then make an informed decision as to which company is the best for you. The following items should be considered as part of the negotiating and decision making process. (Yes, you can negotiate a better deal with a Health Insurance Company that is "buying business")

1. You can negotiate the premium rates with the insurance carrier for single person, employee and spouse, and family coverage.

2. You can negotiate with your broker to reduce their commission, thereby reducing the health coverage premium.

3. You can negotiate a longer fixed term for the initial premium rates to stay in effect. The standard is 12 months, however it is possible

to negotiate up to 24 months or more, depending upon how much the insurance carrier wants your business.

You can employ other cost-saving measures that will affect employee's coverage and the employee's cost of coverage. The following represent other ways for your company to reduce the overall cost of health insurance coverage.

1. You can negotiate different levels of individual deductibles and the overall policy limits with your health insurance carrier. Most insurance companies already have prepackaged policies with different levels of deductibles. If you are successful in changing the individual deductibles and limits, you must communicate this to your employees in writing before the effective date of the change.

2. You can simply increase the amount that employees contribute to their health coverage plans.

3. If you are convinced that this will not be acceptable to your existing employees, you can increase the amount that new employees will contribute to their health coverage plans without affecting existing employees as of the effective date of that change.

By increasing the amount of the employee contributions to their health plan as in paragraphs 2 and 3 above, employees can save a portion of that increase by eliminating FICA taxes, (currently 7.65%) and income taxes on the contribution amount if you have adopted a Cafeteria Plan. Employers save by reducing their health premium costs by the increase in the amount of employee contributions. They also eliminate the matching FICA taxes, (7.65%), on those same premium dollars funneled through the Cafeteria Plan. (See my Chapter on "CAFETERIA PLANS")

You should be extremely wary if your broker suggests that your company sponsor a partially self-funded health insurance plan. I

normally do not recommend partially self-funded health insurance for small to medium-sized companies because of the costs, both known and unknown, and the complexity of these kinds of plans. Please read the following carefully.

PARTIALLY SELF-FUNDED INSURANCE, WHAT IS IT?

There are two types of partially self-funded insurance. First, there is the individual company provided partially self-funded insurance that I do not recommend for small to medium-sized companies. This type of insurance requires that the company purchase stop-loss and stop-limit insurance from an Insurance Company provider. The Stop Limit is the threshold at which medical claims become payable by the insurance carrier for the remainder of the policy year for an individual. Insurance coverage under a Stop-Loss policy is the threshold at which no payments are made by the insurer until the sum of all claims paid within the year exceeds a predetermined limit or aggregate. Generally speaking, this insurance is expensive for small companies because it is difficult to negotiate loss limits that make any economic sense. Your company will also have to hire a Third Party Administrator (TPA) to facilitate the payment of claims. A TPA is a company that accepts the responsibility for administering some or all of an employer's benefit programs for a fee. Additionally, the company will have to pay for and provide health insurance booklets and provider information to its employees. Of course, the company pays for all the claims that are not covered by the stop-loss and stop-limit insurance purchased from the insurance provider.

Another important consideration is that claims are not paid at the time that they are incurred. There is **a "tail period" that extends from 90 to 120 days after the coverage ends in which claims that were incurred prior to the end of coverage are actually paid.**

AN ILLUSTRATION OF A PARTIALLY SELF-FUNDED INSURANCE BOONDOGGLE

I remember quite well a situation that developed with a medium-sized company that I was associated with as a CFO. Prior to my coming on board, the company decided to provide partially self-funded health insurance to their employees. They purchased stop-loss and stop-limit insurance with excessively high limits from an insurance company at some considerable expense. The company also had to hire a Third Party Administrator (TPA) to facilitate the payment of claims. Additionally, we had to pay for and provide health insurance booklets and provider information to our employees. During the entire year that we were partially self-funded, we never reached the limits of our stop-loss insurance, which means that our company paid for each and every claim. In effect, because of the naïveté of management, the insurance provider was able to take advantage of this lack of knowledge. Also, our employees became extremely dissatisfied with the actions of the TPA and the way they handled claims. This dissatisfaction grew to the extent that our union employees were ready to strike if we continued with that TPA. Additionally, as we computed our overall costs of being partially self-insured, we discovered that we had paid over 20% more in overall costs as compared with being fully insured by a health insurance company. This of course did not include any of the indirect costs of lower employee morale created by the actions of our TPA. There was only one logical course of action, and that was to terminate our partially self-funded plan, and get quotes from several third party health insurance company providers. By locating an insurance company that was adding to its book of business, we were able to save over 30% of the overall health insurance costs that we experienced with the partially self insured plan. We even saved over 10% of the cost of health insurance in the year prior to initiating this partially self-funded plan.

AN EXCEPTION TO THE GENERAL RULE REGARDING SELF-FUNDED OR PARTIALLY SELF-FUNDED PLANS

FOR COMPANIES THAT ARE DESPERATELY IN NEED OF CASH, HERE IS AN IMMEDIATE CASH FLOW BENEFIT:

A one-time positive cash flow benefit results from a change to a partially self-funded health insurance plan that can assist companies that are starved for cash. As the tail period of 90 to 120 days extends the coverage payment period beyond the ending date of the policy, the reverse effect occurs at the starting date of a partially self-funded plan. Consequently, you can expect to see only 30% of your average monthly claims experience being paid out in the first month, 60% in the second month, 90% in the third month and average monthly claims payments after that time. It doesn't take a rocket scientist to figure out that you will save 120% of your average monthly claims experience in cash the first three to four months. As long as you stay with a partially self-funded plan the "tail period" continues. However, if you change your insurance plan from a partially self-funded plan to a third-party plan requiring average monthly payments, the additional cash expended to cover the "tail period" will approximate the amount of cash saved during the initial 90 to 120 day period.

ANOTHER CASH SAVING IDEA – ESTABLISH A SELF-FUNDED VISION INSURANCE PLAN:

This is a high visibility (pardon the pun), low-cost scheduled benefit self administered plan that contains an overall payment limit for the purchase of contact lenses or eyeglasses, frames and a vision exam once every two years. Since each benefit in the plan has a specific payment limit and there is an overall payment limit, there is no implicit risk that would require stop-loss or stop-limit insurance. If you already have a vision plan provided by an insurance company, you should also consider changing to the self-funded vision plan as described above and save 75% to 85% of your insurance premium! You may also be able to trade this relatively insignificant benefit in terms of cost, for the reduction or elimination of a much higher cost benefit.

IMPLEMENTING A SELF-FUNDED VISION PLAN

I met a Human Resources Vice President from one of our major casinos in Las Vegas at a seminar several years ago. While we were discussing a number of issues, she told me about a self-funded and self administered vision benefits program that they had inaugurated a few years before. This plan was costing them significantly less than a third party insurance plan. I asked her to kindly e-mail me a copy of their vision plan. I further simplified the plan I received so that the scheduled benefits had a specific payment limit for each purchase of contact lenses, eyeglasses, frames and a vision exam once every two years. This self administered plan also had an overall payment limit of $150 once every two years for the purchase of any item or combination of items listed above. Of course, a condition of reimbursement required the employee to provide invoices and proof of payment. An interesting outcome of the institution of this vision plan was that there were virtually no problems resulting from the administration of the plan over the course of several years. And the cost, which has averaged less than $2,000 each year, was about 10% to 15% of the cost of a third-party vision insurance plan!

SUMMARY

Yes, you can win at the Insurance Game if you are prepared to play the game! By getting the best quotes from insurance companies who want to add to their book of business, you can substantially lower your portion of the cost of employee health insurance. And, you can further reduce your costs by negotiating your broker's commission, increasing deductibles, and increasing the employee's contribution to their health plans. If you already have a vision plan provided by an insurance company, you should also consider changing to a simple self-funded vision plan with defined benefits as described above and save at least 75% to 85% of your insurance premium!

CHAPTER 38

CAFETERIA PLANS – IT'S A WIN/ WIN SITUATION FOR YOUR COMPANY AND YOUR EMPLOYEES

CAFETERIA PLANS, WHAT ARE THEY?

Section 125 Plans are sometimes referred to as Premium Only Plans (POP Plans) or Cafeteria Plans. Cafeteria Plans are one of the most underused employee benefits for small businesses today. These plans simply allow employees to withhold a portion of their salary on a pre-tax basis to cover the cost of qualifying insurance premiums. These plans will reduce payroll tax liabilities for both the employee and employer. They are authorized under IRS Code Section 125, which allows employees to make cafeteria plan deduction elections to pay their portion of medical, dental, vision and disability insurance premiums using pretax or tax-free dollars. Your company can purchase documents which provide everything that you need to establish a simplified Section 125 POP Plan for as little as $99.00. And, the administration of this simplified Cafeteria Plan does not require an expensive outside administrator. You may, however, require some assistance in setting up this plan. Your insurance broker or the insurance company itself may provide the plan documents and assistance to you free of charge.

HOW DO YOUR EMPLOYEES BENEFIT FROM PARTICIPATION IN A CAFETERIA PLAN?

Assuming a 15% federal tax rate and the current 7.65% FICA rate, employees save a minimum of 22.65% to as much as 40% of their pre-tax Section 125 premium deductions in federal payroll taxes. The actual tax savings will also include city and state income taxes on all contributions employees use to pay for their portion of insurance premiums. Under a Section 125 Cafeteria Plan, your employee's take-home pay is increased. This helps to reduce the high cost of providing health coverage for family members.

HOW DOES AN EMPLOYER BENEFIT FROM THE ADOPTION OF A CAFETERIA PLAN?

Employers benefit by eliminating the same 7.65% FICA rate as the employees. Depending on the employee individual salary limits, the employer may also save on Federal and State unemployment taxes. Employers may also qualify for workers compensation insurance reductions, but this is governed by individual state regulations.

WHAT TYPE OF BUSINESS CAN ADOPT A CAFETERIA PLAN?

Just about any small business, to include sole proprietorships, C corporations, S corporations and LLCs, are qualified to adopt and initiate a Cafeteria Plan.

WHAT ARE THE REQUIREMENTS TO START A CAFETERIA PLAN?

1. You will need a Section 125 Plan Document that you can probably obtain from one of your health or disability insurers. You will have to sign your plan document and have it available for an IRS or DOL audit. There is no actual filing requirement.

2. You will also need a corporate Board of Directors Resolution to Adopt the Section 125 Cafeteria Plan which you should keep on file along with the Plan Document.

3. You will need a Section 125 Summary Plan Description to distribute to your employees along with an Election Form that they will have to sign and return.

4. You won't need a Third Party Administrator (TPA) to administer a Section 125 Premium Only (POP) Plan.

5. You will be required to complete Section 125 non-discrimination testing forms annually. Most all of these sample documents, forms and resolutions are available through your broker from your benefit insurance providers without cost.

WHEN IS THE BEST TIME TO START A CAFETERIA PLAN?

A Cafeteria Plan can be started any time during the year. However, the best time to start a Cafeteria Plan is either at the end of the calendar year, or the date when your group health insurance plans renew. Remember to give each employee a summary cafeteria plan description and an election form to be signed and returned prior to the start date of the plan.

SUMMARY RECOMMENDATION

If you have employees who are paying a portion or all of their medical, dental, vision, or disability insurance, and you don't already have a Cafeteria Plan in effect, complete the items listed above. Then, initiate your plan at the beginning of the next month, and start saving money for you and your employees courtesy of Uncle Sam!

CHAPTER 39

401k RETIREMENT PLANS - THE PROS AND CONS

WHAT IS A 401k PLAN?

A 401k plan is a retirement plan that was created by the IRS tax code section 401(k) in 1978. 401k plans have become very popular because contributions to 401k plans can be made with pre-tax earnings and the funds are allowed to grow tax-free until retirement. 401k plan providers have essentially improved their products over the last several years regarding more flexible investment products, decreased administrative costs and better plan administration. To initiate a 401k plan it must be sponsored by your company. The plan permits your employees and your company to make pre-tax retirement contributions to the plan. Don't forget that if you, as an owner, are also an employee of your company, you can benefit from the inauguration of a 401k plan. So even though your company might not be matching any employee contributions, you and your employees will still have the benefit of contributing tax-free dollars to your 401k company plan.

RECOMMENDATION: If you have a payroll service in place that can handle the increased payroll administration of a 401k plan, and you have the time available to begin a search for a 401k plan provider, why wait? Make the decision to move ahead with the implementation of a 401k plan. However, if you don't have the time to initiate a 401k plan now, consider implementing it at the beginning of the next calendar year. It's a great benefit for you and your employees. And unless you have more than 100 employees eligible for the plan, it isn't that difficult to report on and administer the plan.

401k PLAN IMPLEMENTATION - HOW DO I GET STARTED?

Establishing a 401k Retirement Plan - A 401k plan document consists of an adoption agreement and the basic plan document containing the operating provisions of the plan. A resolution of the company Board of Directors, the signed adoption agreement and the plan document are required to initiate the plan. You must also notify the employees with a Summary Plan Description (SPD) written in plain English without a lot of legalese so that the SPD can be easily understood. Most 401k providers have a template that they use to prepare the SPD for you.

The information that must be provided in the SPD includes:

1. The identification number and location of the plan
2. Contact information for the plan sponsor and trustee
3. A description of what the plan provides for employees and how it operates
4. At what age and when are employees eligible to participate in the plan
5. The size and timing of employer matching contributions, if any
6. The vesting schedule for employer matching contribution, if any
7. How to apply for and receive 401k loans, if applicable
8. How are interest rates on employee 401k loans calculated and a description of the repayment terms
9. How to qualify, apply for and receive hardship withdrawals
10. Withdrawal procedures for rollovers and for retirement
11. Circumstances under which employees may lose or be denied benefits
12. The employees rights under ERISA, including a description of the appeals process

Of course, if the plan provisions are changed or modified, your employees must be notified in writing of a revised SPD, or in a separate document called a summary of material modifications (SMM).

RECOMMENDATION: I would strongly recommend that you adopt the IRS maximum allowable limits for the entering age, length of service, union membership and nonresident alien status. In general, an employee must be allowed to participate in a qualified plan after meeting the following minimum requirements:

1. The employee has reached age 21
2. The employee has at least one year of service. A year of service is generally a minimum of 1,000 hours of service performed for the company during the plan year, and
3. The employee is not already covered under a collective bargaining (Union) agreement.
4. The employee is not a nonresident alien.

SHOPPING FOR A 401k PLAN PROVIDER

Assuming that you have completed the basic information necessary to create a 401k plan document, you are ready to go shopping for a plan provider. The following listing of plan provider requirements should assist you in your search.

1. Choose a retirement plan provider that has flexibility regarding investment choices and can adapt a plan to your company's current and future needs.
2. Choose a plan provider that will furnish you with a prototype IRS 401k plan document without an additional charge.
3. Choose a plan provider who will offer you a bundled set of services. Some providers unbundle every bit and piece of the administration of the plan at your expense. They even require you to farm out certain administrative responsibilities to a TPA. Be sure that you are aware of any extra charges for services that are not part of a bundled package.
4. Typical 401k provider fees for the initial setup can range from $500-$2500 for a small plan. The cost of annual administration will be fixed fee of about $1000 per year plus a participant charge averaging $25 a quarter.
5. Have your plan vendors submit to you a comprehensive quote for their services to include a 401k setup, plan document, SPD and their annual administration fee.

6. Have your plan vendors disclose what they are charging the plan participants as investment management fees for their products. You will be surprised at the results, and how much they vary. Remember that the plan administrators who charge the participants more for their services are not necessarily the ones who provide the best services.
7. Choose a plan vendor who will conduct quarterly 401k review meetings at your premises, and will also conduct new employee participant meetings on your behalf.
8. Look for ease of plan use, online access to participant accounts, and the willingness and ability of the plan vendor to conduct employee training meetings.
9. Will the plan vendor be available for consultations with management without additional charges?
10. Get a list of local references from each retirement plan provider so that you can check the reference's satisfaction with all aspects of the 401k plan provider.

401k EMPLOYEE CONTRIBUTIONS - A SUBSTANTIAL TAX ADVANTAGE FOR YOUR EMPLOYEES

During 2009, if you are under 50 years of age you can contribute $16,500 or 100% of your W-2 earnings, whichever is the greater, to a 401k plan on a tax-deferred basis. If you are 50 years of age or over, the contribution limit is $22,000. In future years, these limit amounts will be indexed to inflation.

401k EMPLOYEE WITHDRAWALS

Withdrawals from a 401k before age 59 ½ will incur a 10% IRS penalty and, additionally, the withdrawals will be taxed as ordinary income. As you can determine, early withdrawals can be extremely burdensome from a tax standpoint, and should not be made unless it is absolutely necessary to do so. After age 59 ½ an employee can withdraw any amount of their 401k funds without penalty but all of the withdrawals will be taxed as ordinary income in the year of withdrawal. This can be advantageous for many 401k participants if they can defer any withdrawals until age 59 ½. When they retire they are typically in a lower tax bracket and can schedule the withdrawal of their 401k funds at a substantially lower tax rate than when they were employed. Minimum annual distributions from 401k funds are mandated by the IRS and start at age 70½. The minimum percentage distributions are computed by the IRS based upon the life expectancy of the participant. Since these withdrawal percentages are computed actuarially, and are updated from time to time by the IRS, we will not spend much time discussing these percentages. **However, it is important to note that if the minimum annual distribution is not taken, the IRS will assess a 50% penalty on the amount of the distribution deficiency.**

401k EMPLOYEE LOANS AND LOAN REPAYMENTS

Most 401k plans have a loan provision which allows employees to borrow 50% of their 401k funds up to a $50,000 maximum without adverse tax consequences. The loan must be repaid over a maximum period of five years. A loan amortization schedule which provides for the payment terms and the amount of the payment should be created when the loan is initiated.

401k LOAN ADVANTAGES:

1. A 401k loan is easy to initiate. It usually only requires a couple of pages to be completed and signed by the employee and the plan administrator.
2. No credit checks are required.
3. The interest rate on the loan is generally much lower than other commercial loans.
4. The term of the loan is generally set to the maximum of five years.
5. The interest that the employees pay on the loan is paid to their 401k plan and it's tax-deferred.

401k LOAN DISADVANTAGES:

1. If you default on paying the loan according to the loan amortization schedule, you can be subject to a 10% penalty

of the loan balance, and the unpaid portion of the loan will be reported as ordinary income for tax purposes.

2. If you terminate your employment with the company, voluntarily or involuntarily, the loan balance will become due and payable. If it is not paid, you will be subject to a 10% penalty. In addition, the unpaid portion of the loan will be reported as ordinary income for tax purposes.

3. You will have less money available to place in other types of investments.

401k EMPLOYER CONTRIBUTIONS

Employers are not required to make matching contributions on behalf of employees to initiate or continue a 401k plan. However, many companies do make contributions to their employees and 401k accounts. A company that can afford it will typically match 50% of the employee's percentage contribution with a maximum match of 3 to 5%. For example, if an employee contributed 8% of their salary to their 401k plan, the company would contribute another 4% on behalf of the employee. In this example, the employee and the company together would be contributing a total of 12% to the employee's 401k retirement plan. However, there is a maximum limit of $245,000 on the amount of W-2 earnings that can be allocated for calculating the contribution for each individual participant in 2009. Also, in 2009 the total of individual and company 401k contributions cannot exceed the maximum limit of $49,000 for each employee participating in the plan. Even so, there is a lot of power in the way the annual contributions in the example above can grow over time into a very significant amount of money! Additionally, having a substantial company match can entice good employees to join the company and will also improve existing employee retention.

401k RETIREMENT PLAN VESTING PROVISIONS

Vesting provisions only apply to the company matching contributions. The employee contributions to their 401k plan are 100% vested at the time the contribution is made. Most 401k plans contain a vesting schedule which requires the employee to be a plan participant for a specified period of time before the company matching contributions are partially or fully vested. The IRS has defined the maximum vesting schedules that a company can adopt as one of the following two schedules:

1. Cliff vesting which is defined as 100% vesting after five years of plan participation, or:

2. A seven year vesting schedule as follows:

     a.   0% vested for the first 2 years.
     b.   20% vested after 3 years.
     c.   40% vested after 4 years.
     d.   60% vested after 5 years.
     e.   80% vested after 6 years.
     f.   100% fully vested after 7 years of plan participation.

Any less stringent vesting schedule, up to and including full and immediate vesting of company contributions, is allowed by the IRS.

401k PLAN TESTING REQUIREMENTS (A SUBSTANTIAL DISADVANTAGE)

Of course, our Congress and the IRS can never allow an employee benefit without standing on their heads to ensure that no officer, director, owner or key employee will advantage themselves to the disadvantage of all other employees participating in the plan. Therefore, all 401k plans are required to undergo a series of annual tests, sometimes referred to as anti-discrimination tests.

The type of tests required for your plan will depend partly on the benefits you provide, as well as the details of your plan document. Some of these tests involve making sure certain limits are not exceeded. Other tests are designed to ensure that Officers, Directors, 5% Owners, Key Employees and others don't get a disproportionate share of the plan benefits. These plan participants are collectively called Highly Compensated Employees (HCEs). An HCE is defined as anyone who makes more than $110,000 in 2009 and will be indexed for upcoming years. The most common compliance tests are the ADP test, ACP test, and the Top-Heavy test. The ADP test (Actual Deferral Percentage test) compares the percentage of salaries that different classifications of employees are contributing to the 401k plan. The ACP test (Actual Contribution Percentage test) compares the percentage of employer contributions into the 401k plan participant accounts for different classifications of employees. And finally, the Top-Heavy test calculates the amount and percentage of the **H**ighly **C**ompensated **E**mployees (HCEs) account values.

401k PLAN TOP-HEAVY TESTING

Some 401k plans that do not discriminate at all in favor of key employees may still provide the majority of plan benefits to highly paid employees or owners of the company because they can afford to participate and are the only participants with long years of service. These plans run the risk of being categorized as "top heavy plans." The IRS considers a plan "top heavy" if the account values for key employees exceed 60% of the account values for all employees. The plan is classified as "super top heavy" if the percentage exceeds 90%. Unfortunately, these restrictions have had the effect of limiting the adoption of 401k plans. In some cases, companies have actually elected to terminate their existing 401k plans because the plan was top-heavy and none of the key employees were allowed to continue their plan contributions. You're more likely to encounter this problem when the company does not make matching contributions to the plan. Most of the non-key employees will have no extra incentive to contribute to the plan. The result, over time, is that the plan will become top-heavy, as defined by the IRS, and the 401k plan may have to be modified or discontinued.

DEADLINE FOR THE ESTABLISHMENT OF 401k PLAN

A qualified 401k plan must be established by the last day of the employer's business tax year. The employer then contributes to the plan for that year and subsequent years as provided for in the plan document.

AN EXAMPLE OF A RETIREMENT PLAN THAT ALMOST FAILED THE YEAR-END TOP-HEAVY TEST

I was hired by a company a few years ago to be their chief financial officer. The company had many problems, one of which was their pension plan. Believe it or not, the plan was an old retirement savings plan and contributions were made in after-tax dollars! In addition, the employer matching contributions were not too generous, and the company had adopted a seven year vesting schedule. As you can imagine, the employees had little incentive to contribute to the plan with after-tax dollars. Consequently, the plan was growing top-heavy. The year after my arrival, I performed a top-heavy calculation, and we were already in excess of the 60% maximum account value for key employees. Since it was determined that we did want to keep the plan, I had to do several things to make the plan viable. One of these was to immediately stop contributions for key employees, and refund their year-to-date contributions. Obviously, this action did not make me very popular with the ownership but it had to be done without delay. Next, we acted to change the retirement savings plan to a qualified 401k plan. The employees could then make pre-tax contributions to the plan. We then sweetened the company matching contributions and made it very easy for employees to participate in the 401k plan by matching their first 1% contribution with a 1% company match. We changed the vesting to a five-year schedule. We also substantially increased employee life insurance coverage if they participated in the company 401k plan. The combination of all these things was particularly successful. By the end of that year, we had doubled the number of non-key employees participating in the plan, and quadrupled the amount of contributions from non-key employees. From that point forward, there was never any danger of this plan becoming top-heavy again!

SUMMARY AND RECOMMENDATION

401k Plans provide substantial tax deferred pension savings for all participating employees. However, employee early withdrawals, loan requirements and loan repayment provisions can be extremely burdensome to the employees. A 401k is moderately difficult for the company to administer because of participant changes, changes in contribution amounts and percentages, and employee loan administration. Additionally, if your company's 401k plan has more than 100 eligible employees at the beginning of the plan year, you are required to have a plan audit. Also, 401k compliance testing requirements are onerous to employers. These tests sometimes result in exactly the opposite of what Congress intended when the enabling legislation was passed. If the 401k Plan fails any of these tests, the Plan may have to be substantially modified. Worse yet, the employer may elect to discontinue the plan. **In spite of the administrative burdens of a 401k plan, the tax advantages for yourself and your employees are so significant that I recommend you adopt a 401k plan as soon as practical.**

CHAPTER 40

GROUP LIFE INSURANCE

GROUP LIFE INSURANCE - A $50,000 TAX-FREE BENEFIT

The Internal Revenue Code Section 79 provides for an exclusion of the first $50,000 of group-term life insurance coverage that is provided under a policy sponsored by an employer. **This is a great benefit for your employees, particularly employees 45 years of age or older, as there are no tax consequences to the individual employees if the amount of their individual group coverage does not exceed $50,000.** Employer provided coverage in excess of $50,000 must be included in the employee's income, using the IRS Premium Table I as shown below, not the actual cost, and is also subject to social security and Medicare taxes. The calculation of the cost of excess coverage and inclusion in employee income and payroll taxes are complex and burdensome to the employee and employer.

Most small companies are not aware that the cost of employer-provided group-term life insurance on the life of an employee's spouse or dependent, paid by the employer, is not taxable to the employee if the face amount of the coverage does not exceed $2,000. This coverage is excluded as a de minimus fringe benefit. As a general rule, if the coverage for a spouse or dependents exceeds $2,000, the excess is taxable and the same Premium Table I is used.

PURCHASING GROUP LIFE INSURANCE

Purchasing group term life insurance is much like buying sugar or flour. Since it is the same basic commodity, don't pay any more for it than you have to. Have your insurance broker shop till he drops to secure the best premium rates. Even when you think you have been quoted the best premium rate, you can still negotiate the rate somewhat lower using your broker as your negotiator. Again, you are looking for an insurance company who wants to add to their book of business. And, believe me they know that group life insurance is very profitable business for them. That's why they want your business!

GROUP LIFE INSURANCE – RECOMMENDATION

This is a great benefit for a company to sponsor, as many employees don't have enough life insurance. Above the usual insurance company entry level requirement of $10,000 of life insurance, it's flexible in terms of the amount of individual coverage you require. For example, let's say that you initiate your group life plan with $10,000 of employee coverage and $2,000 of spouse or dependent coverage. You can also segregate your coverage, have two or three tiers, and cover your officers and directors to the maximum tax-free limit of $50,000. **However, my strong recommendation is that you "Keep It Simple". Don't allow the plan to exceed the $50,000 employee limit or the $2,000 spouse or dependent limit. Also, don't allow the employees to pay for group life coverage in excess of the coverage that is provided by the employer.** If your employees desire additional coverage, they can purchase that coverage by enrolling in a non-employer sponsored individual plan, paid for by payroll deductions. As a small company, you really don't have the time to deal with the intricacies of having to compute your employee's taxable fringe benefits under your group life insurance plan, and complicating your payroll by having to include payroll taxes on these fringe benefits. If you still want to have life coverage in excess of the limits for your employees, I have included IRS Premium Table 1 showing the assumed cost of the excess coverage.

TABLE I. UNIFORM PREMIUMS FOR $1,000 OF GROUP-TERM LIFE INSURANCE COVERAGE

Cost per $1,000 of coverage for one month using 5-year age brackets

Under 25 . . . . $0.05	45 to 49 15
25 to 29 06	50 to 54 23
30 to 34 08	55 to 59 43
35 to 39 09	60 to 64 66
40 to 44. 10	65 to 69 . . . . 1.27
	70 and above 2.06

CHAPTER 41

WORKERS COMPENSATION INSURANCE

WHAT IS WORKERS COMPENSATION INSURANCE?

Workers compensation insurance is essentially a no-fault insurance policy required by law to be paid for by employers for the protection of their employees while engaged in the employer's business. It also protects companies from being sued by employees because of workplace conditions that cause an injury or illness. Compensation insurance premium rates vary according to the nature of the employee's job classification and the company's experience modification rate. The amount is based on the employer's payroll, usually reported on a monthly basis to the compensation insurance carrier. The cost of purchasing mandatory compensation insurance is a serious concern for many businesses. A recent survey by the Washington chapter of the National Federation of Independent Business found that workers compensation costs were one of the top three "most serious problems" for small business owners, trailing only the cost and availability of liability and health insurance. Workers' compensation has been criticized as an expensive component of doing business. The system is made even more expensive by employee fraud. The system was designed to provide the employer and the injured worker with a fair and equitable resolution of a workplace injury. However, my experience of over 35 years is a testament to the fact that some employees pretend to be injured on the job simply to receive compensation benefits. They are quite successful at manipulating a system that is rigged in favor of the employees. There is a presumption among some administrative judges that all employers have 150 IQs, ("intelligence quotients"), and are sitting in a smoke-filled room planning and plotting ways to take advantage of their employees. In many cases the reality of the situation is the reverse of the assumption. In fact, there are 150 IQ employees who are very successful at taking advantage of their employers under workers compensation laws and the very liberal administration of those laws. I call these individuals "Workers Compensation Specialists". Unfortunately, these individuals and their ambulance chasing attorneys are catered to by the system. However, the system has generally been effective in compensating injured employees fairly, keeping them employed, and emphasizing the necessity of safety in the workplace.

AN EXAMPLE OF AN EMPLOYEE TAKING ADVANTAGE OF THE WORKERS COMPENSATION SYSTEM

Although I have encountered a number of cases of suspicious employee conduct with regard to Workers Compensation claims, there is one case that stands out in my memory as the most egregious example of taking advantage of the system. An employee was just hired as a mechanic. He had worked for another company where he had apparently filed a Workers Compensation claim for a back injury. He then filed two more claims for back related injuries with the new company. In examining the last claim that was filed, it was duly noted that there was no evidence that this supposed injury occurred on the job! Two witnesses, including the employee's supervisor, stated in writing that the individual showed no sign of injury at all, not even as much as a grimace, when the supposed incident occurred. In addition, there was no report made of the injury by the employee until two days later. Despite these facts, the employee was awarded compensation benefits on appeal. (Not surprising, as most Workers Compensation Appeal hearing officers are extremely liberal!) The employee later left the company to work again for his former company in another state. Shortly thereafter, the employee filed another workers compensation claim with his former company relating to a new back injury and received a full disability rating from that state. By the way, he was still receiving Workers Compensation payments from the first company mentioned for the suspicious back injury claim referred to above! This story illustrates exactly why your company should be covered by a Workers Compensation carrier that is diligent in following up and investigating suspicious claims. With the Workers Compensation Appeal Board working diligently on behalf of the claimant, it's reassuring to have someone else in your corner working on your behalf!

NOT ALL WORKERS COMPENSATION INSURANCE IS CREATED EQUAL!

There are a number of providers of workers compensation insurance. They range from state mandated and funded programs to private insurance company programs, and partially self-funded group programs. You will find that state programs are not very proactive about safety and do not stress accident prevention to any great degree. At best, they are representative of the typical bureaucratic boondoggle we encounter with other state and federal agency programs. Insurance company programs vary greatly, but generally speaking, are better than state mandated programs with regard to proactive accident prevention. Partially self-funded insurance programs are usually the best at providing effective accident prevention programs at no direct cost to the insured. This is an important consideration, because sooner or later your success at preventing accidents will enable you to lower your Workers Compensation costs by reducing your Experience Modification Rate. Your Experience Modification Rate is a claims experience factor that is applied to your overall Workers Compensation rate subtotal to arrive at your net Workers Compensation cost. Obviously, you want your Experience Modification Rate to be as low as possible.

SELF-FUNDED INSURANCE, WHAT IS IT?

There are two types of self-funded insurance. **First, there is the individual company provided self-funded Workers Compensation insurance that I do not recommend at all for small companies**.

This type of insurance usually requires that the company purchase stop-loss and stop-limit insurance from an Insurance Company provider, and pay for all of the other claims that are not paid for by the insurance company through the stop-loss and stop-limit claims. The Stop-Limit is the threshold at which Workers Compensation claims become payable by the insurance carrier for the remainder of the policy year for an individual. Coverage under a Stop-Loss policy is the threshold at which no payments are made until the sum of all claims paid within the year exceeds a predetermined limit or aggregate. Generally speaking, this insurance is too expensive for small companies to obtain loss limits that make any sense. Additionally, in most states, there are substantial financial requirements that would preclude most small businesses from self funding their workman's comp insurance.

Secondly, there is group or association partially self-funded Workers Compensation insurance that I highly recommend for your consideration as a small company.

To protect the companies in the group from any catastrophic losses, the group will typically purchase Stop-loss and Stop-limit insurance from a third-party insurance carrier at a reasonable premium cost. This will limit any large group losses from Workmen's Compensation claims.

WHY USE A SELF-FUNDED GROUP TO INSURE YOUR WORKERS COMPENSATION LIABILITY INSURANCE?

The following services are generally included in your self-funded group membership without cost.

PREVENTATIVE SAFETY SERVICES

1. Assistance in your safety program design and maintenance.
2. Convenient, no-cost or low cost safety training and seminars.
3. Reduced injury exposure through proactive safety management, assistance, guidance and regular on-site safety inspections. Don't underestimate this service. If you ever have a serious

reportable OSHA accident, I guarantee you that you will need this documentation for OSHA.
4. OSHA representation for serious accidents and upon request, for OSHA safety inspections.

CLAIMS MANAGEMENT

1. Claims oversight by the Group, utilizing an on-staff case manager.
2. Aggressive investigation of questionable claims.
3. Reduced medical costs through provider network utilization.

ANCILLARY SERVICES

1. Pre-Employment Screening including previous worker compensation history, social security number and previous employment verification.
2. Credit checks and other services at a minimal cost.
3. Employer representation in the appeals process of a claim by an attorney paid for by the Group.
4. Certificates of Workmen's Compensation Coverage provided upon request.
5. Assistance in separating personnel issues from claims' issues.

FINANCIAL ADVANTAGES OF GROUP MEMBERSHIP

1. Strict underwriting to select the best companies as candidates for membership.
2. Stop-loss and stop-limit third-party insurance company coverage provided by the group.
3. Substantially lower Workers Compensation Rates.
4. Lower experience modification factors.
5. A one-time initial advance assessment is usually required.
6. Monthly assessments are paid in arrears based on actual payroll. Because using actual payroll supports an accurate monthly computation, there is little or no change in premium as a result of the yearly audit.

7. In some states, there can be an additional 33% savings on the premium portion of overtime rates, assuming a 50% overtime premium.

8. Since the Group is Non-Profit, there is a reduction in overall premium of about 18%, representing the average insurance company profit. Also, there is no 5 to 10% commission paid to an insurance broker. These savings and efficient administration create surpluses which are returned to the members as dividends and rate reductions.

AN EXAMPLE OF PARTICIPATION IN A PARTIALLY SELF-FUNDED GROUP

Prior to 1996, there were no viable options for a small business in Nevada. You had to participate by law in a state funded program or a private third party insurer that was recognized by the state. In 1996 that law changed and we were able to move to Pro Group Management, a partially self-funded Workers Compensation Insurance Group. Over the next 12 years, in addition to all of the advantages listed above, we were able to save well over $250,000 on our Workmans Compensation premiums!

SUMMARY RECOMMENDATION

As soon as possible, find a partially self-insured group that services your industry and location. With them, you will get assistance in accident prevention, claims management, pre-employment screening, and administration. *And, more importantly, you will start saving 20 to 30% of the cost of your Workers Compensation insurance each month!*

CHAPTER 42

PAYROLL PROCESSING COST REDUCTIONS

The act of entering and paying a payroll is the last thing that occurs in a sequence of events leading up to the payroll itself. Many other activities occur beforehand, such as processing new hires, changes in payroll status and rates, and terminations processed by your designated payroll administrator. Many important decisions affecting administrative costs have to be made regarding the set-up and administration of the payroll function. A list of the more important payroll decisions are listed below:

1. **What will my payroll schedule be? Will I have a weekly payroll, a biweekly payroll, a semi-monthly payroll, or a monthly payroll?** I think a lot of employees would like to have a daily payroll to smooth out their cash flow. However, you must keep in mind that the more payrolls your company has per month, the higher the cost of payroll administration as there is that much more work to do.

RECOMMENDATION: If you can manage it, I would recommend that you adopt a semimonthly payroll. This way your employees don't have to wait much more than two weeks for their pay, and your accounting department only has to process two payrolls a month. Another great time-saving feature of a semi-monthly payroll is that the accounting department does not have to compute and process a payroll accrual. Compare paying a weekly payroll which requires 4.33 payrolls per month along with a payroll accrual each month-end, with a payroll having two payrolls a month and not requiring an accrual. You have reduced your overall payroll administrative cost by at least 60%! This is true whether you do your payroll internally, or you have a payroll service company such as Paychex process your payroll for you.

2. Should I process my payroll internally or send it to an outside payroll service company?

RECOMMENDATION: For small businesses, I strongly recommend that you have your payroll done by an outside payroll service company. The smaller your payroll is, the more time, money and aggravation you'll save. The payroll service company will also input your new hires, terminations, payroll changes, take care of lost checks, and even operate a separate bank account so that you don't have to worry about confidentiality or perform payroll bank account reconciliations. I would also recommend that you make your payroll tax service responsible for paying all of your payroll taxes. The better payroll tax services will also prepare a report for your Worker's Compensation monthly premium, upon request. They will prepare and file your quarterly IRS Form 941 and annual Form 940, in addition to filing any required state and local tax forms. I do not recommend that a small business assume the responsibility for paying the various tax deposits and filing the required government reports on time. The interest and penalties on one or two late deposits a year will probably pay for a year's worth of the payroll tax service charges. And, don't forget that the IRS can levy a 100% tax penalty based upon the amount of the unpaid payroll taxes due. I wouldn't consider an internal payroll system unless my employee count substantially exceeded 100. It's just not worth taking the risk. A payroll tax service is relatively inexpensive compared to the internal time required for payroll processing and reporting and the increased internal control that goes hand-in-hand with an internal payroll system!

3. Which outside Payroll Service Company should I utilize to process my payroll?

RECOMMENDATION: I would recommend Paychex, Inc. as your small business payroll service provider. Paychex has a good reputation for servicing small business customers with a flexible array of products at a reasonable price. My own experience with them has been good. You can get information about Paychex at **www.Paychex. com**. Unfortunately I can't in good conscience give you the same recommendation for some other nationally known payroll services.

4. Who should be placed in charge of the payroll function?

RECOMMENDATION: I would recommend that you assign the function of payroll administration to your CFO or controller. If they don't already know, remind them in no uncertain terms that payroll information is confidential, and is not to be discussed with any employee who does not have a need to know. By the way, it is much easier to keep payroll information confidential when you're using a payroll service provider. If you are, the payroll information is entered directly to them, and all the payroll reports, checks, check stubs, and other payroll related information come from them to one person, the CFO, controller or other person you have designated to process and record the payroll information.

5. I don't contribute to any of my employee benefit plans. Should I consider setting up an IRS Section 125 Cafeteria Plan?

RECOMMENDATION: You are in the best possible position to save tax dollars for your company and your employees. If you initiate a cafeteria plan, both you and your employees will save the 7.65% FICA tax and your employees will also save state and federal withholding on their cafeteria plan contributions. Please read my Chapter titled "CAFETERIA PLANS - ITS A WIN-WIN SITUATION".

6. Should I get involved with the time, trouble and complexity of setting up a 401k plan for my employees when the company can't afford to provide an employer match at this time?

RECOMMENDATION: Keep in mind that you and all your managers are also "employees" and can substantially benefit from the inauguration of a 401k plan. In 2009 if you are under 50 years of age you can contribute $16,500 to a 401k plan on a tax-deferred basis. If you are 50 years of age or over, the contribution limit is $22,000. In future years, these limits will be indexed to inflation. So even though your company will not be matching any employee contributions, you and your employees will still have the benefit of contributing tax-free dollars to your 401k company plan. If you don't have the time to initiate a 401k plan now, consider implementing it at the beginning of the next calendar year. It's a great benefit for you and your employees, and unless you have more than 100 employees eligible to enter the plan, it isn't that difficult to report on and administer. Please read my chapter titled "401k PLANS - THE PROS AND CONS".

SUMMARY RECOMMENDATION

Have your CFO or Controller administer your payroll and process your payroll semi-monthly through a recognized, responsive, and responsible outside payroll service provider. Take full advantage of Cafeteria Plans and 401k Plans if you have not already initiated them.

CHAPTER 43

SUPPLIES INVENTORY - A BASKET OF SAVINGS

There are many different kinds of supplies that are inventoried by all kinds of businesses. For example, an automobile dealer will inventory small hardware, various automotive bulk fluids, shop towels and rags, solvents, rubber gloves and other items specific to automobile repair and maintenance. A CPA firm, on the other hand will have a large inventory of forms, stationery and office supplies. However, all businesses of any size will keep certain common items in their supplies inventory. These items can include all types of forms, stationery, envelopes, timecards, company brochures, advertising materials, stock business cards, cleaning supplies, printer ribbons and inkjet cartridges, and the list goes on. It is possible to save a substantial amount of money in a year on these supply purchases.

A money-saving idea - When purchasing supplies, get banded volume discount quotes from your vendors. To prepare yourself to get your best price on all types of forms and stationery and other supplies, you must do few simple calculations. Determine your economic order quantity (EOQ), which is nothing more than your maximum order amount, by performing the following calculation:

1. Determine your monthly usage of the forms, stationery or other supplies than you intend to order. For example, let's say you use an average of 2,000 imprinted envelopes each month.

2. Determine the maximum number of months of that supply item that you can reasonably store without expanding storage capacity.

For example, let's say that you are willing to store six months of the imprinted envelopes.

3. Then, calculate the total number of the imprinted envelopes that you are willing to store in inventory by multiplying your monthly usage by the number of months. (6 x 2 = 12,000 envelopes)

4. Have you suppliers/vendors send you quotes for imprinted envelopes based upon ascending banded volume levels

Quantity	Price/thousand	Quantity	Price/thousand
0-1,000	$100/thousand	1,000-3,000	$80/thousand
3,000-5,000	$60/thousand	5,000-10,000	$50/thousand
over 10,000	$40/thousand		

5. Based on the example above, the Economic Order Quantity (EOQ) of these envelopes would be 10,001, based upon a quote of $40/thousand. If you had been ordering 10,000 envelopes in the past in quantities less than 3,000, you would have paid $800 (10 x $80). By ordering over 10,001 envelopes at once, your cost is reduced to $400. This represents a savings of $400 or a 50% savings over the prior cost of 10,000 envelopes ordered piecemeal.

Recommendation: To keep it really simple, choose an overall limit for the number of months you are willing to store discounted supply items in inventory. If that limit is six months, simply inform the employees responsible for purchasing that they can purchase up to six months usage of any supply item as long as the discount for volume purchases is 10% or better. **Imagine your annual savings, when you use this purchasing procedure for all of your forms, stationery and other consumable supplies!**

Another money-saving idea – Ask your vendors to store your excess forms, stationery and other orders at their location until you're ready to have them delivered. In many cases, your vendors will actually store your excess quantity orders until you are ready to take delivery of them. All you have to do is ask them! Even in the case of out-of-town or out-of-state vendors, they may have local representation and storage capability near your location. This off-site storage frees up more of your own storage space to be used for other discounted supplies.

Tip: Always inform any employees who are responsible for purchasing office supplies of the following events so that they may adjust any forms or stationery purchasing volumes accordingly:

1. Any name changes.
2. Any address changes.
3. Any logo or trademark changes.
4. Any advertising campaigns or other activity that would require a higher volume of purchases.
5. Any other changes would affect supply inventory purchases.

Another Tip: What can you do with the supply of forms and stationery that, because of any of the changes above, are now unusable for most purposes?

1. Internal forms that are outdated because of name and address and trademark or logo changes can still be utilized until they are exhausted.
2. Envelopes with dated addresses or logos/trademarks can be used to mail accounts payable checks until they're gone.
3. Old stationery with current addresses can be utilized in a direct-mail campaign.
4. Envelopes, such as statement mailers, can be stickered with labels having current address information.
5. Old stationery can be used as a statement mailer to show the new address.

The point here is that you don't have to throw away your old forms and stationery supplies. The only limit to your usage of outdated forms and stationery is your own creativity.

SUMMARY

There is truly a basket of savings in the way you purchase forms, stationery and other consumable supplies. By getting banded volume discounts from your vendors and ordering a six months supply of the items you need, you should be able to save a minimum of 10% to 30% of your supplies costs. And, if you happen to get caught with some outdated forms and stationery, there are numerous ways to use them up. A few of those ways have been listed above.

CHAPTER 44

RECORDS STORAGE MANAGEMENT AND CONTROL

Records Storage Management – This is an area that you don't give much thought to until you need to retrieve critical records. Then it hits you like a ton of bricks! You have no records management system in place, and either you can't locate the necessary records or, worse yet, they've been thrown out with the trash. I will give you some ideas concerning the control and management of records and, in my opinion, the best ways for a small business to approach this problem. But first, why do we have to be concerned about records management and retention at all?

1. **First and foremost, you must comply with state and federal records retention laws** - To keep it simple, I would recommend the following records retention for the following classifications of records:

   a. **All Corporate Records** – Corporate records such as articles of incorporation, corporate by-laws, stock record books, and shareholders and directors meeting minutes must be kept permanently.

   b. **General Ledgers, General Journals, Financial Statements, Tax Returns, Audit Reports, Applicable Chart of Accounts, Cash Schedules, Checks and Bank Statements, and LIFO Records** – Keep these documents permanently.

   c. **Personnel Files** – Keep these documents permanently.

    d. Accounts Receivable and Payable Records, Cash Vouchers, Sales Records Subsidiary Journals, and Physical Inventory and Reconciliation Records - Keep these documents for 4 years to avoid any problems with federal or state tax audit requirements, even though there is only a three year retention requirement.

    e. Fixed Asset Property and Equipment Records - Keep these documents for 4 years after disposition to avoid any problems with federal or state tax audit requirements, even though there is only a three year requirement.

    f. Payroll Records – I would recommend that you keep these records on file for seven years to be safely within all federal and state records retention guidelines which are conflicting and numerous.

2. **Manage and organize your records so that you can easily retrieve a record out of storage** – Management of your records is most easily done as you box up the records going to storage, as follows:

3.

    a. **Organize your records in a logical fashion** – Don't just dump different unrelated records into a box and then have to engage in the equivalent of "dumpster diving" to find anything! Organize your records by category. Then sort within that category, by date, by number, or by name. You can then start boxing your records.

    b. **List the records that are in the storage box on the front of the box in the appropriate location** - The major assumption here is that you are using boxes made for records storage, preprinted for this purpose.

c. **Assign to each box a unique identifying number** – Do this so that the box that contains the record that you want to access can be easily retrieved.

d. **Record the box number and contents on a master listing** - When you have completed your listing of the batch of records going to storage, make a few copies for your file.

An Unbelievable Story About Inadequate Records Storage - When I came to work for this company which had been in business for 15 years prior to my arrival, their records storage was comprised of a huge number of boxes of all sizes, types and varieties stuffed with records. Some of the contents were indicated on the boxes, and some of the boxes had no indication of contents at all. All these boxes, many of which were falling apart, were jammed into a cargo ship container 8' by 8' by 40' without any attempt at organization. As you can imagine, the container was hot and dirty and inhabited by mice and black widow spiders! What an unbelievable mess! And, if you wanted to find anything specific, good luck! It took us a few months of weekend work to sort through this jungle, and toss out records that were no longer required to be kept. Then, we had to select the records we needed to retain, sort them and then re-box those records for retention. During this process we filled up an 8' by 6' by 20' dumpster with trash and old records that were no longer required!

4. **You will minimize any adverse litigation risks and tax consequences by having your required records available for inspection**- If you have a Department of Labor (DOL) Audit regarding payroll or personnel issues and you have no supporting records, you are presumed guilty until you prove yourself innocent! If you are involved in civil litigation, the burden of proof is usually on you. And, what happens when the IRS or State Sales Tax Agencies want to audit your sales from three years ago and you don't have all the necessary

records? By retaining your records in an organized fashion, you can protect yourself from the presumption that you have done something wrong by being able to prove otherwise.

A True Story About the Tax Audit From Hell – A number of years ago we were audited by an IRS auditor who, in addition to everything else, was conducting a comprehensive LIFO audit. You may not know about LIFO which is a Last-In-First-Out inventory valuation method. Unfortunately, LIFO is also a "can opener" that allows the IRS to go all the way back to the year you adopted LIFO and check your LIFO indexes and calculations for all of the interim years! We had to go into our old records and produce 13 years worth of LIFO inventory, indexing and calculations for the IRS auditor. Luckily, I had just finished reorganizing the 15 years of records that were jammed into the cargo container referred to above, and we were able to successfully complete the audit.

5. **Protect your critical records from loss or damage** – You can accomplish this by storing critical records on site in a locked room designated for records storage. I strongly recommend that, if space permits, you keep the last 4 years of the records needed for an IRS, DOL, or State Sales Tax Audit along with LIFO records from the time you adopted LIFO on site and available for audit purposes. You can also make copies of your permanent corporate records, and store them offsite, with the originals accessible on site.

6. **Write up and distribute a Records Retention Policy Letter** – The letter should address the following items:

   a. A listing of the records to be stored.

   b. The length of time the records are to be stored.

   c. The location of the records being stored.

d. The personnel having access to the records.

e. The records custodian charged with safeguarding the records, moving them in and out of storage, and complying with your records retention policy.

7. **Insure that you have a secondary magnetic media back-up for your paper storage** - In this age of advanced computer technology, there is no excuse for not having a computer back-up on a CD or USB flash drive for your ledgers, general, sales and payroll journals, schedules, inventory, cash journals, interim and final financial statements, and anything else you want to save.

a. Believe it or not, you can now buy a 1 Terabyte (That's 1,000 Gigabytes, Folks!) Hard Disk Drive from Seagate for as little as $89 plus shipping. This giant sized storage capability makes it possible and practical to store all of your prior year's records requirements on your current computer.

b. You can also transfer this information to a USB flash drive capable of saving up to 128 Gigabytes of data. You can recycle your flash drives off-site using a bank safety deposit box for storage.

c. If you utilize a computer systems provider, they probably already offer a service to store old computer records electronically off site. There are also third party providers who offer this service.

8. **Minimize the costs of storing your records** – There are several ways that you can reduce the cost of records storage and still have all of the benefits of a managed records retention program.

a. **Keep the last 4 years of records on site.** It shouldn't take up too much of your space, and most everything you need to access will be at your fingertips.

b. **Utilize a recognized records storage management company for your permanent records storage requirements.** This will be relatively inexpensive, since most of the   records you send to storage will be stored permanently.

c. **After the 4 year retention cycle, destroy all records that have a 4 year retention requirement or less.** Do this **before** you send the remaining records to your records storage company. Then send the records that have a five year or greater retention requirement to your storage company. This should be done once a year, immediately after you have completed your year-end financial audit. This saves you all of the acquisition, storage and destruction charges regarding records with a records retention requirement of 4 year or less.

d. **Use the records listing sent by your storage company to destroy records past their retention cycle.** Periodically, at minimum once a year, your records storage company should send you a suggested listing of records past their retention cycle. I said they should send the destruct listing, because sometimes they don't. It's up to you to insure they do! Use this listing to mark for destruction all of the records you no longer have to keep. This will keep your records growth to a minimum.

SUMMARY

There are many reasons to properly store records, but the number one reason has to be retrieval of those records when you need them for internal purposes. An important secondary reason is the need to produce records for audits of all types, whether they are internal audits, external audits such as your CPA annual audit, franchisor audits, or governmental audits. The third reason relates to legal matters that require you to support your position as the plaintiff or defendant. Your records may also be requested by third parties in unrelated legal matters, as you are the custodian of those records. In order to be able to retrieve those records, you have to be able to find them. That assumes that the records are boxed and numbered in an organized fashion with visible labels on each box displaying the contents. If you keep 4 years of the required records on site, you will be sending a minimal amount of your records to storage, thereby saving on external storage costs and making that space available for other important uses. **To close this chapter, regardless of the posted requirements for records retention, if you think you're going to need it, keep it!**

CHAPTER 45

UTILITY COST CONTROL

Utility costs are the largest facilities-related expense item according to researchers. And because of substantial planned increases in utility costs, your utility expense will only grow, unless you become proactive about inaugurating effective energy cost reduction programs. A company wide strategy to implement utility cost reductions can reduce your company's energy expense by at least 10% to as much as 30% or more. And in these tough times, a penny saved is a proverbial dollar earned!

To reduce energy costs, companies must take an overall approach to achieving energy efficiency. Energy savings can be achieved throughout your company. There are many things you can do to improve your energy efficiency. For example, if you have an older building, it probably harbors many energy inefficiencies that cry out for remediation. Here are a few cost effective recommendations that will assist you in the development of an effective energy efficiency policy, and the identification of cost effective energy reduction projects.

1. **Develop an Energy Usage Baseline** – You can use this baseline to measure the effectiveness of your energy efficiency programs. The baseline should include all of your separate energy usage and costs by meter for the prior 12 to 24 months, plus a multiplier for any recent or proposed cost increases.

2. **Develop a Utility Cost Reduction Policy and Strategy** - A comprehensive approach to developing an energy strategy includes an analysis of energy wastage. Have an energy audit conducted by a professional energy engineer to identify

possible energy efficient solutions, evaluate those solutions using cost/ benefit analyses, and suggest a detailed plan for implementation of the projects selected.

3. **Order an Energy Audit For Each of Your Facilities** – You can check with your utility companies to see if this service is provided free of charge. If not, I'm sure they can recommend a qualified energy consultant who can provide this audit to your company at a reasonable charge.

4. **Analyze the Audit Recommendations for Older Buildings** – Older buildings are notoriously inefficient energy consumers. If you have an older building, at least a few of the following items are contributing to energy inefficiency.

POTENTIAL PROBLEMS

   A. Heating and air conditioning ductwork that is under insulated or not insulated at all.
   B. Insufficient roof and sidewall insulation.
   C. Old buildings that are leaking hot and cold air like a sieve.
   D. Old and inefficient heating and air conditioning units.
   E. Improperly sized air intake and outflow vents.
   F. Old thermostats that can't be programmed.
   G. Hot water pipes without insulation and hot water heaters without thermal jackets.
   H. Inefficient and insufficient lighting.
   I. Other areas needing improvement that are too numerous to mention.

POSSIBLE SOLUTIONS

   A. Increase the R rating of your ductwork to a minimum of the current building code requirement. Don't implement this until you have checked the adequacy of your air vents, as this could affect the size requirement of your ductwork.
   B. Increase the R rating of your attic and sidewall insulation to a minimum of the current building code requirement. Start with the attic insulation, as it is the easiest and least

expensive way to save on energy costs and has the shortest cost recovery period.

C. Have an energy audit performed to expose building air leaks, and plug up those leaks!

D. Consider replacing old and inefficient heating and air conditioning units with new units that are much more efficient. The old air conditioning units are not only inefficient, but if they are over 10 years old, you have probably lost another 10% to 15% of the original EER (Energy Efficiency Rating) due to wear and tear on the units. If you have a smaller building, you probably have an air cooled air conditioner. Consider replacing it with a water cooled unit as they are much more efficient, particularly in hot arid climates like the desert southwest.

E. As part of your energy audit, have your air intake and outflow vents inspected for proper sizing and placement. If recommended, have your vents resized and, if necessary, relocated.

F. Replace old non-programmable thermostats with new programmable thermostats. This is another no-brainer which can be done at a negligible cost. Just get it done, program the thermostats for your location to best conserve energy, and enjoy the savings!

G. Insulate accessible hot water pipes, air ducts and wrap hot water heaters with a thermal jacket. Don't waste time thinking about this one. Just do it!

H. Replace all of your incandescent and regular fluorescent lighting fixtures with high efficiency fluorescent lighting to achieve a 50% to 67% reduction in your baseline lighting costs.

A Personal Story Regarding Energy Savings - This story is illustrative of several of the items mentioned above and that is why I chose it. My wife and I recently bought an older home that was terribly inefficient with regard to heating and cooling costs. Our electric bills in the summer were outrageous at $557/month, and it was impossible to cool the house down to a reasonable comfort level even when running the air conditioner full time. After having a heating and air conditioning specialist look at our system, it was determined that our intake and outflow air vents were improperly sized, one main air intake was not properly located, the other main intake had only a 2 inch plenum rather than the 6 inches recommended, our air ducts were mismatched and improperly sized with a lower insulation value than recommended, the thermostats needed replacing, and our 16 year old air conditioners were not performing at anything near peak efficiency. After correcting all of the problems above and replacing our old air conditioners with 2 Freus water cooled air conditioners, our electric bill dropped to $147 the next month for a $400/month savings in the summer. We received rebates from the electric company and income tax credits totaling $3,500, reducing our net project cost to about $7,000. And best of all, after completing the work we could easily reduce the summer temperature in our home to a comfort level without having to run the air conditioners more than several minutes at a time!

5. **Consider Using Your Waste Oil to Heat Your Building** – Essentially, this provides "free heat" to your premises, once you have recouped the cost of the waste oil burner unit.

6. **Offer Bonuses to Employees for Energy Conservation Ideas** – The ideas have to be implemented and result in an energy cost savings. The bonus should be based on the actual amount of energy savings achieved in a predetermined time frame, normally one year.

7. **If You are in a Hot and Dry Area Requiring Landscape Irrigation, Consider Switching to Desert Xeriscaping or Low Water Use Landscaping** – Replacing grass lawns and shrubs that have to be irrigated with desert type landscaping can save a substantial part of your water bill. Your sewer bill may be based on your water usage, so by reducing one you automatically reduce the other. Check with your water company as they may offer rebates to convert regular landscaping to low water usage landscaping, and the rebate may cover the entire cost of the conversion.

8. **Check With Your Utility Companies to Determine Your Eligibility for Rebates** – Many utility companies offer substantial rebates for energy conservation that can significantly defray your cost to implement those energy efficient projects. If you decide to qualify for any of their rebate programs, make sure you have a clear understanding of what is required, along with your vendor. Insure that your vendors have pre-qualified your projects with the utility companies and have filed final paperwork required for the rebate before you have made your final payment to them.

9. **Perform a Cost/Benefit Analysis (CBA) of Your Potential Energy Projects** – Don't waste time analyzing simple items, such as putting a thermal jacket around a hot water heater tank. Just do it! For other more expensive projects, determine the net cost after rebates, the annual energy savings, and the payback period in years (net cost divided by the energy savings). Then list your projects by descending energy savings with a payback period of less than 3 years, and implement as many of those as you can afford within your capital budgeting constraints.

10. **Insure that You Get 2 or 3 Bids From Qualified Vendors for Your Energy Projects** - You can further reduce your energy project expense by getting at least 2 or 3 bids from different vendors. Everything else being equal, choosing the lowest bid.

11. **Don't Forget to Include Maintenance Savings in Your Project Analysis** – In some cases your maintenance savings can actually exceed your energy savings. There are also intangible but nevertheless real benefits to take into consideration, as described in the following true story.

A True Story About an Energy Project – I chose this particular energy project because it encompasses a number of the items discussed above. We were operating a fabrication shop in an older building having about 20,000 square feet of space. The lighting in the building was not only inefficient but substantially inadequate, to the point of being a safety hazard. In addition, the maintenance costs of continuing with that lighting were estimated to be at least $2,000 to $3,000 per year. We decided to opt for a high energy efficient fluorescent lighting system that would give us an average of 36,000 to 38,000 hours of actual usage before requiring replacement. Our initial bid to completely replace the lighting with more powerful and efficient fluorescent lighting was $22,000. After receiving several more bids, we chose the low bid of $18,000, thereby shaving $4,000 off the cost of the original bid. We were also eligible for an electric company rebate of $4,000, further reducing the net cost to $14,000. We estimated that we would achieve an annual electric utility bill reduction of $5,000. When combined with the smaller estimate of $2,000 in maintenance savings, the overall expense reduction was $7,000 per year, and the payback period based on the net cost of $14,000 was only 2 years! The decision to proceed with this project was a classic no-brainer. We also increased the amount of production floor lighting by 400% compared with what we had before starting the project! While the increased lighting was an intangible benefit, and therefore it was difficult to estimate a specific dollar value for it, you knew intuitively that the substantially increased lighting would certainly increase production efficiency and help to prevent industrial accidents.

SUMMARY

There are numerous ways to contain and even reduce utility costs. Many of these utility cost reductions are subsidized by utility company rebates and federal and state tax credits. Start with an energy audit to determine what you need to do to reduce your utility costs. Then create a utility cost reduction plan and prioritize the individual projects incorporated into the plan by the net monetary benefit of the project and the cost recovery payback period. After you have a detailed plan for implementation of these projects, don't waste time. Just get started!

CHAPTER 46

TRAVEL AND ENTERTAINMENT EXPENSE CONTROL

Travel and Entertainment (T&E) Expenses – There are always meetings requiring travel that you absolutely have to attend. Some of these would be seminars where your company is one of the presenters, and conferences and expositions where your company is an exhibitor. Sometimes, it is convenient to be able to attend a conference where you can see your major customers, vendors and competition all at the same time. When you have good reasons for travel, why spend more money than you have to on T&E. To reduce your T&E costs to a minimum, here are a few ideas that will save you money.

A. **Don't travel!** – This kind of sounds like an oxymoron, but do you really have to make that trip if other avenues are available to you. Here are several suggestions that may help you to make that decision.

1) **Consider Web Conferencing** – Take a good look at Web Conferencing as an alternative to travel. It will allow you to do almost everything you can do in person except "press the flesh" and take your customer to lunch! One of the best companies offering this service is Cisco's Webex Meeting and Conferencing Center. They have special low priced plans for small businesses, great training and support facilities and obviously, excellent security measures. You can do everything that you could do in a face to face meeting and more! You can have audio, video, discussions, power point presentations, web access and access to all of your computer files available to you. Access to any these

items can be temporarily shared at your Webex meeting with one or all of the participants. These are powerful tools that may be hard to duplicate in another meeting room if you are traveling away from your office. WebEx has an excellent 15 minute on-line tutorial available if you would like to check out its capabilities.

2) **Consider an open-ended phone call** – Perhaps all you really need is an open-ended phone call with your customer or vendor. Set this up in advance so that you have a floating agenda to guide your conversation and make it productive. If you then decide that you still need a personal meeting, at least both of you will be better prepared for it. And, better yet, both of you may decide to have the meeting at your location!

B. **Schedule your meetings to coincide with client or vendor visits to or near your area** – Perhaps your clients, vendors or others are traveling to or near your city to attend a seminar, convention or for another purpose. Arrange to meet with them at a time convenient to them before or after their other meetings. With the money you save, you can easily afford to take them out to a nice lunch or dinner!

C. **Schedule meetings with clients, vendors, or others to coincide with your other planned visits near their offices -** Arrange to meet with them at a time convenient to them before or after your other meetings. With the money they save, they can afford to take you out to a nice lunch or dinner!

C. **Designate one of your employees as your Travel Director** – Perhaps your secretary or receptionist could fill this assignment. All travel plans should be administered by this person and approved by you. That way, you have no unnecessary unapproved travel.

E. **Control the costs of approved travel** – Instruct your travel director to go online and book the best deals on airline tickets, hotels and car rentals. You might be able to get a company contract rate from a hotel chain or car rental agency that is better than anything you can get online.

F. **Institute a Travel Policy** – Communicate your travel policy to your employees in writing. Let them know that you will only reimburse business related expenses, not personal items. Sorry guys, no more cocktails and xxx rated movies in the hotel at night at company expense!

G. **Require employees to use hotel shuttles** – Hotel shuttles are free and taxis are expensive! If a rental car is necessary, this should have been arranged in advance by the travel director and scheduled for airport pick-up of the traveler by the rental agency.

H. **A standard Travel & Expense (T&E) form must be filed for reimbursement** - Let your employees who travel on behalf of the company know that they must file a standard T&E form for reimbursement. Also, inform them that any attempt to have personal expenses reimbursed may result in disciplinary action. The form should go to the Travel Director for initial approval, and to you for final approval before being reimbursed.

SUMMARY

Some business travel is necessary for almost every company. However, by following the simple guidelines above should enable you to substantially reduce your travel and entertainment expenses, and still accomplish all of your business objectives.

CHAPTER 47

AUDIT COST CONTROL

As in controlling legal costs, controlling audit costs is even more dependent upon choosing the right CPA firm, since it is a one-time fixed-fee event each year. The audit price should be negotiated prior to starting the engagement at a fixed price agreed upon by you and your CPA firm. The fixed price should be clearly stated in the engagement letter from your CPA, along with an expected date of completion. Please read my chapter on choosing the right CPA firm. Assuming that you have done your homework and selected the right CPA firm, the only way to save substantial time and money is to plan and prepare for your audit prior to the auditor's physical arrival on site, as indicated below.

AUDIT PLANNING MADE SIMPLE

1. **Communicate significant changes** - Well before the audit starts, communicate any changes in ownership, management, location, product lines, union contracts, significant customer additions or deletions, legal activities, or other important changes in your business with your auditor.

2. **Secure your auditor's approval before adopting any accounting method or estimate changes** – Always seek your auditor's approval before changing depreciation methods, inventory valuation methods, reserving methods or other existing accounting methods. Make your auditor a member of your team! **Don't blindside your auditor with unapproved accounting method changes!**

3. **Start an audit file** – Keep all significant information regarding your upcoming audit in this file and send a copy to your auditor.

4. **Clarify with your auditor the working paper format for general ledger account reporting** – With this template, you can prepare and assemble all the required audit information in advance.

5. **Schedule your audit date** – Discuss with your auditor the arrival date for the audit team, the length of the engagement, and the expected date of completion.

6. **Schedule your staff for the audit dates agreed to above** – You don't want key accounting or financial personnel taking vacation or other discretionary leave during the audit period.

7. **Individually assign to all staff their required audit work, with mandatory completion dates prior to the audit** - All general ledger accounts, account schedules showing the account detail, and account reconciliations should be listed in this master schedule. Identify the person responsible for the reconciliation and the mandatory completion date. Also schedule and complete any special reports that you know your auditor will request prior to the engagement.

8. **Substantiate any significant year-to-year operational variances** – Have an explanation ready for any significant variances in account balances or operational results. Remember, your auditor only gets to take a good look at your books and records once a year! He needs your input!

9. **Be honest and open with your auditor** – When you are asked questions, answer them honestly and forthrightly. If you are aware of information that is germane to the completion of your audit, don't wait to be asked the question. Volunteer the information and discuss it with your auditor.

A TIME AND MONEY-SAVING TIP – *If you are not going public in the next five years, and you have no other requirements to have an audit, consider a review as a less expensive and time consuming alternative. The only substantive differences between an audit and a review are as follows:*

1. *Auditor Observation of Physical Inventories* – Here the auditor evaluates the inventory taking process and is on site to observe the physical inventory count. The auditor will also do a stratified sample test count of certain inventory items and compare the test count to your actual count. This comparison will help to verify the accuracy of your overall inventory taking process.

2. *Auditor Confirmation of Receivables* – The auditor will independently confirm your receivables by sending out confirmation requests, usually with your month-end statements. If your auditors do not receive a high enough percentage of confirmations returned, they will typically send out a second request to customers who do not reply the first time. When the desired percentage of confirmations has been received, the auditors can then assess the overall collectability of your receivables.

If you can live without the two items above, you can save time and money by having a review instead of an audit. You will still receive nearly all the beneficial effects of having an audit!

AN EXAMPLE OF EXCELLENT AUDIT PREPARATION

How you can prepare for an audit or review and keep the time, disruption, and expense of the engagement to a minimum – During my tenure as the chief financial officer with a smaller medium-size company, we would prepare all of the audit working papers for several companies prior to the audit, along with the draft Financial Statements, a listing of all the general ledger accounts and other schedules and information necessary to complete the tax returns. We would then Fed-Ex this comprehensive package, which we called an **"audit in a**

box" to our auditors. The auditors then had ample time to review this information prior to their arrival on site. Therefore our audits only required 3 to 4 days of on site audit work. The accounting staff had no additional work during the audit, as a result of all of the preparation done beforehand. Some of our management staff were always curious about the progression of the audit. They would ask how it was going and whether I was concerned about the results. I would tell them that since we had already completed a thorough internal audit, we had nothing to worry about. Our outside auditors should simply confirm what we had already done. Because we essentially completed a pre-audit before the auditors arrived and made our own internal audit adjustments, we had a string of 12 years without the need for any audit adjustments from our CPA firm! This comprehensive audit preparation saved the company considerable time, money and disruption of staff.

SUMMARY

First and foremost, you must choose a CPA firm that is right for you. Please read Chapter 11 titled "CHOOSING YOUR CPA FIRM". Then, if you prepare for your audit by following the suggestions above, you should end up with the lowest cost highest quality audit possible, with minimal disruption of your time and that of your staff.

CHAPTER 48

CONTAINING AND REDUCING LEGAL COSTS

EFFECTIVE WAYS TO UTILIZE YOUR ATTORNEYS AND REDUCE YOUR LEGAL COSTS

1. **Hire the Right Attorney!** – Please read Chapter 9 titled "CHOOSING YOUR CORPORATE ATTORNEY". This selection process is where the major portion of your legal cost and quality control starts and ends. **If you skip this critical step, you can wind up with unbelievably high legal fees for shoddy performance delivered late or not at all.**

    An Illustration of High Legal Fees for an Estimate – Some time ago, my partners and I needed a legal opinion concerning a sale of realty with a wrap-around mortgage. We engaged a firm, one of the best in town, that we had good results with in the past. However, we didn't know the attorney who was assigned to our project. We asked him for an estimate of fees to render an opinion in this matter. What we didn't ask him for was his cost of rendering an estimate! A month later, we had a bill for $5,000 from this knucklehead and nothing to show for it. The moral of this story is to take nothing for granted when you are dealing with an attorney or an attorney firm you don't know. Insure that there is no charge for an estimate of costs!

2. **Ask Questions!** – Don't be shy about asking questions concerning items that may have legal implications. There are many legal questions that can be answered over the phone, but only if they're asked! When you have identified a potential legal problem, don't hesitate to call your attorney. If you ask

the right questions before a legal problem arises and follow your attorney's advice, expensive litigation can be avoided.

3.   **Standard Business Contracts** - Have your corporate attorney create any contracts for you that are specific to your business. If you already have such contracts in place, have them reviewed by your attorney. Negotiate a fixed price for this service.

   A Perfect Example of a Problem Contract - A number of years ago, I was hired as the V.P. Finance for a management company. I quickly noted that the company, by contract, had to perform cash proof audits on demand for its clients. This was not only peculiar but also extremely expensive and time consuming. I was prompted by this requirement to review the management contract, which was based on time and materials plus a management fee. After my review, I asked the President what legal firm had written the management contract, which was very heavily weighted in favor of the customers. I told him that it looked like one of our customer's attorneys had in fact written the contract. He thought about it for a moment and then said that "It was written by our first major customer 12 years ago." No wonder they weren't making any money! I quickly drafted a fixed cost contract including a management fee that allowed us to retain any savings that we achieved, and eliminated the need for those onerous cash proof audits. Of course, I had our corporate counsel review the contract before we utilized it. Once we had transferred all of our clients to our new fixed cost contract, our profitability and peace of mind soared!

4.   **Fixed Project Fees** – When you have a legal project of known length and complexity, always get a fixed contract price (No ups- No extras) from a number of attorney firms competent to handle the project before making a decision to go forward. Get all the things that you have agreed to in writing from your attorney firm in the form of an engagement letter that spells out the expected work product, the expected completion date, and the fixed cost of the project.

5. **Join Your Industry Organization and Utilize Their Attorneys** – You will generally be able to utilize attorneys representing your industry or trade organization at a much lower hourly fee. They are also experienced in and knowledgeable about your industry. This saves you even more time and money in successfully dealing with your potential legal problems.

6. **Settle Disputes Without Litigation** – If at all possible, avoid expensive and time consuming litigation. There is absolutely no percentage in it for you or your opponent. In fact, the only parties who always win in litigation are the attorneys. If you are looking for a guideline, I would say that any potential litigation that your attorney estimates you don't have at least a 60% chance of winning should be settled. Regarding other legal matters where your percentage of success is higher, offer sweetened terms to your opponent that discount the time and cost of litigation. This keeps you out of the courtroom, and allows you to put your full attention to making money for your business.

An Example of Unnecessary Litigation Caused by Ego - We had a client who had several problems regarding some extensive repair work done by us for his company. We made a number of concessions to include an additional $2,000 reduction in his bill. After this was negotiated, the customer agreed to pay the remainder of the bill, but then reneged on his promise. We were forced to start litigation proceedings in order to collect on this account. Prior to the start of litigation, we again met with the customer to see if we could come to an agreement. We offered him a 50% discount on his billing, which surprisingly, was unacceptable to him. I told him at the time that this was silly on his part, as the only winners would be the attorneys. Sure enough, the case went to court and we were awarded most of our claim plus interest and legal costs. All that our customer ended up with was a court order to pay us and a fat legal bill! The moral of the story is when you get a good settlement offer in a legal matter, take it and don't let your ego get in the way!

7. **Utilize Standard Legal Forms for Common Legal Issues**
    - There are many legal issues of a generalized and mundane
    nature that have to be addressed by your company almost every
    day. These items can include the creation of notes receivable,
    both secured and unsecured, limited powers of attorney,
    employee loan documents, pension plan loans, real property
    leases, purchase and sale agreements, simple non-disclosure
    agreements, and other legal documents commonly used by
    your company. Unfortunately, if you were to utilize outside
    counsel to create all of these common documents each time
    you needed them, you would generally find the following:

    1. The documents would not be created in a timely fashion.
    2. The documents may have to be sent back and forth to your
        attorney a few times to have corrections made.
    3. If you were in your attorney's office at that time, you
        would probably find that a paralegal was actually creating
        these common documents instead of your attorney.
    4. You would end up paying much more than you should for
        the creation and redrafting of these documents.

A MONEY-SAVING IDEA REGARDING COMMON LEGAL FORMS

Find a company that specializes in the sale of standard legal forms and
documents. Have them give you a catalog that indexes all of the legal
forms that they have for sale. You can purchase these forms from
any office supply store that carries legal forms in whatever quantity
you need. Then, have the standard legal forms that you intend to use
reviewed by your attorney, revised if necessary and downloaded to
your Controller in an M/S Word format. Your controller can then
input the variable information on the form each time they are used,
and send a file copy to your attorney. The advantage here is that you
will be able to modify the variable information in those forms on
demand, utilizing a common word processing program. Your forms
will then be available in minutes rather than days with less investment
of your time than it would take to communicate this information to

your attorney, and at a fraction of the cost. This way you are not constantly reinventing the wheel, paying your attorney to modify common legal forms at substantial cost to you! So in situations where common legal forms can and should be utilized, by simply entering the variable information yourself, you win all the way around!

NOTE: The person modifying these standard legal forms must have some minimal amount of legal training. That is why I have suggested that your Controller or CFO be directly involved with the use, modification and approval of these common legal forms.

8. **Prepare an internal draft document -** If possible, prepare an internal draft for any non-standard legal documents that you require. This will allow you to collect and organize your thoughts and determine what, in your opinion, the document should contain before you send the document to your attorney for review.

TIP - Remember, your attorneys bill you by the hour, charging you $200 to $500 for their services. If you or one of your staff has the ability to draft specific legal documents, you can accomplish the following:

1. Organize your thoughts as to the framework of legal document that you require.
2. Input all of the variable information, such as names and addresses, into the draft document without your attorney having to ask for it.
3. Because you have provided your attorney with a basic draft document for review, you will receive your finished product much more quickly.
4. You will reduce your attorney's billing hours and save a substantial amount of money when you provide your attorney with a draft document to simply review, rather than create it from scratch.

A PERSONAL EXAMPLE OF PROVIDING DRAFT DOCUMENTS TO YOUR ATTORNEY

I am not an attorney, but by experience over the years I have attained some sort of paralegal status. In many cases, both in business and personally, I have provided draft letters and documents to our attorneys for their review. In about 30% of those cases, I was given the green light to use or send the documents without any additions, deletions, or corrections. It can be done, and you don't have to be a Philadelphia lawyer to do it!

SUMMARY

Again, you can save a substantial amount of your legal costs, but it all starts with choosing the right attorney. Join your industry organization or association. Utilize them by having your industry association attorney review your standard business contracts. Purchase most of the common legal forms that you use, and have them reviewed by your attorney for suitability. Any changes should be incorporated in a Microsoft Word document. For any other non-standard communications, forms, contracts or other complex legal documents, prepare a draft of the document using the information you already have. Also include any other provisions you would like to have the document contain. For example, if it's a legal letter you require, create a draft letter and send a copy to your attorney for review. If you follow the suggestions contained in this chapter, you will promote more effective legal representation. This will save you a substantial amount of time and also minimize your legal costs.

CHAPTER 49

THE PROPERTY & CASUALTY
INSURANCE GAME

THE GAME

Property & Casualty (P&C) Companies play the Insurance Game the same way as Health Insurance Companies. They are either adding to their book of business, (buying business), or reducing business, (shedding existing customers). When they reduce their book of business in a geographic area, they accomplish this by increasing their premium or not writing new business! It really doesn't matter what your specific claims experience or loss ratio has been. Good, bad or indifferent, your premium will increase substantially. If, however, the Insurance Company is increasing its book of business in that area, they will discount their premium, and even take on risks that were less than acceptable beforehand. By taking advantage of this knowledge, you can save hundreds of thousands of dollars over several years without sacrificing your coverage or quality of product.

PROPERTY & CASUALTY INSURANCE - PREPARING TO PLAY THE GAME

If you are purchasing Property & Casualty Insurance, you must start the process at least 120 days in advance. **As a necessary part of your preparation to receive quotes from other P&C insurance companies, you must first request copies of your claims loss reports for the last three to five years**. You must have this information on hand before starting the process. If you wait until your broker or agent asks you for it, you will be wasting a lot of time, and you may miss out on the possibility of getting a favorable quote. Loss reports can be requested from your current broker or directly from your current or past P&C insurance company. If you don't have a broker who is a "general agent", an agent who can represent multiple insurers, I would suggest you locate one. If you are currently purchasing your insurance from a "captive agent", an agent who is employed by only one company, have him quote the policy also. Your captive agent will know that you are shopping the policy, because you have requested loss reports. Instruct him to have his company sharpen their pencil and give you their best competitive quote. Your agent should be able to get a renewal quote from your existing carrier about 60 days from policy expiration. At least 30 days prior to that, you need to instruct your general agent or broker to shop your policy with other P&C providers. If you have any specialized risks that limit your coverage to only a few P&C companies, make sure that your agent or broker knows this up front. Tell him to ensure that the company who will be quoting the insurance is not only aware of the specialized risks, but is willing to make a quote on that basis. Also, let him know that you are looking for a company that is "aggressively buying business" and is willing to offer you the very best rates for comparable coverage. Ideally, you will be receiving several competitive bids to choose from.

PROPERTY & CASUALTY INSURANCE - PLAYING THE GAME TO WIN

Believe it or not, you can negotiate with your Property and Casualty Insurance Company and your broker to reduce your premium as follows:

1. Your first objective should be a reduction in the quoted cost of your P&C insurance as compared with your prior year. Don't let the fact that your current P&C insurance company has already given you a current quote deter you from asking them for a more competitive quote. Let them decide if they want to keep your business or not!

2. Examine your deductibles. If you have a low deductible on certain coverages that are highly unlikely to result in a claim, have that area of the policy quoted again with a higher deductible.

3. Review all of your physical damage coverage. There may be segments of your policy where you could save considerable premium cost by self-insuring.

4. Review of all of your required bond coverage. There may be bonds that you are being charged a premium for that are no longer necessary and can be deleted from the policy.

5. Review all of your real property coverage to ensure that it is accurate. Any real property no longer owned or occupied by your company should be removed from the policy.

6. Review your business interruption insurance. Make sure that the coverage is based upon a realistic estimate of needed income, plus 10%. If it is substantially in excess of that amount, consider reducing the coverage.

7. Review all of your insurance coverages in advance of your renewal date with your broker each policy year for potential savings.

TWO EXAMPLES OF PROPERTY AND CASUALTY PREMIUM REDUCTIONS

Recently, the P&C Company that had been insuring our company for over 30 years waited until the last moment and then increased our premium over 25%. We had already gotten competitive quotes from two other companies, and were able to save 25% and more by moving to a new company. After two years with the new company, they decided to increase their premiums significantly. Our old company quoted the policy at a very competitive rate because they knew that we were shopping the insurance. Obviously, we then made the decision to move our P&C insurance back to the original company at a substantial savings.

The most egregious example in my memory of outrageously high premiums compared with very low risk occurred a number of years ago. It involved physical damage or loss coverage on 18 Motorola two-way radios. The best quote that I could get from the insurer was about 60% of the market value of the radios, which amounted to $5,400 in total. This equated to a complete loss on 11 of the 18 radios we had! Since the insurer was competitive in all other respects regarding the policy, and the radios were in separate vehicles that were not parked in the same location, it became evident that we should self-insure these radios. In the years that we did so, we did not experience any loss whatsoever, saving the company $5,400 each year! This experience did not reflect well on the underwriting department of that insurance company regarding their excessive rating of this risk!

SUMMARY

If you know the Insurance Game and how it's played and, with your Insurance Broker's assistance, you are prepared to play the game, there is no reason why you can't substantially reduce your P&C premiums and win the game!

CHAPTER 50

INCOME TAX EXPENSE REDUCTION

HOW TO REDUCE YOUR FEDERAL INCOME TAX EXPENSE

1. **Write off any doubtful asset before your tax year-end** - Keep your Balance Sheet lean and mean by writing off any doubtful assets. An example of an appropriate year-end write-off would be a customer receivable account that you have sent to legal or collections, is in bankruptcy, or that you have serious doubts about being able to collect.

2. **Take full advantage of any Section 179 asset purchase deductions** – Purchase qualifying assets before the 2009 year-end to be eligible for the Section 179 expense deductions. As of 2009, the limit is $125,000 plus cost of living adjustments (COLA).

3. **Check your eligibility for any Income Tax Credits in 2009** – There are a substantial number of income tax credits you could be eligible for. A partial listing would be Social Security Tax Credits for food and beverage establishments, Disabled Access Credits up to $5,000 if you incurred expenses in providing handicap access to your business, Work Opportunity Credits if you hire individuals from certain classifications, Solar Energy Credits, Research & Development Credits, Hybrid Vehicle Tax Credits, and a number of other Income Tax Credits. Along with your CPA, plan to get all of the income tax credits you're entitled to.

4. **If you are a cash basis taxpayer, delay receipts until next year** – If you report your taxable income on a cash basis, defer revenue receipts into the new tax year.

5. **If you are a cash basis taxpayer, accelerate business expenditures in the current year** - If you report your taxable income on a cash basis, pay all of your expense invoices in the current year.

6. **Delay profitable depreciable asset sales until next year** - If you are contemplating asset sales that exceed your taxable basis, delay those sales into next year. You might consider a rental agreement to bridge the time gap, making the sale contract effective next year.

7. **Sell unprofitable depreciable assets this year** – If you are contemplating selling assets with a tax loss, complete the sale in your current year.

8. **If they can actually make a contribution to your business, hire family members in order to distribute some of your income** - Keep in mind that if the family member is not contributing to the business in a meaningful way, you might be better off paying the tax!

9. **Maximize your company contribution to your retirement plans** – This strategy is only effective when most of the contributions go to your own retirement plans.

10. **If Your Income Tax Payable is Less Than Your Estimated Payments, File Your Income Tax Return Early** – File your Income Tax Return as soon after your tax year end as possible to receive your refund quickly. Also, if you had a net loss in 2008, do not pay any estimated tax for 2009 until you are sure you will have income to report for that year.

11. **Schedule your tax planning early in the tax year** - Schedule your tax planning with your CPA prior to the beginning of your tax year, not at the year end when you can't change what

has already occurred. I suggest that you have a tax planning session with your CPA firm for next year while they are still on premises and before the current year's audit field work is completed. This way, you know for sure that you are ahead of the game in planning tax strategy for the upcoming year.

12. **Inform your CPA of any significant events after your meeting** - If there are any significant events affecting your business after your tax planning session, discuss those events with your CPA to determine any mid-course tax planning recommendations.

SUMMARY

It is not my purpose to enumerate all of the tax strategies that you can utilize, or the numerous tax credits you could be eligible for that will reduce your corporate tax expenses. There are too many variables such as your type of business, the tax laws of the city, county or state where you are actively engaged in business and other important factors to consider. However, the strategies above are applicable to most businesses and stress advance and mid-year tax planning with your CPA to insure that your tax reduction strategies are successful.

SECTION 9

CONTROL OF ASSETS AND WORKING CAPITAL

CHAPTER 51

CONTROL OF CASH AND CASH EQUIVALENTS

CASH MANAGEMENT AND CONTROL

The management and control of cash is extremely important to the long term success of your business. The control of cash starts with the way your bank accounts are established. If you only have one company, you will need a minimum of one general and one payroll bank account. If you have more than one company and one payroll, you'll need separate bank accounts for each company and each payroll that you have. Signature cards should be on file with your bank for each company, with updated information for each check signer. Instead of having your banking relations spread over a number of banks, I would suggest that you consolidate your operational banking with one bank for the following reasons and ease of operation.

A CASH SAVING AND MONEYMAKING IDEA - Ask your bank to set up an automated sweep account that will collect all of your bank account balances nightly. Then instruct your bank to invest these sweep balances in a money market account that should enable you to collect some interest on your account. Since your bank balances are generally higher than your ledger balances (this positive difference is called the "float"), you actually get paid interest on your ledger balance plus the float. Depending upon the average amount of your cash bank balances, the interest can amount to a substantial amount of money over 12 months. I would advise you in this time of credit stress to invest your excess funds in a government money market account, secured by US government obligations. By utilizing your sweep account, you won't have to worry about the current FDIC insured limit of $250,000, as you will have established only minimum balances in your general and payroll bank accounts.

A "LOAN ON DEMAND" IDEA - If you have not already set up a line of credit with your bank, begin the process with your bank now to institute a line of credit with reasonable limits. You might be thinking that "right now I don't need a line of credit". You may be right, but because you don't need a line of credit now, this is exactly the time that you to apply for a line with your bank. Because, believe me, when you need a line of credit, it's difficult if not impossible to get one approved by your bank. The reason for this is very simple. When you need a line of credit, your business is probably under financial stress and your bank knows this, or will know it when you provide them with the financial information they require. So set up your line of credit now, when you don't need it!

TIE THE TWO TOGETHER WITH AN "AUTOMATED LOAN ON DEMAND"

Last year, I was able to get our bank to tie our sweep account balance directly to our line of credit! To illustrate the advantage of doing this, let's say that for some unknown reason, your sweep account opens with a negative bank balance. With no positive balance in the sweep account to clear checks, wire transfers and other items, you could be looking at some considerable financial embarrassment. However, since the line of credit will fund the sweep account up to the line of credit limit, the prospect of the sweep account going negative is highly unlikely. By the way, this extra protection was added at no additional cost to the company!

CASH RECEIPTS - WHAT IS "CASH"

The term "cash" includes currency, coin, checks, money orders, wire transfers, credit card receipts, and anything else that is deposited into your bank account. You will either control your cash receipts properly, or you can expect some of that cash to head out the door in one or more of your employees' pockets. Therefore, I would recommend the following policies and procedures be instituted regarding the control of your cash receipts.

1. **IMPORTANT - Mail must be opened by an employee who does not have any direct responsibility for cash, cash deposits, cash disbursements, cash receipts or bank reconciliations**.

2. Then, you must require individual accountability for all cash received or utilized in the business, including cash receipts, and petty cash funds.

3. A pre-numbered company invoice or other receipt for cash, such as a receipt for an accounts receivable payment should be initialed by the person receiving the cash, and transferred to the person responsible for the daily cash reconciliation.

4. Access to cash should be restricted at all times to the person responsible for the daily cash deposit. The person should be provided a lockbox, a safe, or both to ensure that the cash is properly safeguarded.

5. If your daily cash deposit represents a significant amount of money that, from a personnel safety standpoint should not be taken to the bank by an employee, an armored car pickup should be arranged to transfer the cash deposit to the bank. All such transfers should be documented to include the date, the amount of cash transferred, and signatures of the company person and the armored car person involved in the transfer. This documentation should be attached to the deposit reconciliation, along with copies of all checks and other cash items that do not represent coin or currency.

6. If, for any reason a timely deposit cannot be made, any cash ready for deposit must be stored overnight in a safe.

7. Written procedures for receiving, recording, reconciling, safeguarding and depositing cash should be prepared and provided to employees with cash handling responsibilities.

8. Employees assigned cash handling responsibilities should receive on-the-job training regarding company cash policies and procedures from a supervisor, and demonstrate that they are familiar with them before allowing that employee to carry out those responsibilities without assistance.

9. Combinations or keys to safes and other storage facilities should be restricted to the custodian of the cash, a designated backup and the controller. Combinations or locks should be changed as needed, or whenever a person with the combination or key leaves the company. Persons responsible for cash should be instructed to maintain confidentiality of safe combinations

10. Cash receipts should not be used for petty cash disbursements, check cashing, or other purposes.

CREDIT CARDS -- AN EXCUSE FOR ABUSE!

Over the last decade, the number of credit card payments has risen dramatically, and the number of employees engaging in credit card fraud has also substantially increased. Even though this is well documented, you don't see much written about controlling this area of potential abuse. So what can you do to control credit card transactions? I have listed some procedures that should keep your credit card fraud problem to a minimum.

Identify and Secure Credit Card Processing Terminals

1. All credit card processing terminals should be inventoried, listing the department, location, manager in charge of daily use, equipment manufacturer, model number, serial number, and location of

credit card supplies. Any changes must be communicated to your accounting department **before** making them.

2. Make a determination as to the number of terminals required in each department.

3. Secure processing terminals during and after working hours to prevent unauthorized access.

4. Assign an individual password to employees authorized to access credit card terminals. By assigning individual passwords, you can help prevent any unauthorized use of these terminals.

5. If unauthorized use is detected, it should be easy to find out which employee password was used.

Credit Cardholder Information

1. Ensure that accurate and valid credit cardholder information is obtained from the person who is the cardholder. The credit card information required to process the transaction is:
   1) Date and Dollar amount of the transaction
   2) Issuer of the Credit Card, Account number, Card Expiration date and the 3 digit security code on the back of the card.
   3) Signature, if the cardholder is present
   4) Other required information

2. When the cardholder is present, use their actual credit card to obtain the authorization, and then process the transaction.

3. If the credit card or the cardholder is not physically present, this transaction presents a much greater risk of nonpayment to the company and special procedures should be utilized. First, obtain all information and verify that information with an authorization from the credit card processing service. Have the cardholder send you a fax with a signed copy of the invoice authorization, verifying

the credit card transaction for the full amount of the invoice. Also, the cardholder must provide you with copies of the credit card, front and back with a signature, attached to the same fax.

Protecting the Cardholder's Information

Credit card information is obtained either from the cardholder with his credit card at the point-of-sale or by the cardholder transmitting information by fax or e-mail. If credit card information is obtained and recorded for future use, the information should be secured and not accessible to unauthorized individuals. This information, once used, should be stored in a secure facility based on the minimum prescribed retention schedule, unless your business requires a longer retention period, then shredded or destroyed thereafter.

Processing Credit Card Transactions

1. Ensure that only authorized staff can process credit card transactions.

2. Whenever the cardholder is present, process credit card transactions by swiping the credit card. This can save your company over 50% of the transaction cost, as compared with manually processing the transaction.

PROCESSING CREDIT CARD REFUNDS

Credit card refunds are particularly susceptible to employee fraud and other abuse. Therefore, the following procedures must be followed to reduce most of the potential for abuse.

1. All credit card refunds or credits must be approved in writing by management.

2. Whenever possible, the customer should be present when processing a credit. The customer should have the original sales

invoice and the credit card receipt. Exceptions to this requirement can only be made by the department manager in writing.

3. Refunds or credits are to be processed to the original credit card number charged, unless the original credit card no longer exists. Any exceptions to this policy must be approved in writing by both department management and the Controller

AN IMPORTANT OBSERVATION: It has been my experience that most employee credit card fraud is committed by utilizing authorized or unauthorized credit card refunds to post a credit to their own credit card. The employee may also post a credit to the credit card of someone acting in collusion with that employee. Therefore, credit card refunds and other credits require more scrutiny and control than most all other credit card transactions.

DAILY CREDIT CARD BATCH SETTLEMENT PROCESSING AND RECONCILIATIONS

Three summary reports should be available each day that provide the following information for the prior day:

(1) A **Batch Detail Report** which lists a summary of each individual card transaction that comprises the batch total.
(2) A **Batch Settlement Report** which totals the credit card activity by day by card type
(3) A **Batch Summary Report** which includes total dollars of sales, voids, and credits, with the quantity of each type of transaction.

Each manager having a terminal in their department must be required to reconcile a Batch Detail Report that lists each transaction in a summary format. These transactions must be reconciled to the individual credit card transaction slips. Management's review must ensure that all refunds and credits are supported with the required documentation, and have been approved by management. The manager must initial and date the batch report to indicate that their review has been completed. Also, the accounting person designated to reconcile the daily credit card activity must ensure that all activity for the prior day has been posted to the general ledger cash account. Any material discrepancies should be brought to the attention of the controller utilizing the appropriate written form.

MONTHLY CREDIT CARD REPORTING AND RECONCILIATION

Just as a bank account must be reconciled monthly, credit card transactions must also be reconciled on a monthly basis, and agree with the monthly bank statements and the credit card issuer statements. The controller must insure that the monthly Credit Card Reconciliation spreadsheet and the accompanying monthly reconciliation summary is prepared and signed by the controller or his designee. This should be a person who is not involved in the daily review or reconciliation of credit card activity. It is extremely important that this reconciliation of credit card activity be completed on time every month-end and reviewed by management. If this activity is not being completed each month-end, you have no positive control of your credit card activity.

Fraudulent or Suspect Credit Card Transactions

Department management and accounting personnel responsible for daily credit card activity and credit card reconciliations must be required to forward information to the controller if inappropriate or fraudulent credit card activity is suspected, regardless of the source of that activity, unless it involves a controller. In that case the information should be forwarded to the company president. Additionally, the controller must analyze any and all accounting information pertinent to the fraudulent or inappropriate transactions, and identify any employees or others who are involved with those transactions in any way.

PETTY CASH DISBURSEMENTS

Control of Petty Cash Disbursements - One of the most significant areas of currency disbursements that are not well controlled in a small business are the petty cash funds. There is only one way to properly control a petty cash fund as follows:

A. Ensure that only one employee has overall responsibility and access to the petty cash box.

B. When a request is made for petty cash fund reimbursement, the petty cash fund should be reconciled as follows:

1. Count the petty cash box to be reconciled, including cash, checks received, petty cash vouchers, and other miscellaneous items, if any.

2. Reconcile petty cash vouchers with the petty cash spreadsheet.

3. Examine the petty cash vouchers, reviewing signatures, amounts, explanations and account number distributions.

4. Check the petty cash spreadsheet addition totals.

5. After the petty cash reconciliation has been completed, insure that the petty cash reimbursement journal has been properly posted to the general ledger.

Petty Cash Time-saving Tip - Consider using a petty cash envelope with a preprinted reconciliation form on the front side. You can use the envelope to hold all of the petty cash disbursement receipts; and any checks received which have necessitated a petty cash disbursement.

OTHER CASH DISBURSEMENTS

Control of Other Cash Disbursements - You may be surprised to learn that many cash disbursements, including large amounts, are not check or currency related. Some of these include automated bank charges and payments, wire transfers and ACH debits which are usually related to tax payments. There are also checks that are one-time vendor payments and Cash on Delivery (COD) payments. Because it would be very time-consuming to set up vendor information for these kinds of payments, generally they are not posted to and paid through the accounts payable system.

One time check payments should be processed as follows:

1. Purchase orders or cash disbursement requests must be initiated for all one time check payments.

2. Packing slips for COD purchases must be signed for by the warehouse person or other employee who has received the goods.

3. Purchase orders for COD purchases must be matched with packing slips and/or invoices by the department that receives the goods and forwarded to Accounts Payable for payment.

4. Process all one time payments by inputting the vendor's name and invoice number. A unique invoice number incorporating the date of the invoice and a portion of the vendor name should be created in the event that there is no invoice number available on the invoice.

5. The invoice should contain a complete description of the items purchased, and each item's cost extended to a total column must appear on vendor invoices to process the order for payment.

6. The Accounts Payable person must ensure that a properly signed and authorized cash disbursement request with all supporting

documentation accompany any one time payment request before actually processing the check.

7. All one-time disbursements should be filed alphabetically by payee name by year. If it becomes evident that certain one-time vendors are being paid periodically, those vendors should be set up in the Accounts Payable master file, and from that point in time normal Accounts Payable procedures should be applied to that vendor.

Control of ACH payments and other wire or electronic transfers: The nature of these electronic transactions is that they are usually initiated by an authorized company officer in accordance with the bank's record of employees authorized to initiate electronic transfers. Dollar limits on any one transaction are also on file with the bank. Because these transactions generally involve only one employee, and are only recorded in the ledger when that employee initiates a journal entry, it is relatively easy for that employee to fraudulently transfer money to their account, or to accounts under their control. Unless the company has an on-line reporting system with their bank, receiving those reports electronically on a daily basis, the company might not know that a fraudulent transfer has occurred until the month-end bank reconciliation has been performed. Therefore, since these transactions are particularly dangerous, it is critically important that safeguards be in place to help prevent fraudulent transactions from occurring. Keep in mind that no control system yet invented can absolutely stop a dishonest employee from committing fraud. However, with the proper control system, you can make it much more difficult for that fraud to be committed. You will also be able to detect a fraudulent transaction much more quickly if your system controls and reporting are in place and are actively being followed. Therefore, the following controls are highly recommended to safeguard electronic bank transactions:

1. There must be at least 2 individuals authorized by the bank to make non-check cash disbursements such as inter-account money transfers, ACH debits and wire transfers.

2. The individuals authorized to make transfers must have separate passwords.

3. Maximum allowable individual transfer limits must be set up with the bank.

4. Any telephone transfers exceeding a predetermined dollar amount must require bank call back verification requiring two authorized individuals to approve the transaction.

5. A written authorization form indicating the date of the transfer, the amount of the transfer, the payee name, the payee bank account and bank account number, the reason for the transfer, company ledger account numbers, and other information deemed appropriate to the transaction, should be completed and signed by the controller and any other individual authorizing the transaction.

6. This information should be posted to the general ledger by the controller or his designee. A copy of the posting journal should be given to the employee responsible for bank reconciliations.

BANK ACCOUNT RECONCILIATIONS

Bank Account Reconciliation Procedures - The following procedures should be utilized by the employee performing your bank reconciliations.

1. Reconcile all bank accounts to their month-end ledger balances.

2. Verify all transfers to payroll and other bank accounts.

3. Verify all credit card transactions as part of the credit card reconciliation previously discussed.

4. Confirm your ledger bank balances to bank statement balances.

5. Confirm the details of any deposits in transit and insure that these items have been credited on the next bank statement.

6. Verify that all reconciling items from the prior bank reconciliation have cleared.

7. Account for all check numbers in the monthly check disbursement report.

8. Prepare a list of checks outstanding at end of the month.

9. Examine check signatures and endorsements periodically.

10. Voided checks should be supported by documentation stating the reason for the void. The documentation should also include the initials of the employee voiding the check.

11. Ideally, the employee charged with the responsibility of performing bank reconciliations should not be involved with daily cash receipts or disbursements.

12. Complete a bank reconciliation form, which begins with the month-end ledger closing bank balance, and details all of the reconciling items to balance to the month-end closing bank balance. All supporting detail for the reconciling items should be attached to the bank reconciliation form.

13. Instruct your controller to review and initial all bank and credit card reconciliations.

A potential overdraft problem - **My bank account cash balances are positive but my book ledger cash account balance is in the red (Negative). Why is there such a difference?**

1. Your bank account balance does not include checks that are outstanding, but will clear the bank in the next several days. The

total amount of outstanding checks can vary from approximately $100,000 to well over $1 million dollars, depending on your company's size and type of business. This amount is the principal component of your "float".

2. Recent ACH transfers within the last 24 hours have not been processed by the bank.

3. Other electronic funds transfers within the last 24 hours have not been processed by the bank. Items one through three can represent a substantial amount of money.

4. Your ledger bank account has not been properly reconciled.

5. Total cash on your financial statement contains account(s) other than cash.

NOTE: Be aware that the aggregated cash accounts shown on financial statements as "cash" sometimes contain accounts other than actual cash in the bank. Ensure that you know exactly what you're looking at, and have your controller reclassify any non-cash accounts to other classifications.

READ AND HEED: It is extremely important that all bank and credit card reconciliations be completed and posted before the monthly financial statements are finalized.

SUMMARY

This chapter stresses the importance of protecting your cash and cash equivalents such as credit cards from theft and internal fraud. I have covered three other important areas; maximizing your earnings with a bank sweep account, obtaining needed cash quickly with a bank line of credit, and protecting your sweep account from going into an overdraft position at your bank by tying your sweep account to your line of credit. Obviously, it is also very important to have accurate and timely reporting of monthly cash and credit card reconciliations, and other daily reports. These reconciliation reports and the attendant follow-up are your best defense against credit card fraud and misappropriation of cash. They will also give you a true picture of your actual cash position at month-end.

CHAPTER 52

CONTROL AND COLLECTION OF ACCOUNTS RECEIVABLE

ACCOUNTS RECEIVABLE - CONTROL AND REPORTING

Written accounts receivable credit policies and procedures are absolutely mandatory in order to control the application for and authorization of new credit accounts, to establish credit limits on those accounts, to set payment and collection policies, and to outline the actions to be taken in case of nonpayment as follows:

SETTING UP A NEW CUSTOMER ACCOUNT

Credit control starts at the front door. If you process your new customer accounts properly, you will substantially reduce your credit risk as follows:

1. A New Account Application must be completed for every customer applying for credit.

2. Unless the business customer meets predetermined credit standards (such as a Dunn & Bradstreet credit rating of 3A2 or better, which signifies a customer having over $1 million in net worth and with a good credit rating), you should get a credit rating report from a third-party provider such as Dun & Bradstreet (D&B).

3. Collect all the credit information that you need to make an informed credit decision along with a recommendation from your Accounts

Receivable person. The controller or other designated manager will then make the decision to extend credit to the customer and set an appropriate credit limit reflective of that customer's business volume and ability to pay.

4. A computerized account should be set up and contain, at minimum, the customers name, address, work phone, fax phone, cellular phone, contact names, authorized purchasers, credit limit, and other special instructions.

5. A letter should be sent to the customer welcoming the company or individual as a new credit customer and stating the customer's credit limit, your company's credit policies. Also include the company contact person and phone number to be called by the customer in the event of a billing problem.

A CUSTOMER RELATIONS IDEA - *You can use this opportunity to invite your new customer to visit your location and meet your management team. Plan to give your customer a reason to increase their business with you during that meeting. A small gift, such as a service discount or a special promotional coupon will show your new customers that you appreciate their business.*

ADMINISTERING CUSTOMER CREDIT ACCOUNTS

Administrative control of customer accounts is a continuing process and obligation throughout the life of the account. The following is a list of general procedures that will assist in the process of controlling the credit account, and safeguarding the customer information attached to that account.

1. As a result of the rather infamous Sarbanes-Oxley Act and other regulations that safeguard customer information, we must ensure among other things that our computer system is protected from unauthorized employees, hackers and other outside incursions.

2. Access to customer information files must be safeguarded and limited to authorized personnel only

3. Access to the company's accounts receivable computer system software must be limited to authorized personnel only.

4. Returns, allowances, discounts and any other customer credits must be approved before issuance by an authorized employee who does not handle cash or accounts receivables.

5. Customer credit invoices must be issued for returned merchandise or services not performed, and supported by proper documentation signed by the receiver of the returned merchandise.

6. Customer complaints should be investigated by a person not responsible for the accounts receivable function.

7. The Accounts Receivable person should not be involved in bank reconciliations.

8. Customer account statements must be sent to the customers monthly as soon after the month-end as possible and mailed by an employee not involved with accounts receivable processing.

An inexpensive advertising idea - When you mail out your customer statements each month, you have an excellent opportunity to include advertising material such as promotional items, discounts and coupon specials at no additional cost for the mailing. Since these items will be included in your statement envelope, your only cost will be the cost of the mailer itself, usually amounting to only a few pennies for each item. It is amazing to me that only a few companies take advantage of this monthly opportunity to advertise to their existing customer base, or use this low cost opportunity to communicate other matters of importance to their customers.

Reporting on delinquent customer accounts - Computerized summary aged accounts receivable reports can be produced on demand, and copies should be made available to each participant in the biweekly Accounts Receivable meeting. In addition, a detailed item report should be available in that meeting for every account that is delinquent (in most companies, defined as over 30 to 60 days old). Also, any delinquent customer notes, written communication or other information, whether computerized or handwritten, should be made available to the meeting participants. All accounts that contain credit balances should be analyzed at least once a month as part of the controller's statement review.

Collecting past due receivable accounts - There is both an art and a science involved in the collection of past due customer accounts. We will discuss first the procedural aspect of past due account collection as follows:

1. Customer receivable past due accounts must be reviewed regularly, and in no case less than twice a month.

2. A member of senior management such as the controller, the president or the general manager should participate in the Accounts Receivable (A/R) review process.

3. Past due or delinquent accounts or unusual items must be investigated in a timely manner.

4. A process must be in place to ensure the collection of past due receivable accounts. This should include the following items:

    A. A courteous form letter that inquires as to the reason for nonpayment of the overdue items, and makes a formal request for payment as of a specific date.

    B. If the items are not promptly paid, a telephone call to the customer or their designated representative should be initiated by the A/R person to ascertain any problems with the invoices, and the status of any payments promised, to include the amount, check number and date of the check being sent.

C. If the account remains delinquent, a 10 day demand letter should be sent by certified mail, return receipt requested, summarizing the action the company will take if payment is not received by a specific date and time. If a payment has been made in the interim, request that your customers include the amount, check number and date of the payment(s) in their response.

5. If the account is still delinquent after these actions, a decision by management is necessary to either send the account to the company attorney, or send the account to a collections agency for collection.

6. Occasionally, some customer accounts are incapable of collection for various reasons. The customer may have gone bankrupt, the company may not be able to locate the customer, or the debt may be small enough that it is not worth pursuing. In this case, the account should be written off to bad debts expense or a reserve account by the controller or an accounting manager not directly related to the Accounts Receivable function.

7 Appropriate documentation should be filed with the customer account and retained after the debt is written off. Some states allow a sales tax credit to be taken based on the original sales tax charge to the delinquent customer. Additionally, future credit should be refused to any customer with a delinquent account or an account that has been written off because of nonpayment.

8. In order to smooth out the effect of bad debt write-offs (the specific write-off method), you may consider setting up an allowance for uncollectible accounts (the bad debts reserve method). To facilitate that method, you have to determine your yearly bad debt expense

total, divide that amount by 12, and expense the result monthly to Bad Debts Expense with a corresponding credit to a Reserve for Bad Debts account. The balance in the reserve account should be analyzed each quarter for adequacy.

A money saving idea that will significantly boost your overdue account collections

I indicated above that monthly customer statements could be utilized as a mailer to advertise directly to the active customer base at little or no cost. A computer generated past due account letter which should be sent to all customers that have delinquent accounts can easily be inserted into your monthly customer statements before mailing. Of course, any letters that you don't want sent to sensitive customers can be sorted out before the letters are inserted in the statement envelope. I would suggest a courteous and personalized letter that indicates the status of the account, the delinquent amount, and a request for a follow-up phone call to the designated Accounts Receivable employee. The cost of making this written contact with all of your delinquent accounts that you choose to include with your month-end statements is negligible! Make no mistake about it, this is a low cost, high results way of collecting your delinquent accounts receivable.

AN EXAMPLE OF HOW TO SIGNIFICANTLY REDUCE THE PERCENTAGE OF DELINQUENT ACCOUNTS OVER 60 DAYS OLD

When I assumed responsibility for the Accounts Receivable as part of my overall administrative duties, over half of the receivables were 60 days past due. In addition, at least half of the customer receivable accounts were in need of reconciliation. Even when the customer balances were correct, the A/R statement contained numerous internal errors that had to be offset. I immediately began to prioritize our overdue customer contacts based on the amount of money that was overdue. I quickly recognized that the total customer A/R reconciliation work required to correct all of the accounts would consume too much time to do all at once. So I reconciled the customer account any time that a payment had to be applied to the account. Over a period of several months, I was able to reconcile and adjust all of the A/R accounts that were out of balance as part of the daily application of cash payments. I was then able to utilize a computer-generated letter making a demand for payment which was addressed to all past due accounts and mailed out with the Accounts Receivable statement. At that point, the A/R person had much more confidence in the company's bookkeeping accuracy, and therefore became more aggressive in their collection efforts. Within one year, we were able to reduce the overdue customer receivable account percentage to less than 10%. Within two years, we further reduced the 60 days past due percentage to less than 3%.

SUMMARY

The timely collection of your customer accounts receivable is a high priority Key Result Area that keeps cash flowing into your company. By following the procedures listed in this chapter, you can substantially reduce your delinquent accounts receivable and increase your cash flow. Also, see my Chapter on "KEY RESULT AREAS".

CHAPTER 53

CONTROL OF INVENTORY

HOW DO YOU VALUE YOUR INVENTORY?

In most businesses, inventory comprises a substantial portion of your current assets. It is truly surprising that more attention is not paid to this important asset. You must first determine how your inventory is being valued. The most common inventory valuation method is first in, first out, also called FIFO. This method assumes that your oldest inventory item is sold first. Consequently, this valuation method is based on the cost of the item at or near the date of last purchase. This method should produce a total valuation that approximates the current cost of all your inventory items. However, there are several problem areas regarding valuation of inventory that you will have to specifically address with your sales manager, general manager and inventory manager. This should be done in a formalized manner at month-end as this can be easily reconciled with the month-end general ledger account balance. There are four major inventory valuation problems that I have addressed below:

1. The first valuation problem area to be addressed is **Obsolete Inventory**. Good examples of this type of inventory are older computers and computer related parts. Generally speaking, if inventory cannot be sold or is not being sold currently or is not supported by the manufacturer any longer, it is by definition obsolete. This inventory should be valued at or near its salvage value, if any.

What to do about Obsolete Inventory. Determine if there is any demand for this inventory by suppliers, rebuilders or local outlets. If there is, determine the price and sell it to reduce your inventory. This will save you shelf space, inventory carrying costs and if you are in the maximum tax bracket, your corporate tax will be reduced by 34% of the write-down amount. Ask your manufacturer if they have any special return programs for obsolete or outdated inventory. If an item has a core credit associated with it, contact the manufacturer, supplier, or rebuilder to see if the core qualifies for a return.

2. The second valuation problem area is **Damaged Inventory**. All damaged inventory that can be sold within a reasonable period of time should be written down to a realistic carrying cost and sold at a discount.

What to do with Damaged Inventory. If the inventory item is damaged beyond repair, consider aggregating these items, selling them for salvage or scrapping them, and filing an insurance claim. If the damage is mainly cosmetic or relating to packaging, reduce the selling price of the item by an appropriate amount and sell it as soon as possible. Again, I can't stress this too much, if the item is a part with an undamaged core, contact the manufacturer, supplier, or rebuilder to see if the core qualifies for a return. Your core credit may well exceed the reduced selling price of the item!

3. The third problem area usually not addressed in the inventory valuation process is non-moving or **Stagnant Inventory**. This represents inventory has not sold within company defined limits. This time frame would normally fall between 90 days and 360 days, depending on the industry, the cost of the inventory item, and the type of inventory. Stagnant or non-moving inventory will generally not be written off if it can be returned to the manufacturer or the supplier. However, we should write down or reserve the amount of stagnant inventory by a factor of 15 to 30%, depending upon the average restocking charge of the manufacturer or supplier. Then, make arrangements to return these items as soon as possible.

This could be done as part of your next supplier approved inventory return. Your task does not end upon the return of these items. You must also compare the return shipment supplier credit to the dollar value of the return shipment, report the difference to accounting and have it posted to inventory general ledger account.

4. The fourth problem area to be addressed is that of **Missing or Lost Inventory**. Of course, you can't record a loss on missing or lost inventory unless you have taken a current physical inventory. Once the inventory has been taken, you can write off the entire amount of the loss on physical inventory and save 34% of that amount on your corporate tax estimate.

What to do about physical inventory losses. Physical inventories should be taken at least once a year, as part of the company's year-end procedures. If you have experienced a substantial loss when a physical inventory is taken, I would recommend taking inventory quarterly until such time as this loss is within reasonable limits. Also consider taking cycle counts, which is another name for expanded bin checks. Ensure that these limited counts are taken several times a month. Any count differences must be reported to management and accounting, and posted to the inventory general ledger account.

IS THERE NEEDED CASH HIDING IN YOUR INVENTORY!

If you adopt the procedures defined above regarding obsolete, damaged, or stagnant inventory, and inventory shrinkage, you will be pleasantly surprised to see the amount of extra cash and decreased income tax liability that is generated by implementing this process. Among other things, you can now afford to purchase at a discount more of the fast moving inventory that your customers are buying, and you now have the space to stock it. That should allow you to stock more saleable products without having to generate any additional cash to purchase inventory!

THE INVENTORY MYTHOLOGY: JUST-IN-TIME INVENTORY VERSUS PURCHASE DISCOUNTS

There is a common misconception held by managers, probably dating back to the high interest rates of the late 1970s and early 1980s, that excess fast moving inventory is very costly to stock. I would like to debunk this inventory mythology and update it to current times. For example, let's say that you stock and sell air-conditioners in Phoenix, Arizona. Typically, you sell $700,000 of air-conditioners and air-conditioner parts during April through September of each year, as they are a seasonal item. You are offered a 10% discount by your vendor on all air-conditioners and air-conditioner parts if you purchase those by March 31st. How much stock should you purchase, if the space to store the additional inventory is not a factor and the opportunity cost of your excess funds is 6% per annum? Depending upon your cash availability, all of the $700,000 should be purchased at a discount.

Your cost of funds is computed as follows:

1. **Compute the average number of months that the balance is outstanding:**
    Six months (April through September) divided by 2, assuming sales are equal for the six-month period, gives us an average balance of 3 months on the entire purchase amount of $700,000.

2. **Compute the cost of holding the excess inventory:**
    Take the average number of months, in this case three divided by 12, times your opportunity cost of 6%, times $700,000. This holding cost totals $10,500. (3/12 = .25 x .06 x $700,000)

3. **Subtract the computed holding cost from the amount of the purchase discount:**
    Subtract the computed holding cost of $10,500 from the amount of the discount, which is 10% times $700,000, amounting to

$70,000. The difference is $59,500, which is your net savings on the purchase. ($700,000 x .10 = $70,000 - $10,500 = $59,500)

I'm sure you'll agree there's no comparison! There are at least two ways to make money. One is to sell high, and the other is to buy low. When you have an opportunity to negotiate a substantial discount on purchases of fast-moving items, assuming that you have cash available to make the purchases and the warehouse area to store them in, make the simple computation above, and start buying at a discount. However, I wouldn't purchase more than a six-month supply of fast-moving inventory in any one category, unless the discount was extremely attractive and you were sure you would be able to sell the entire discounted inventory within the estimated time period.

THE NEGATIVE RESULTS OF UNMANAGED INVENTORY

When I joined this company as a Chief Financial Officer, our inventory ledger balance was $865,000. This amount of inventory should have been more than sufficient for a company of our size to service its customers. Our inventory was scheduled to be taken in another 45 days, so I printed a no-bin report (a part without a bin location). The report disclosed that we had 21,000 parts on hand, and of those, only six thousand parts showed a bin location. This situation was totally out of control, and without swift remedial action, inventory taking would have been a practical impossibity. I strongly encouraged the parts manager to enter bin numbers into the parts master file over the next six weeks. By the time we were scheduled to take inventory, we had 15,000 parts with bin numbers and 6,000 parts without bin numbers. Certainly, this was far from an ideal situation for taking inventory when the first 110 pages of our physical inventory count report had no bin number attached to the parts. We began that inventory on a Thursday evening, and did not finish until Monday morning at about 3:00 a.m. The net value of our physical inventory totaled $730,000. We had to reduce our general ledger inventory account by $135,000 and post an equal amount to our physical inventory loss account! To add insult to injury, we did not even have a profit for that year to offset the amount of this loss.

Upon examining quality of this inventory which was now valued at $730,000, I discovered that only $250,000 of this inventory was selling with any degree of frequency (At least one sale in the last 12 months). The remainder of this inventory, $480,000 had not sold within the last two years and could be classified as stagnant or obsolete inventory. I knew then why we didn't have sufficient inventory to satisfy our customer's needs. We required an active inventory of at least $750,000 to accommodate our customer's purchases. Years of neglect had created a situation where we only had about one third of the active inventory required to properly service our customers. In order to return this stagnant inventory to the manufacturer, we had to overcome several complications.$280,000 of the stagnant inventory was not eligible for a return. In addition, we were limited to an annual return of 8% of our yearly inventory purchases for those parts which were eligible for return. I arranged to participate in a special return program that allowed us to return, over a period of several years, all of the ineligible stagnant inventory balance of $280,000 without any deduction or restocking charge. In the next few years, we were also able to return $200,000 of the parts that were eligible for return. We had to pay a 15% restocking charge of 15%, or $30,000, for those returns. During this same time period, we were able to increase our active inventory to an amount in excess of $840,000 and were in a much better position to service our customer requirements. Also, another significant advantage resulting from better inventory control over time was the reduction in the number of our active inventory parts from 21,000 to just over 7,000. This enabled us to reduce the number of parts in our inventory by 14,000, eliminate a parts clerical position and save about $40,000 per year in personnel costs.

BIN CHECKS AND CYCLE COUNTS, WHAT ARE THEY?

All inventory items for sale must have a bin or location number entered in the inventory master file. As an illustration, to perform a bin check, all item numbers from bin 100 to bin 110 would be listed. The list would display at a minimum, the bin number, the item number, the item description, and the quantity on hand. Assuming an average of 10 items per bin, there would be 100 items on the list to count. This could easily be done by the swing shift or the night shift person in their spare time. A cycle count is generally done the same way. However cycle counts will include a lot more bins based on different selection criteria.

CREATING A SCHEDULE TO PERFORM CYCLE COUNTS

In order to effectively schedule interim inventory counts, your inventory bins must be designated as containing fast, medium, or slow moving items. You may want to count your fast moving items 4 to 6 times each year, your medium moving items 2 to 4 times each year, and your slow moving items 1 to 2 times each year in addition to your annual physical inventory. Therefore, it is necessary to create an inventory bin layout showing the location of all bins, a description of the number and kinds of items in those bins, and the speed of inventory movement of those bins. After creating your inventory bin layout, you need to design a schedule that will allow you to count all of your bins as determined by their movement speed designation during the year.

THE BENEFITS OF COMPLETING REGULAR BIN CHECKS

There are many benefits that will accrue to your company when you regularly schedule inventory bin checks. Among these benefits are:

1. It substantially improves the accuracy of your day-to-day perpetual inventory. This improved accuracy will assist your sales persons to better service your customers.
2. It allows you to more accurately determine when you have had an inventory loss.

3. It allows you to order more accurately, thus saving money and ensuring that you have the items on hand that your customers are buying.
4. It should enable you to more easily track and find the causative factors that have created any physical inventory loss. Most likely, this will lead to uncovering employee theft, sloppy record keeping, or both.
5. And last, but not least, let's not forget the theft deterrent factor. When your employees know that you are counting your inventory frequently, they are much less likely to develop "sticky fingers".

SUMMARY

Unless you are electing **LIFO,** the **L**ast **I**n **F**irst **O**ut inventory valuation method for tax purposes, you should be using the **FIFO** inventory valuation for book purposes. The **F**irst **I**n **F**irst **O**ut method will give you a true picture of your inventory valuation after you have written down or written off any impaired inventory. Inventory carrying cost should be adjusted to market value when the inventory item is determined to be obsolete, damaged or stagnant and not selling. You should have already written off your entire missing or lost inventory as part of your inventory cycle counts and your annual physical inventory. *When you have identified impaired or stagnant inventory that can't be returned to the manufacturer or supplier for credit, you should turn it into cash as soon as possible by reducing the selling price to a level where it will sell. I guarantee you that stagnant or impaired inventory will not become more valuable sitting on the shelf and taking up valuable space!*

CHAPTER 54

ACCOUNTS PAYABLE CONTROL AND REPORTING

Accounts payable (A/P) are a form of short-term credit, usually not longer than 60 days, that your suppliers or vendors offer to your company by allowing you to pay for a product or service after it has been invoiced and received. This is an important form of credit for your company in these difficult times. The amount can be determined by the balance in your general ledger accounts payable account at month-end. When your vendor invoice arrives it is matched to the packing slip and purchase order, and if all is in order, the invoice is paid. This is commonly referred to as a three-way match. To properly track accounts payable, record your invoices and credits, and make payments to your vendors, you must have a computerized accounts payable system. Your A/P system will help you to accurately record these transactions, keep track of them, and prevent duplicate or erroneous payments. **It has been my experience that less than 50% of small companies properly record and reconcile their accounts payable, leading to numerous errors in payments of invoices, and Credit Memos.** Credit Memos are receivables from your vendors and suppliers payable to your company that sometimes never get processed or collected!

SETTING UP A NEW VENDOR ACCOUNT

Many fraudulent schemes have involved payments to nonexistent vendors, or actual vendors who are in collusion with company employees. To substantially reduce fraudulent vendor payments, you must control potential new vendor authorizations at the front door before the vendor account is actually set up in the computer system master A/P file.

1. If you already have an A/P system in place, request a vendor master file listing and analyze it for suspicious vendors. These are vendors that you don't know or have not done business with in the past, or have suspicious addresses, telephone numbers, or contact persons in the vendor master listing.

2. Require that a new vendor information form be initiated by the manager requesting vendor credit, and be approved by you, the controller or the general manager.

3. Require that the following information be provided on the new vendor information form:
   a) The vendor name and address and telephone/fax/e-mail numbers.
   b) The goods and services that this vendor will provide.
   c) The payment terms for this vendor.
   d) The overall credit limit for this vendor.
   e) Company personnel authorized to charge for purchases from this vendor.
   f) Vendor contact person's names, telephone and cellular numbers.
   g) Special instructions, if any

4. If the new vendor information form has been approved, the vendor will probably require a credit request form from the company. This form will include most of the information listed above. If this is not the case, send a letter to the new vendor listing the payment terms, credit limit, and company personnel authorized to charge for purchases.

5. Assign the new vendor a vendor number and input the new vendor information in the A/P vendor master file.

6. Inform all appropriate employees that the new vendor number has been set up and is ready for use.

7. Update your vendor information file periodically with new or changed information and, if appropriate, communicate that updated information to employees authorized to charge on this account.

ADMINISTERING ACCOUNTS PAYABLE VENDOR ACCOUNTS

Administrative control of A/P accounts is a continuing process and obligation throughout the life of the account. The following is a list of general procedures that will assist in controlling the account and the vendor information attached to that account.

1. Purchase orders must be initiated for all vendor accounts that are not fixed payments such as vehicle installment payments, mortgage payments, contract payments such as property lease payments, insurance payments, taxes, utility payments and other periodic payments that simply have to be made on time.

2. Packing slips must be signed for by the warehouse person or other employee who has received the goods.

3. Purchase orders must be matched with packing slips and invoices by the department that receives the items and forwarded to Accounts Payable for payment.

4. All vendor invoices must be input by using either the vendor's invoice number or creating a unique invoice number in the event that no invoice number is available.

5. The invoice should contain a complete description of items purchased, and each item's cost extended to a total column must appear on vendor invoices to process the invoice for payment.

6. The Accounts Payable person must apply any unused credit memos for that vendor to any invoices set up for payment. Credits received, where there are no open invoices to be offset against, will be sent to the vendor with a request for prompt payment.

7. If there is a need to stop payment on a vendor check, department managers should notify the Controller immediately by phone and then submit a stop payment notice in writing. This notice must be signed by the manager and must explain why the payment should be withheld. Additional written notification will also be required to reschedule a payment.

8. Prior to any vendor payment being made for the prior month, the Accounts Payable person must reconcile each vendor statement with the accounts payable vendor detailed balance report to ensure the accuracy of the amount to be paid. Any invoice or credit memo differences should be researched. Requests should be sent to the vendors to identify any such charges or credit memos and copies of this information should be sent to the Accounts Payable person when received. Accounts Payable should determine the status of any unprocessed items within forty-five days. This will enable them to pay valid invoices within a 60 day time frame. On the other hand, if the vendor charges are in error, the vendor should issue a credit memo for the invoices that are either eliminated or reduced in amount before payment is made.

9. A Check Disbursement Request Form must be completed prior to processing the check, and must accompany the check along with all of the supporting documentation when sent to the check signers for signature. The Form must be signed by the requesting manager, have an authorized signature approval, and must show the following minimum information:

    a. Payee's full name and vendor number, if any.
    b. Account number to be charged.
    c. A description of item(s) purchased.

d. The purpose of the expenditure.

e. Adequate instructions for disbursement of the check to the vendor must be included (mail to payee, return to the department manager, hold for vendor pickup or other instructions.)

A MONEYMAKING IDEA - NEGOTIATE A PROMPT PAYMENT DISCOUNT WITH YOUR VENDORS

- You may be able to negotiate a discount of 1 or 2% of the invoice amount with your vendors for prompt payment, usually within 10 days of the invoice date. This assumes that you have the cash available to make these payments early. Although 1 to 2% doesn't sound like much, over the period of a year, this can amount to a total of $10,000 to $50,000 or more, depending on the size of your business. Keep in mind that this prompt payment discount does not have anything to do with other purchase discounts already negotiated. It simply adds to the total amount of the discount.

ANOTHER MONEYMAKING IDEA THAT WILL INSURE COOPERATION FROM YOUR ACCOUNTS PAYBLE PERSON IN NEGOTIATING VENDOR DISCOUNTS

It has been said that you can't develop a meaningful incentive program for your accounts payable position. I disagree and will give you the following simplified incentive program for accounts payable that will work to the benefit of the company and incentivize the Accounts Payable person to achieve the highest amount of vendor prompt payment discounts possible as follows:

1. If you don't already have one, set up a general ledger account number that will allow you to track all of your prompt payment discounts.

2. Set up a bonus program for your Accounts Payable person that will pay, on a quarterly basis, 5% to 10% of the prompt payment discounts posted during the quarter.

You will notice substantial positive results at the end of the first or second quarter that this incentive program is in effect. We achieved a prompt payment discount savings of well over $50,000 the first year that this program was instituted. And, our Accounts Payable person realized an incentive bonus of over $5,000! This is another win/win idea that you, your vendors and your Accounts Payable person will love.

SUMMARY

By following the procedures outlined above you can control your Accounts Payable so that only authorized vendors are set up, and only authorized invoices get paid on time to those vendors for the correct amount. You can also negotiate terms and prompt payment discounts with your vendors and share a percentage of those prompt payment discounts with your Accounts Payable person. Don't allow yourself to be placed in the same category as many other companies. Unfortunately for them, they don't know who they are paying, what invoices they are paying, how many times they have paid it, and what credits or discounts they may be entitled to that they have not yet received!

CHAPTER 55

FIXED ASSET MANAGEMENT & CONTROL

WHAT ARE "FIXED ASSETS"

Fixed Assets are assets that singly or as a group, have a cost that exceeds a predetermined amount, are used in your business, and have a useful life that exceeds one year. Land is one of the few Fixed Assets that is not depreciated and is generally shown at its purchase cost. Most all other Fixed Assets, such as buildings and equipment are depreciated, or expensed over the productive life of the asset to a salvage value, if any. I would recommend that any asset under $1,000 in cost be expensed in your current year. Likewise, any asset that has a productive life less than 12 months should be written off over the number of months of expected use. This will eliminate the unnecessary paperwork involved in tracking and depreciating small dollar value assets. This decision has nothing to do with the expected life of the asset. For example, an outside concrete cigarette butt receptacle filled with sand may last the life of the building, but its cost may not exceed $150. Write it off to expense!

PROCEDURES FOR PURCHASING FIXED ASSETS

1. This procedure will not apply to the purchase of fixed assets less than the $1,000 cost threshold above. However, it will apply to assets costing over $1,000 with a productive life more than 1 year.

2. A committee should be established to approve fixed asset purchases, consisting of the President, General Manager and the CFO or controller.

3. A Fixed Asset Requisition Form should be developed and contain the following information:
   a. Item description
   b. Item cost
   c. Reason for purchase
   d. Item department and location
   e. Fixed Asset Account Number
   f. Estimated monthly payment, if financed
   g. Estimated annual depreciation expense
   h. Estimated salvage value, if any
   i. Estimated useful life of the asset
   j. Preferred Vendor if any, and a reason for the preference
   k. Requirement for 3 quotes or bids to be attached to the Requisition Form, unless there is a special situation pre-approved by the committee.
   l. The Department Manager's name, signature and date are required on the Requisition Form before submission.

A Fixed Asset Requisition system, along with your Fixed Assets Committee, effectively places the control of your Fixed Asset purchases where it belongs, right up front!

PROCEDURES FOR ORDERING AND RECORDING FIXED ASSET PURCHASES AFTER APPROVAL

Prior to ordering and paying for the Fixed Asset, the following procedures should be followed.

1. A Purchase Order should be initiated for the Fixed Asset purchase and signed by the department manager with an approved Fixed Asset Requisition attached. Copies should be sent to Accounts Payable.

2. When the Fixed Asset is received by the department, the packing slip should be initialed by the department manager

and sent to Accounts Payable with a copy of the Purchase Order.

3. Invoices will be received by the Accounts Payable person who will attach the Fixed Asset Requisition Form, Purchase Order, and Packing Slip to the Invoice and forward it to the Controller for account coding and entry into the Fixed Asset Control and Tracking System.

4. The Controller or his designee will insure that a metallic, sequentially numbered label is placed in a conspicuous location on the Fixed Asset and record the Fixed Asset information in the software tracking system.

PROCEDURES FOR TAKING AN ANNUAL FIXED ASSET INVENTORY

1. The Controller should forward an inventory worksheet to each department manager, listing all the departmental tagged assets in sequential order. Fixed Asset Physical Inventory Instructions should be attached to the worksheets. A member of the fixed asset committee should observe the physical inventory.

2. After the completion of the Fixed Asset Physical Inventory, the Controller will be responsible for completing a reconciliation of physical differences in the count compared with the inventory worksheet.

3. The Controller should immediately report any lost, stolen or misplaced assets to the department manager and the Fixed Asset Committee.

4. A reasonable attempt should be made to find out what happened to the lost or stolen assets and why they were not better secured. Any misplaced assets should either be returned to the original department or recorded in the department of use.

SUMMARY

All of these procedures may seem to be quite a lot to digest, but it's the only way you will establish firm control of your Fixed Assets. You will save money by purchasing only those assets that have been approved for purchase. You will also save money by purchasing those assets at the best price possible. Finally, you will reduce pilferage to a minimum, because everyone in your company will know that you are tagging, counting, and controlling your fixed assets.

SECTION 10

CHANGE MANAGEMENT, SUMMARY & FORECAST

CHAPTER 56

MANAGING CHANGE

One of our founding fathers, Ben Franklin, has been quoted as saying *"The definition of insanity is doing the same thing over and over and expecting different results."* Currently, the question is not whether you are going to experience change, but how well you will manage it. There are a number of change agents, both internal and external, that will affect you as a small business owner. You will have to successfully manage these changes and insure that your requirements for change do not spiral out of control. The good news is that this is one area where small businesses have a decided advantage. Small businesses by their very nature are more innovative and flexible, and can respond to change and innovation much more quickly than larger companies.

EXTERNAL AND INTERNAL SOURCES OF CHANGE

There are many sources that mandate change, both internal to your organization and from external sources. We will cover the external change agents first.

EXTERNAL CHANGE AGENTS

1. **Governmental** – You can compile quite a listing of governmental sources of change, particularly if you are doing business in multiple states and jurisdictions. I have listed some of the more important governmental agencies below.
   A. Federal Agencies such as the IRS, the Department of Labor (DOL), and OSHA.

B. State Agencies such as the Department of Corporations, State Income and Sales Tax Agencies, and State Licensing Boards.

C. Counties and Cities may duplicate state agencies listed above. In addition they will have their own zoning and building codes to consider.

An example of the mindless despotism of the bureaucracy - Today, much of the change you have to deal with in a small business is mandatory. It is dictated by nameless, faceless bureaucrats who act as if they are responsible to no one but themselves. An excellent example of this peculiar form of bureaucratic idiocy involves taxable passenger car leasing in Nevada. To insure that no business escaped their clutches, these crafty bureaucrats used the telephone directory as their source for companies involved in passenger car leasing. Any company unlucky enough to have "lease or rental" as part of its name received 2 quarterly report forms to fill out for the state and the county. Our company did not lease or rent any passenger cars, but were still required to file the reports. Even after several contacts asking that we be removed from their list, we still had to file 8 negative reports every year! What could they possibly care about the waste of time involved for them and for us relating to the way this change was implemented by them?

2. **Regulatory** – These are independent regulatory bodies such as the Securities and Exchange Commission (SEC), the National Association of Securities Dealers (NASD), and the National Association of Insurance Commissioners (NAIC).

3. **Franchisor Requirements** – If you are a licensed dealer for any brand name, such as a Ford dealership, you will have to deal with a number of franchisor requirements for change.

4. **Lender or Investor Requirements** – Your investor or banker may have additional financial requirements that may require substantial changes in reporting your business operations to be in compliance with those new requirements. These changes

are not uncommon in this current environment of tight credit restrictions.

5. **Competition Driven Changes** – These are changes driven by your competitors in the form of improved or innovative products, services, delivery capability or other items that are currently unique to the competition. These improvements may require you to transform your operations accordingly.

6. **Customer Driven Changes** – These are product, service, or other changes requested or mandated by your customers that you may have to address.

7. **Market Forces** - A substantial increase or decrease in your sales volume can require you to modify your business plan and upsize or downsize your organization.

You would certainly agree that the first 4 of the external changes listed above; governmental, regulatory, franchisor, and lender related changes, are mandatory and must be complied with. Changes relating to the competition and your customer needs are voluntary on your part, but it is often necessary to address those changes if you want to retain or increase your customer base. Changes relating to market forces are reactive unless you are a prophet with the ability to predict the future. Your response will probably require some major changes to your company operations.

INTERNAL SOURCES OF CHANGE

1. **Problem Resolution** – Resolving a substantial problem, such as a quality control failure, may require substantial operational and procedural changes.

2. **Additional Capital Requirements** – You may need additional funding for expansion, acquisition or working capital which may necessitate changes in the operation and financial reporting of your business.

3. **Updating Inefficient and Outdated Operations** – Making a decision to update your plant, equipment and inefficient workforce will require substantial change in your company. Just ask the management of GM and Chrysler how difficult this can be, if they are still entities operating out of bankruptcy as of the publishing of this book!

4. **Product Innovation and Improvement** – Just about any product innovation necessitating a substantial outlay of funds will require significant changes in your company operations.

5. **Business Plan Requirements** – There may be other large projects in your business that, by their size and complexity, will require substantial change in your business in order to implement them.

The first of these internally driven changes is a reaction to a new problem. The next 2 changes can be proactive or reactive depending on the circumstances that initiated the need for change. The last 2 changes are the result of a purposeful business plan and therefore would be classified as proactive. Obviously, you would like to have as much change as possible be as a result of your proactive decision making made in accordance with your business plan.

TYPES OF CHANGE

Routine Changes – This kind of change relates to changes that are well known in advance, such as the 401k contribution limits which change every year. They are reasonably easy to implement and don't require any substantial changes within the company. They are most likely mandatory changes that must be implemented, but are an integral part of conducting business.

Mandatory Changes – These are required changes that you must comply with. However, they are substantial enough that they may require some major or minor planning and modifications in order to implement them.

Discretionary Reactive Changes – These changes are usually based upon external circumstances, but are not mandatory. They are implemented as a result of a reactive management decision to resolve an existing problem, whether that problem was externally or internally generated.

Discretionary Proactive Changes – These changes are usually based upon your company's business plan and are discretionary. They are implemented as a result of a proactive internal management decision to plan ahead. These are the best kind of changes for the company to implement as the business plan has been approved by the Board of Directors, and the implementation planning has been communicated to your managers and employees. More importantly, Discretionary Proactive Changes should result in more efficient and effective operations, increased sales, and improved profitability.

PLANNING FOR AND IMPLEMENTING CHANGE

There are three tracks to change implementation, depending on the type of change to be implemented.

Routine Changes – To implement routine changes, simply communicate the changes in writing to the affected managers, and have them copy you back with proof that the change has been implemented. As President Regan said concerning arms negotiations with the Russians, **"Trust but Verify"**.

Mandatory Changes – These are required changes that are not a subject for discussion as to whether you must comply with them. However, these changes require some major or minor planning and modifications in order to implement them. Since no discussion about the reason for the change is required other than "It's Mandatory" the following abbreviated plan for implementation will be sufficient.

1. Communicate the required change to all affected managers.

2. Have those managers develop an action pan to implement the required change.
3. Determine the resources (Manpower, Money, and Materials) necessary to complete the project.
4. Appoint a Manager in Charge of the implementation.
5. Develop a Schedule for Implementation.
6. Schedule periodic reporting of progress in implementing the change in writing from the designated project manager.
7. When completed, have the designated project manager fill out a Project Completion Report, backed up by evidence that the project has, in fact, been completed.

Discretionary Changes – Whether these changes are based upon external circumstances or on your business plan, the planning and procedures for implementation are the same.

1. Develop a Project Plan with your manager's input and consent.
2. Determine the resources (Manpower, Money, and Materials) necessary to complete the project.
3. Present the Project Plan to your Board of Directors for approval.
4. Communicate the approved Project Plan to all your managers.
5. Develop a Project Implementation Schedule with your manager's input and buy in.
6. Have the manager develop action pans to implement the project on time and within budget.
7. Appoint an overall Manager in Charge of the project implementation.
8. Schedule regular reporting of the progress in implementing the project orally and in writing from the designated project manager. Formal progress reports should be required at the quarterly Board of Directors meetings.
9. When completed, have the designated project manager fill out a Project Completion Report, backed up by evidence that the project has been successfully completed.

HOW TO DEAL WITH RESISTANCE TO CHANGE

Employee Fears - First we must examine why employees fear change?

1. They feel that implementing the change will require a lot of work.
2. They feel that the change will be a "waste of time and effort"
3. They feel that information regarding the change will not be properly communicated.
4. They feel that they will have little or no input in planning for the implementation of the change.
5. They think there will be inadequate training regarding the change.
6. They think that their managers are not dealing with the potential problems that implementing the change can produce.
7. They feel that they will "lose control" by implementing the change.

Strategies to Negate Those Fears - Now that we have examined our employee's fears, let's look at some effective strategies to deal with those fears.

1. Let your employees know that you have taken into account their work schedules in your implementation planning.
2. Have your managers stress the expected real benefits of the change implementation.
3. Have departmental staff meetings to fully explain the proposed change.
4. At those meetings, have your managers solicit feedback and implementation ideas from your employees. You might consider awarding a prize for the best employee ideas.
5. Schedule specific individual and departmental hands on training for managers and employees to help them prepare them for the change. This can be done inexpensively by utilizing tutorial software or by using interactive online training.
6. Be honest about any potential problems that may be created by the proposed change, and how you have planned to address them.

7. Agree with any valid concerns the employees have regarding "control issues". Stress that the company's concern now is how to successfully implement the change and that they can play an important role in that implementation.

SUMMARY

The rate of change affecting any business from all sources has increased dramatically in the last several decades, along with the advent of the computer and the movement toward a global economy. And mandated change emanating from governmental institutions still seems to grow unfettered by any necessary correlation to common sense. For small businesses in particular, this trend has encroached upon the time that management has available to spend on business planning and has hindered the ability of management to advance their own agenda for change. Therefore, it has become increasingly important for you to assign a high priority to your own business planning and to be proactive about the management and scheduling of discretionary changes in your company.

SUMMARY

A FEW CLOSING REMARKS

From the beginning, the focus of this book has been to provide the owners and managers of small businesses everywhere with a blueprint for professional and profitable business management. There is a scarcity of practical, no nonsense books about the management problems inherent in organizing and managing a small business. I elected to start this book with a Chapter titled "HOW TO COPE WITH THE GREAT RECESSION OF 2009" because there is no doubt that we are 18 to 21 months into a deep recession that promises to extend well into 2010 and beyond! In that chapter, I summarized some ideas that can be implemented quickly and should help you, as a small business owner, to survive this recession. Most of these ideas and suggestions are covered in greater detail in subsequent chapters.

The second section of this book, ORGANIZING YOUR BUSINESS FOR SUCCESS, was designed to take you through the process of forming and organizing your business, hiring the best management team possible, professionally terminating underperforming managers, and managing your business through your Board of Directors. As I indicated earlier, *"Once you begin to manage through your Board of Directors, you will feel the power that you get from being proactive and being out in front of your business decisions. It is a welcome change from being reactive and always feeling like you're behind the eight ball in everything that you do with your business. And, once you have tasted the economic rewards of real participative corporate management, you'll never go back to the old way of doing things."*

In the third section, ASSEMBLING YOUR TEAM OF ADVISORS, I cover the creation of an Outside Advisory Board, and how to choose your corporate attorney and CPA firm. *For some reason, very few small businesses, who have the greatest need for professional advice, will take advantage of the expertise that an Outside Advisory Board can offer. As a small business owner, don't let this opportunity to form an Advisory Board slip away from you.* There is also a special chapter regarding the pitfalls of Arbitration. *"If you have a good case and a good attorney representing you, stay away from arbitration if you are not legally bound by contract to arbitrate a dispute."*

The fourth section is about the title, BUSINESS CONTINUATION PLANNING. I first cover two very important planning areas for small businesses, Disaster Planning and Business Succession Planning, where the planning is either inadequate or not done at all. In the Chapter on Disaster Planning, I cover 8 pre-planning items that are so critical to the survival of your business that I strongly recommend you address those items even before you complete a comprehensive disaster plan. In Business Succession Planning, we discuss family succession from a common sense standpoint. Remember that your business should not become a family playground. As I stated, *"Business acumen is not transferred through the genes, but is forged in the hot fire of tough business experience and difficult decision-making."* Family member or not, begin training up your successor to take your place now! You never know what day will be your last day at the office!

The fifth section, "SUCCESSFUL BUSINESS PLANNING" is the heart and soul of this book. I start with a chapter on Corporate Goal Setting, because all of your planning efforts start here. If you have set the right goals and objectives, your success in achieving them is dramatically increased. Regarding business planning, *"I cannot stress enough the importance of goal setting. It sets the tone and direction of your corporation. It allows you to set objectives that are consistent with the overall goals that you have established. And, like a lighthouse beacon on a dark and stormy night, it keeps you on the right track to achieve those goals."*

Then, I move on to discuss Key Result Areas (KRAs), what they are, how to measure them and how to utilize KRAs in your business planning. Finally, we discuss the process of Management by Objectives (MBO). In order for the MBO process to be successful, *your objectives must be realistic, attainable, consistent with other company goals and objectives, specific, measureable in terms of costs and benefits, and must contain time schedules for implementation and a process for receiving objective feedback at measured intervals.* MBO reporting should be done monthly, but at minimum quarterly at the Board of Directors Meeting in a formal report updating the progress of the project and proposing any mid-course corrections.

The sixth section is all about ANALYZING FINANCIAL STATEMENTS. Your Financial Statements are your business scorecard. They tell you where you've been and how well you have done. Therefore, Financial Statements must be accurate and timely. *"If your company's financial statements are inaccurate because your financial controls are virtually nonexistent, your company is like a ship without power and without a rudder. You don't know where you are, you don't know where you've been, and you certainly don't know where you're going! And if you don't know where you're going, any errant wave will get you there. However, you may not like the journey and you certainly won't like the destination, when you are dashed against the financial rocks of bankruptcy."*

Assuming that you have accurate Financial Statements to work with, you can now analyze your Financial Statements. However, always keep in mind the following: *"Financial analysis is like doing a postmortem on dead meat"!* In other words, when you review accurate financial statements, you are engaging in a historical analysis of the past performance of the company. Nothing you can do in the present will change that past performance. *Obviously, if all you do is analyze past performance and do not utilize the results of that analysis to modify or improve future results, you truly are wasting your time!*

The seventh section is devoted to INCREASING SALES AND IMPROVING GROSS MARGINS. In following chapters, sales pricing strategies, product & service innovations and improvements, product availability and selection, advertising and promotion, quality, guarantees and warranties, reputation and customer service, and location and customer convenience are covered. One of the best strategies for sales and gross margin improvement and increased cash flow is contained in Chapter 29 as follows. *Since almost everything is working in your favor, you can become your own Extended Warranty Provider. You will collect the entire extended warranty premium in advance, to cover a relatively low failure rate for most electronic equipment and appliances.* Further, your liability for product repair or replacement will only begin after the expiration of the manufacturer's warranty. This warranty expires in 90 days to 1 year after the sale of the product. It's a sweet deal for you and can also benefit your customer if you service the extended warranty properly! Also, if you are a manufacturer or fabricator, Chapter 32 titled "COST OF SALES REDUCTION STRATEGIES" lists many ways for you to reduce your overall product costs.

The eighth section covers EXPENSE REDUCTION STRATEGIES. Chapter 33, the first chapter in this segment, summarizes a basket full of potential expense reductions. Seventeen of these expense reduction strategies are then covered in detail in separate chapters. If you have already incorporated all of these expense reduction strategies into your business, my hat is off to you. You are really on top of your game! If you haven't, start with the easiest and least costly expense reduction ideas and don't waste valuable time in getting them implemented.

The ninth section is concerned with the "CONTROL OF ASSETS AND WORKING CAPITAL". There are a substantial number of small businesses that pay little or no attention to the accurate reporting and control of assets and liabilities. As a result, small business owners like you, who have worked hard to make your business a success, wake up to the unpleasant reality that the profit you thought you had before an audit has evaporated after all of the negative audit adjustments. It's very disturbing to realize that you have hemorrhaged away all of your profits because you have exercised little or no control of your assets and liabilities. The control procedures outlined in Chapters 50 through 54 of this section may seem a bit cumbersome. However, it's the only way you will establish firm control of your Cash, Accounts Receivable, Inventory, Accounts Payable and Fixed Assets. If you introduce these controls, you will reduce fraud, theft, loss and pilferage to a minimum, because everyone in your company will know that you are reconciling, reporting, tagging, counting, and controlling your assets. You will protect and safely invest your cash, collect your outstanding receivables on time, count your inventory and record any necessary adjustments, and mark-to market and sell any impaired inventory. You will correctly pay legitimate invoices to approved vendors only, and collect any vendor credits that are due to you. You will also save money by purchasing only those assets that have been approved by you for purchase at the best price possible. Finally, you will sleep better at night, knowing you have your business under control!

The last section briefly covers "CHANGE MANAGEMENT" which could easily be the subject of another book! *Currently, the question is not whether you, as a small business owner, are going to experience change, but how well you will manage and control it. The rate of change for any business from all sources has increased dramatically in the last three decades, along with the advent of the computer and the movement toward a global economy. And mandated change emanating from governmental institutions still seems to grow unfettered by any necessary correlation to common sense. For small businesses in particular, this trend has encroached upon the time that management has available to spend on business planning and has hindered the ability of management to advance their own agenda for change. Therefore, it has become increasingly important for you to assign a high priority to your business planning and to be proactive about the management and scheduling of discretionary changes in your company.*

A FINAL WORD – My purpose for writing this book has been to provide you with a practical guide to small business organization, planning, profitability and control. My objective is to assist you in the successful management of your small business in turbulent economic times. To that end, I have provided you with a substantial number of practical no-nonsense ideas and suggestions that should help you, as a small business owner or manager to profitably manage your business. You should be able to implement a few of these suggestions in your business to increase sales and gross margins, decrease expenses, and implement the controls that will enhance your profitability. If you are successful in accomplishing any of these things, then the purpose of my book will be fulfilled!

FORECAST

A BRIEF GLIMPSE INTO THE FUTURE

I see dark and troubled economic times ahead for the United States. Unfortunately, the free spending politicians we have elected to represent us in Washington have shown little or no fiscal responsibility. Some people would like to place the blame for this financial debacle on "we the people". This is not true, because no matter whom "we the people" elect, Democrat or Republican, they seem to be heading, perhaps at different rates of speed, for the same cliff which will inevitably have our country descend into national insolvency. This is an important consideration for any small business owner, because you will **not** be the beneficiary of any national bailout plan. You are not large enough to qualify, and you have probably not contributed enough money to national political campaigns to have any politician act on your behalf! Of course, if you were AIG, you might be the recipient of $180,000,000,000, yes that's 180 billion dollars in bailout funds that could have been used to buy up illiquid mortgage backed securities as was originally intended. Even if our leaders faced up to reality and started to restore some fiscal sanity to our national economic governance, it would take decades to climb out of this mountain of debt that our spendthrift government has created. Unfortunately, with the budget busting Economic Stimulus Plan we will have added several thousand feet to that mountain! This does not factor in the costs of a national health plan now before Congress, which is expected to add trillions of dollars more to the deficit. Therefore, during the remainder of 2009 and most of 2010 we can expect to see the following events occur:

1. Foreclosures will continue to rise and commercial and residential real estate values will continue to fall. Because of this increase, more banks will fail this year and next.

2. Chrysler and GM, two of our "Big Three" automakers have already filed for bankruptcy protection this year. Even though Chrysler and GM have emerged from bankruptcy, the multiplier effect of these huge business failures has yet to be fully absorbed by our economy.

3. Unemployment rates will continue to rise into the double digits nationally because we are still losing jobs, not creating them.

4. More large and medium-sized businesses will cut back or drastically curtail employment.

5. More workers will be underemployed at lesser wages than they previously earned, or be working less than 40 hours a week.

6. Small retail and wholesale businesses will declare bankruptcy or simply disappear.

7. Cities, Counties, and States will have to drastically curtail their profligate spending or face insolvency, as California is just beginning to understand.

8. More of our manufactured goods will be produced by other countries, most notably China.

9. Interest rates will begin to rise as small business loans become increasingly more difficult to qualify for, and our nation continues to increase its reckless deficit spending.

10. Consumers will continue to curtail their spending, until they see a sustainable turnaround in our economy.

11. Government tax and revenue receipts at all levels will continue to fall thus amplifying the trends listed above.

12. Tax rates will have to be raised by local, state and federal governments at a time when businesses and individuals are least able to cope with the tax increases.

The effect of all of these events will be disastrous for our economy and will have a negative impact on almost all businesses in the United States.

END NOTES

IT'S NOT TOO LATE!

RECESSION RELATED PROTECTIVE MEASURES YOU CAN TAKE NOW!

Unless you have a car repair facility, a grocery store or some similar type of recession resistant business like Wal-Mart, you will be experiencing the effects of this deep recession. Here are some things that you, as a small business owner, can implement now to protect yourself and your business?

1. *Insure that your business structure is set up to protect you and your family's assets in the event of a bankruptcy*. Sole proprietorships or general partnerships will not protect your personal assets in bankruptcy. See Chapter 2 on "**CHOOSING YOUR TYPE OF BUSINESS ORGANIZATION.**"

2. *Operate your business lean and mean!* See Chapter 1 on "**HOW TO COPE WITH THE COMING RECESSION**" and all the other chapters regarding increasing sales, reducing cost of goods sold and decreasing expenses.

3. *Professionally manage your business.* Read Chapter 7 on "**MANAGING THROUGH YOUR BOARD OF DIRECTORS**".

4. *Manage by Objectives.* Read the segment on "**SUCCESSFUL BUSINESS PLANNING**" starting on Page 37.

5. *Adopt a policy of having a "<u>living budget and forecast</u>".* Simply put, this means that your quarterly budget and forecast should be updated with the substantial changes you can expect in the economic climate in your area and your company's current business conditions. In this fast changing economy, you need updated information to know where you're heading!

6. *Institute control of your assets and liabilities.* Read the section on **"CONTROL OF ASSETS AND WORKING CAPITAL."** And then implement the necessary controls.

7. *Increase your cash position.* Read Chapters 53 and 54 on **ACCOUNTS RECEIVABLE** and **INVENTORY CONTROL** for suggestions regarding the collection of overdue accounts receivable, and selling or returning impaired or excess inventory. There are many other suggestions throughout this book relative to increasing your net income that will translate into improved cash flow when implemented.

8. *Place any cash, cash equivalents or short-term investments in government guaranteed accounts.* Don't play with the money that you need to operate your business. Make sure that your CDs, money market funds and other short-term investment vehicles take full advantage of the new federal $250,000 FDIC guarantee limit. If you have more than that amount in any single bank account, set up a second or third account with other banks.

9. *Pay out any excess cash that is not necessary for the operation of your business.* If your company is fortunate enough to have a substantial amount of cash in excess of your current and future business requirements, pay yourself and any other owners a bonus to reduce this excess cash. This is a protective measure that will put the cash in your pocket, and not at risk in your company. You will also be able to deduct this bonus as a company expense for tax purposes, if you are fortunate enough to have any income to offset against it!

You still have some time to protect yourself and your small business from the effects of the deep recession we are currently experiencing. But, time is running out. Start implementing your business recession plan now!

INDEX